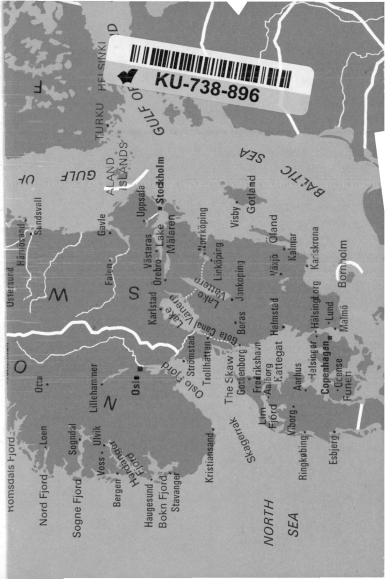

Collins Phrase Books

FRENCH
GERMAN
ITALIAN
PORTUGUESE
SPANISH
SCANDINAVIAN
RUSSIAN
GREEK
YUGOSLAV
DUTCH
LATIN AMERICAN SPANISH

COLLINS
PHRASE BOOKS

L. E. Robertson

COLLINS
PHRASE BOOKS

SCANDINAVIAN

Edited by
LAILA MYKING

COLLINS
LONDON AND GLASGOW

First Published 1959
Latest Reprint 1983

Cover photographs for cased
edition by courtesy of
J. Allan Cash Ltd. (top)
Colour Library International Ltd. (bottom)

ISBN Cased 0 00 433907 X
ISBN Limp 0 00 433927 4
© William Collins Sons & Co. Ltd. 1959

Printed in Great Britain
Collins Clear-Type Press

CONTENTS

INTRODUCTION

Norway, Denmark and Sweden possess many similarities which may lead the visitor to wonder why their peoples remain firmly, almost obstinately, individual. To the rest of the world these three countries often proclaim themselves to be one unit —Scandinavia; but at the same time each is careful to emphasise its own national identity. Many attempts have been made to sum up the different attitudes in outlook by drawing attention to the influences of history or the contrasting geographical features. Perhaps one of the best of these attempts combines both the geographical and historical influences. The Norwegians are an Atlantic people looking westwards, the Danes are a Continental people tied to the mainland, and the Swedes are a Baltic people with an eye always to the east and Russia.

In relation to its geographical size each country has a small population. Each possesses a capital city with a very large population. Sweden and Norway are long, sprawling countries, with great contrasts in landscape; Denmark is flat and fertile. For the nature-loving visitor Sweden has perhaps the most variety to offer, though Norway's fjords are unsurpassed in beauty, and Copenhagen has been justly described as "The Paris of the North".

In all three countries the standard of living is high. Scandinavian architecture, interior decoration and design are among the best in the world. The ordinary citizen in Scandinavia enjoys the results of these in his daily life.

The Scandinavians are cultured, progressive and civilised. Superficially they are undemonstrative, and some people may find them a trifle reserved at first. But to the holiday-maker they offer every kind of pleasant vacation, and they are very proud and pleased to welcome the stranger.

INFORMATION

Norway:
    The Norwegian National Tourist Office, 20 Pall Mall, London, SW1Y 5NE.
    The Norway Travel Association, H. Heyerdahlsgate, 1, Oslo:

Denmark:
    The Danish Tourist Board, 169/173 Regent Street, London, W1R 8PY.
    Banegårdspladsen 7, Copenhagen.

Sweden:
    The Swedish National Tourist Office, P.O. Box 4XD, London, W1A 4XD.
    P.O. Box 7306, S-10385, Stockholm, 7.

PRELIMINARY REQUIREMENTS

Citizens of the United Kingdom do not require visas for any of the three countries. Nationals of India and Pakistan require visas for Sweden. Valid passports are essential for all three countries.

The addresses of some of the Consulates are:

Norwegian:
25 Belgrave Square,
London SW1X 8QD.

Reynolds & Co.,
Rutland House,
148 Edmund Street,
Birmingham B3 2LB.

509 Tower Buildings,
Water Street,
Liverpool, L3 1BA.

54 Pilgrim Street,
Newcastle-on-Tyne, NE1 6TJ.

86 George Street,
Edinburgh.

140 Hope Street,
Glasgow, G2.

Danish:
67 Pont Street,
London SW1X 0BQ.

15 Hazelbank,
King's Norton,
Birmingham, B38 8BT.

24 Fenwick Street,
Liverpool, L2 7NE.

9 Park Terrace,
Glasgow, G3.

50 East Fettes Avenue,
Edinburgh, EH4 1EQ.

Swedish:

23 North Row,
London W1R 2DN.

Crown Works, Rubery,
Birmingham, B45 9AG.

Room 407,
India Buildings,
Water Street,
Liverpool, L2 0Q2.

Clayton House,
Regent Centre,
Gosforth,
Newcastle, NE3 3HW.

6 John's Place,
Edinburgh.

16 Woodside Crescent,
Glasgow, G3 7UT.

ROUTES TO SCANDINAVIA

By Air: There are many regular flights from London, Manchester, Glasgow and Dublin to the capitals and other large cities of Scandinavia. DEA and SAS run daily services to Oslo, Copenhagen, Gothenburg and Stockholm.

By Sea: Newcastle-Bergen (Bergen Line)—19 hours. Five sailings a week during the summer season.

Newcastle-Oslo (Fred Olsen Line)—37 hours. Three sailings a week during the summer season.

Harwich-Kristiansand (Fred Olsen Line)—22 hours. Three sailings a fortnight during the summer season.

Harwich-Esbjerg (United Steamship Company)—18 hours. Six sailings a week during the summer season.

Newcastle-Esbjerg (United Steamship Company)—19 hours. Three sailings a week during the summer season.

N.B. From Esbjerg there is a special train to Copenhagen which takes approximately 5 hours.

London (Fenchurch St.)-Tilbury-Gothenburg (Swedish Lloyd)—40 hours. Three sailings a week during the summer.

Hull-Gothenburg (Ellerman's Wilson Line)—36 hours. Three sailings a fortnight.

Immingham-Gothenburg (Tor Line)—25 hours. Three sailings a week throughout the year.

By Rail: London (Liverpool Street) to Harwich, thence boat to Hook of Holland (7 hours), and thereafter train on to

Copenhagen daily (27 hours). Connections from Copenhagen to Oslo, Stockholm and Gothenburg.

Current time-tables, fares and other costs should be checked at the travel agencies.

CURRENCIES

Travellers from the United Kingdom must comply with British regulations concerning the foreign currency allowance. In 1971 the personal foreign currency allowance for United Kingdom citizens journeying to Scandinavia was £300 a year. Travellers' cheques may be cashed without difficulty at all banks, travel agencies, most hotels, and at the booking offices of some of the larger railway stations.

The currency in each of the three countries is based on the decimal system. There are 100 øre or öre to the Norwegian and Danish krone and the Swedish krona. In 1971 one Norwegian crown and one Danish crown were each equivalent to 6p. The Swedish crown was equal to 8p. In all three countries prices are written thus:

> kr 35.80 (35 crowns 80 øre or öre).
> kr   7.50 (7 crowns and 50 öre)

Prices less than one crown thus:

> 75 øre (or öre) or 0.75kr or kr 0.75.
> 35 øre (or öre) or 0.35kr or kr 0.35.

When referring to each other's currency the countries write:

> N. kr. 60 (60 Norwegian crowns).
> D. kr 60 (60 Danish crowns).
> Sv. kr 60 (60 Swedish crowns).

Two of the countries regulate the amount of banknotes which may be imported or exported by the visitor.

Norway: A limit of 800 N. kroner may be taken out but any amount may be brought in.

Sweden: A limit of 6,000 Sv. kronor may be taken out and 6,000 Sv. kronor may be brought in.

CUSTOMS

In all three countries the main concern of the Customs officials is in the importation of liquor and tobacco. British subjects may take in one bottle of spirits, one bottle of wine and 200 cigarettes (or the equivalent in tobacco) without paying duty. Other items such as cameras, radios, jewellery, nylons, etc., may be taken in provided they are for personal use.

TRANSPORT

It is important to remember that distances between towns in Sweden and Norway are very great. From the northernmost tip of Norway and Sweden to Malmö in the south is 1,000 miles. Parts of the countries are very mountainous as well, so that great attention has been paid to methods of getting about. There is an enormous choice of different kinds of travel for the visitor by bus, train, boat and aircraft. There are many special "round trip" tickets on all types of transport during the summer. Some of these runabout tickets extend from country to country. The Swedish State Railways have about a hundred special cheap tours, and several circular trips which include Denmark and Norway. There are rebates for families and cheap tickets for children. Each of the countries publishes a summer route book with a section in English. These are designed to help the tourist enjoy the Scandinavian countryside as fully and cheaply as possible. One can save a great deal of money and see a great deal of Scandinavia by studying these route books.

In Scandinavia trains are extremely clean, the great majority being operated by electricity.

Norway: There are two classes, I and II, on both day and night trains and fares are based on a sliding scale. On main routes, e.g. Oslo–Bergen, Oslo–Trondheim, it is advisable to book one's seat in advance. One purchases a "sitteplass". There is a small additional charge for this. On all main-line trains there are restaurant cars. Night trains have sleeping berths (I and II class). It is important to book a sleeping berth well in advance. There is a free baggage allowance of 75 kilos (170 lb.).

Denmark: There are two classes, I and II, on day and night trains. Some trains are diesel-powered. The longest train journey from Copenhagen to the furthermost part of Denmark takes only six hours. Most Danes travel II class. First-class fares are usually 50% more than class II, but the farther you travel the cheaper (proportionately) the fares become. Major connections between Copenhagen and other mainline stations are by "lyntog" or "lightning" trains and it is advisable to book a seat in advance. Restaurant cars are put on main-line trains; and there are excellent eating facilities on the train ferries. There is a free baggage allowance of 25 kilos (56 lb.), and thereafter the charge depends on the length of the journey and the weight of the baggage.

Sweden: Two classes, I and II. Fares are based on a sliding scale so that the farther you travel the less it costs per kilometer. Second class is very comfortable. Sleeping berths and eating facilities are as for the other two countries. Hand luggage may be taken free. It is customary to register heavier baggage. The cost of registration depends on the distance to be travelled and the weight of the luggage. On express and certain other trains a seat ticket is necessary.

During the summer, SAS (Scandinavian Airlines System) operate frequent direct flights between the three capitals. But in addition there are many excellent services connecting the smaller towns of the three countries.

Many excellent bus tours are available in Scandinavia. There are also buses (often owned by the State Railways) connecting remote hamlets with each other and with the railway stations. Trams and trolleybuses operate in the main cities, and fares are quite cheap. Stockholm has an Underground system and Gothenburg has excellent trams. Taxis are available in most towns. Their prices are roughly 15% higher than in London.

It is important to mention boat services in Scandinavia. In Norway in particular frequent daily services from village to village in the fjords often provide the most (or only) satisfactory form of travel. The boats are comfortable and usually have good dining facilities. Trips in these boats give superb opportunities of seeing the various fjords.

In Sweden the Göta Canal deserves mention. This canal has been cut from Gothenburg to the two great central lakes, and thence to Stockholm. Small luxurious steamers take three days to navigate in either direction over the whole length of the Canal. This is a very popular way of seeing central Sweden.

MEALS

Norway: Meals are good and food is abundant. The open sandwich (smørbrød) is particularly recommended: bread and butter topped with smoked salmon, shrimps, beef, liver-paste, cheese and many other delicacies. The fish in Norway is always fresh, often alive a few minutes before you order it. Trout (ørret), salmon (laks), cod (torsk) and halibut (kveite) are all excellent. Among the more exotic foods are ptarmigan (rype) and reindeer (dyrestek), often served with sour-cream sauces. For English visitors the puddings are disappointing, but there are two notable specialities in the sweet line, namely cloudberries (multer) and cream, and a soft sponge cake filled with whipped cream and fruits known as Bløtkake. There are two national cheeses which Britons regard with undeserved suspicion—goat cheese (geitost) and "old cheese" (gammel ost). The former is a pale chocolate colour and is slightly sweet; the latter is very strong and is a cousin of English Stilton. Both should be tried at least once.

Breakfasts at many hotels are excellent and monumental, consisting of a huge cold buffet and the conventional English breakfast in addition. Coffee is drunk by Norwegians in preference to tea, but tea is readily obtainable. Afternoon tea is not served, but coffee is taken at any hour and in the afternoon is served with cakes.

The Government owns all the liquor shops (Vinmonopol) but the visitor may buy at them without restriction. Restaurants have to be licensed to sell wine and spirits. Wine is of high quality and often costs less than in Britain. There is a local spirit known as "Aquavit" which is drunk when one eats smørbrød. It is very powerful.

Denmark: Danish food is world-famous and is first-class. Breakfast is in the "continental" style, but there is no difficulty in obtaining porridge and bacon and eggs. Danish coffee is very good, but tea is also available. Lunch is usually taken at midday, and in hotels and restaurants will often consist of cold buffet. This is a table set with many dishes of fish, birds, meats, cheeses, etc. Danish rye bread is served with the meal. One helps oneself, piling one's plate. Dinner is taken around six in the evening. From about half-past nine in the evening many Danes take more coffee and open sandwiches. After-noon tea is not taken but, Danish coffee and Danish pastries are consumed at any time.

Copenhagen has many famous restaurants. Some of these offer as many as fifty different types of smørrebrød. There is one restaurant which has more than two hundred different types of open sandwich on its menu.

Danish beer (Carlsberg and Tuborg) is among the best light beer in the world. Danish Aquavit is served with beer and open sandwiches. It is not customary to drink Aquavit with-out food to accompany it.

Sweden: Swedish food is good. Many visitors will have heard of the Swedish "Smörgåsbord", a vast table covered with delicacies. But today this is not readily found in Sweden. Instead most restaurants serve half a dozen substantial *hors d'œuvres* type dishes as a preliminary to the meal. If one wishes, one can still specially order a "Smörgåsbord". In August Swedes eat "kräftor" (crayfish) and crayfish parties out of doors are very popular. Swedish herring, smoked eel, and smoked reindeer are all worth trying. There are many kinds of bread; and in particular "hard breads". These are similar to Ryvita. On Thursdays Swedes traditionally have pea-soup with pork in it, followed by pancakes.

Breakfast is in the continental style. Lunch and dinner are

taken at much the same time as in England. Throughout the day the "konditori" (café) is popular, selling various soft drinks, and tea, coffee and chocolate, with open sandwiches and pastries.

Modern self-service grill bars are to be found all over the country and one may get a good cheap meal quickly at these.

The Government owns the liquor shops (Systembolaget), and restaurants require licenses to serve wine and spirits.

TIME

In Norway during the *Summer:* G.M.T. + 1 hour.
In Norway during the *Winter:* G.M.T. + 1 hour.
In Denmark and Sweden all year: G.M.T. + 1 hour.
All time-tables are printed on the 24-hour system.

TIPPING

Norway: 10% service charge is added to hotel bills (sometimes 15%). No further tips required for chambermaids. Hall porters can be tipped if they have been helpful. A crown a day and not less than 3 crowns is a fair guide. In restaurants 10% is added to the bill automatically, but many people make the bill up to the nearest crown. Taxi-drivers are not usually tipped, though again one may make the fare up to the nearest crown. Cloakroom attendants, 35–50 øre. Luggage porters will tell you their fee and you pay them that and no more.

Denmark: Hotel and restaurant bills include service charges (15%) and Value Added Tax (15%). No further tipping is required, except in the case of special services rendered by the hotel porter. In ladies' and gentlemen's rooms the tip is usually 1 crown. Taxi-drivers expect 10–15% of the fare. Railway and ferry-boat porters expect D.kr 1.75 to 2.40 per piece of luggage.

Sweden: 15% service charge is usually included in the hotel bill, so it is not necessary to tip the chambermaid or other staff. Restaurants add $12\frac{1}{2}$% to the bill. Taxi-drivers and hairdressers expect a tip of 10–15%. Cloakroom attendants should receive 1 crown per coat; a porter 3 crowns for the first two items of baggage and 1 crown for each one thereafter. For small services it is not usual to offer a tip of less than 1 crown.

AMUSEMENTS

In all three countries the cinemas show British and American films. The sound-track is not usually dubbed, and only the sub-titles are in one of the Scandinavian languages. Performances are at fixed hours, not continuous. Seats are often booked in advance. There is a strict "no smoking" rule in concert halls, theatres and cinemas throughout Scandinavia.

Norway: Amusements are mainly out of doors. In the winter, skiing and skating. In the summer, swimming, sailing, walking and motoring in the mountains. Football is played in the summer. Fishing in Norway is excellent. The National Theatre in Oslo is worth a visit.

Denmark: Much of the amusement centres on Copenhagen, which is delightful for the visitor throughout the year. The Tivoli Gardens are open from May to September with open-air traditional pantomime, a fun-fair, park and concert hall. There are many good bars and night clubs. The ballet enjoys a good reputation. Football is played in the summer. The sandy beaches on Zeeland and in North Jutland offer excellent bathing.

Sweden: Skiing in the winter. Sailing on the west coast and in the archipelago outside Stockholm in the summer. Swimming, particularly on the west coast. Fishing in many places. Football and athletics during the summer months. Throughout the year there are excellent opportunities for listening to good music in Stockholm. There is fine opera and ballet.

MOTORING

The British tourist can acquire information and the requisite documents from the Automobile Association or the Royal

Automobile Club. The three corresponding Scandinavian organisations publish good touring books for the motorist in their respective countries. Their names are:

Norway:
 Kongelig Norsk Automobilklub, Tolltonswent Room 610, Grensen 3, Oslo.

Sweden:
 Kongelig Dansk Automobil Klub, Sturegaten 32, Stockholm.

Denmark:
 Kungliga Automobil Klubben, Frederiksborgade 18, Copenhagen.

In 1971 the price of petrol was between 35p and 40p a gallon in the three countries; e.g. in Norway it was N.kr. 1.49 øre per litre.

In all three countries the rule of the road is RIGHT.

In all three countries the laws relating to driving after having been drinking are very strict. If the police suspect a driver of being even slightly "under the influence", he is liable to have a blood-test taken. If alcohol above a certain percentage is found to be present in the blood, the driver may be severely punished. In Norway, for example, over 0.05% alcohol in the blood (about a large whisky and soda) makes the driver liable to up to three weeks' imprisonment.

SOME PLACES OF INTEREST

Oslo—Vigeland sculptures in Frogner park. The Viking ships at Bygdøy, the Kon-Tiki raft, the Town Hall.

Bergen—Fløyen (cablecar ride with view over Bergen), the Fish market and Bryggen (Hanseatic quay). Trollhaugen, the house in which the composer Edward Grieg lived.

West Norway—The fjords; the Stave church at Borgund in Sogn dating from 1150.

Copenhagen—The Tivoli Pleasure Gardens. Langelinie and

the statue of the Little Mermaid of Hans Andersen. Rosenborg Palace.

Frederiksborg—The Palace.

Helsingør—The Castle (the Elsinore Castle of *Hamlet*).

Odense—The birthplace of Hans Andersen.

Stockholm—The Djurgården Park and Skansen open-air folk museum. The Town Hall, one of the finest examples of twentieth-century civic architecture in the world. The Old City. Millesgården.

Gothenburg—Scandinavia's largest harbour. Liseberg amusement park. Trädgårdsföreningen (Garden). Älvsborg fortress.

Island of Gotland—Visby, a town of great charm and historical interest with fine roses and ancient ruins.

Lapland and the Midnight Sun—SAS operate night flights to the Arctic Circle and back in June and July. The Swedish State Railways operate a nine-day excursion in a special luxury train to the Arctic Circle, Narvik in Norway and back to Stockholm.

FORMS OF ADDRESS

In all three languages there are two forms of "you". One is used between friends, the other is more impersonal and is used generally. The former is somewhat like the old-fashioned English intimate form "thou". In this book the impersonal form of "you" has been used throughout. In Norwegian and Danish this is "De"; in Swedish "Ni".

In Scandinavia there are no absolute equivalents of Sir, Madam. It is safe to use "Herr" for Mister, and "Fru" for Mrs.

Shop assistants, telephone operators, maids and waitresses may be addressed as "Frøken" in Norwegian and Danish, and "Fröken" in Swedish.

There is no single word for "Please" in any of the three languages. But one of the most useful phrases is "Vær så god" in Danish and Norwegian and in Swedish "Var så god". This phrase is used whenever something is being offered or handed over; it is a polite way of saying "Here you are" or "Please accept this" or "Please begin to . . . (e.g. eat)".

THE THREE LANGUAGES

The three languages are in many ways very similar. The reader will see at once the close resemblance they have to each other, but in this book he will also see the substantial differences in pronunciation. Many words are spelt in the same or a very similar way, but, unfortunately for the visitor, are pronounced quite differently. Grammatically all three languages are much the same. A knowledge of German vocabulary is very helpful when learning one of the three languages.

Norwegian is really the "bridge" language. A Norwegian usually has very little trouble in being understood in either of the other two countries. But to make matters confusing for the foreigner the Norwegians insist on having two distinct languages, each with a different spelling and pronunciation. One is called "New Norwegian" (Nynorsk) and is spoken and written in country districts and by certain scholars, the other is called "National Norwegian" (Riksmål) and is spoken in the large towns. In this book Riksmål has been used. Most Norwegian newspapers and books are written in Riksmål.

Danish is the most difficult language of the three to pronounce. The Danes speak softly, swallow parts of their words, and slur the endings of many of them. The language is often spelt in the same way as Norwegian (or one should say Norwegian is often spelt in the same way as Danish), but the pronunciation is quite different.

Swedish is spoken in a crisper, more singsong way than Danish. The reader will see that often Danish and Norwegian have the same word for a thing, and Swedish has a different word. Pronunciation in Swedish is not difficult, but one must pay attention to the way in which the Swedes stress the syllables of their words.

SCHEME OF PRONUNCIATION

The pronunciation of each of the languages varies widely within each country. There are many dialects. This book is based on the standard pronunciation in each country. Because there are such wide differences and yet so few people (the total population of Norway is only 3¼ million, Denmark 4 million, and Sweden 7 million), it is not easy to talk of a "standard" pronunciation, but the pronunciation scheme set out in this book will generally be understood anywhere in each of the three countries.

Read the transliterated words and phrases as if they were English words and phrases. The scheme of pronunciation has been kept as simple as possible and unfamiliar symbols have been avoided, but it has been necessary to formulate a few simple rules where the sounds cannot be accurately represented in English. These rules have been made common to each of the three languages, and are:

ö	represents	"u" as in fur
aw	„	aw as in saw
ee	„	ee as in feel
oo	„	oo as in look, book
ay	„	ay as in day
ah	„	a as in rather
ă	„	a as in Northern English "lad"
eh	„	e as in bell
ü	„	ü as in German "über" or French "lune", rather like saying English ee with rounded lips

ch in *Norwegian* is pronounced as in cherry but with the lips
   drawn back.
ch in *Swedish* as ch in cherry in the normal way.
th in *Danish* transliteration is pronounced th as in "then".
   The symbol – above a vowel indicates a long vowel.
   The symbol ˘ above a vowel indicates a short vowel.
   The symbol ′ denotes the stress is placed on the syllable
      immediately preceding.

*I wish to express my grateful thanks to Mr. Peter Ramm
and Mrs. Agnete Hort for their valuable assistance in compiling
and correcting the Danish and Swedish texts. I should like to
thank also Anthony Abrahams who helped with the Introduction,
and patiently acted as an English guinea-pig in matters of
pronunciation.*

I. M.

PHRASES IN COMMON USE

Yes, No.

| Ja, Nei | Ja, Nej | Ja, Nej |
| *yah, nay* | *yah, ny* | *yā, nay* |

Please, Thank you.

| Vær så vennlig, Takk | Vær venlig, Mange tak | Var snäll, Tack |
| *vair saw ven'-lee, täkk* | *vair ven'-lee, mangh'-eh tähk* | *vår snell, tåk* |

Excuse me.

| Unnskyld meg | Undskyld mig | Ursäkta |
| *ðŏn'-shüll may* | *oon'-skül my* | *oor-saik-tä* |

Pardon me, What did you say?

| Unnskyld, Hva sa De? | Undskyld, Hvad sagde De? | Förlåt, Vad sade ni? |
| *ðŏn'-shül, vah sah dee* | *oon'-skül, vath sāh dee* | *för-lawt', väd sä nee* |

Good morning.

| God morgen | God morgen | God morgon |
| *goh mor'-en* | *go mor'-en* | *goo morron* |

Good evening, Good night.

| God aften, God natt | God aften, God nat | God afton, God natt |
| *goh af'-ten, goh nàtt* | *go åhf'-ten, go nåht* | *goo äf-ton, goo nätt* |

Good-bye.

| Farvel | Farvel | Adjö |
| *fåhr-vel* | *fåhr-vel'* | *a-yð* |

Do you speak English?

| Snakker De engelsk? | Taler De engelsk? | Talar ni engelska? |
| *snåkk-er dee ehng'-elsk* | *tah'-ler dee ehng'-elsk* | *tä-lär nee ehng-el-skä* |

I do not speak Norwegian, Danish, Swedish.

| Jeg snakker ikke norsk, dansk, svensk | Jeg taler ikke norsk, dansk, svensk | Jag talar inte norska, danska, svenska |
| *yay snåkk'-er ick'-kĕ norsk, dahnsk, svensk* | *yi tah'-ler ick'-ke norsk, dansk, svensk* | *yä tä-lär in'-tĕ norskä, danskä, svehn-skä* |

| Norwegian | Danish | Swedish |

I do not understand.

Jeg forstår ikke	Jeg forstår ikke	Jag förstår inte
yay for-stawr ick′-kĕ	*yi for-stawr′ ick′-ke*	*yā fur-stawr′ in′-tĕ*

Will you please speak more slowly.

Vil De være så vennlig å snakke langsom-mere	Vil De være venlig at tale langsommere	Vill ni vara snäll och tala långsammare
vill dee vair-ĕ saw ven′-lee aw snäkk-ĕ lahng′-som-mĕ-rĕ	*vill dee vairĕ ven′-lee at tah′-le lahng′-som-me-re*	*vill nee vā-rä snell ock tā-lä long-säm-mä-rĕ*

Write it down, please.

Vær så vennlig å skrive det ned	Vær venlig at skrive det ned	Var snäll och skriv ner det
vair saw ven′-lee aw skree-vĕ deh ned	*vair ven′-lee at skree′-ve deh neth*	*vär snell ock skreev nëhr dëh*

You do not understand me.

De forstår meg ikke	De forstår mig ikke	Ni förstår mig inte
dee for-stawr may ick′-kĕ	*dee for-stawr′ my ick′-ke*	*nee fur-stawr′ may in′-tĕ*

What time is it?

Hva er klokken?	Hvad er klokken?	Vad är klockan?
vah air klock′-ken	*vath air klock′-ken*	*vād ëh klock′än*

Is it time to go?

Er det på tide å gå?	Er det på tide at gå?	Är det tid att gå?
air deh paw tee′-de aw gaw	*air deh paw tee′-the at gaw*	*ëh dëh teed att gaw*

I must go.

Jeg må gå	Jeg må gå	Jag måste gå
yay maw gaw	*yl maw gaw*	*yā mosstĕ gaw*

It is late.

Det er sent	Det er sent	Det är sent
deh air sehnt	*deh air sehnt*	*dëh ëh sëhnt*

It is early.

Det er tidlig	Det er tidligt	Det är tidígt
deh air teed′-lee	*deh air teeth′-leet*	*dëh ëh tee-dit*

Norwegian	Danish	Swedish

Am I interrupting you?

Forstyrrer jeg Dem?	Forstyrrer jeg Dem?	Stör jag er?
for-stür'-rer yay dem	*for-stür'-rer yi dem*	*stör yå ēhr*

Are you ready?

Er De ferdig?	Er De parat?	Är ni färdig?
air dee fair'-dee	*air dee påh-råht'*	*ēh nee fair-dee*

As soon as possible.

Så snart som mulig	Så snart som muligt	Så snart som möjligt
saw snahrt som moo'-lee	*saw snahrt sum moo'-leet*	*saw snärt som möy-lit*

Please bring me . . .

Vær så vennlig å bringe meg . . .	Vær venlig at bringe mig . . .	Var snäll och ge mig . . .
vair saw ven'-lee aw bringĕ may . . .	*vair ven'-lee at bring my . . .*	*vär snell ock yĕh may . . .*

Come here.

Kom her	Kom her	Kom hit
kom hair	*come hear*	*komm heet*

Come in.

Kom inn	Kom ind	Kom in
kom in	*come in*	*kom in*

Don't do that.

Ikke gjør det	Lad være med at gøre det	Gör inte så
ick'-kĕ yör deh	*lath vai'-re meth at göre deh*	*yör in'-tĕ saw*

Don't forget.

Glem ikke	Glem det ikke	Glöm inte
glem ick'-kĕ	*glem deh ick'-kĕ*	*glöm in'-tĕ*

Fast.

Hurtig	Hurtig	Fort
Hoor'-tee	*hoor'-tee*	*fohrt*

How long must I wait?

Hvor lenge må jeg vente?	Hvor længe skal jeg vente?	Hur länge behöver jag vänta?
vohr leng-ĕ maw yay ven'-tĕ	*vor laing'-eh skal yi ven'-te*	*hoor leng-ĕ be-hö-ver yå ven'-tă*

Norwegian	Danish	Swedish

Will it be long?

Blir det lenge?	Vil det vare længe?	Dröjer det länge?
bleer deh lĕng-ĕ	*vil deh vah'-re laing'-eh*	*dröy-er deh leng-ĕ*

I am busy.

Jeg er opptatt	Jeg har travlt	Jag är upptagen
yay air opp-tătt	*yi hahr troult*	*ya ēh op'-tā-gĕn*

I am in a hurry.

Jeg har det travelt	Jeg har travlt	Jag har bråttom
yay hahr deh trä-velt	*yi hahr troult*	*yā här brot-tom*

I am hungry, thirsty.

Jeg er sulten, tørst	Jeg er sulten, tørstig	Jag är hungrig, törstig
yay air sŏŏl'-ten, törst	*yi air sool'-ten, tör'-stee*	*yā ēh hoong-rig, tör-stig*

I am tired.

Jeg er trett	Jeg er træt	Jag är trött
yay air trĕtt	*yi air trait*	*yā ēh trött*

I am glad.

Jeg er glad	Jeg er glad	Jag är glad
yay air glāh	*yi air glath*	*yā ēh gläd*

I am annoyed.

Jeg er irritert	Jeg er irriteret	Jag är ond
yay air ir-ree-tehrt'	*yi air ir-ree-teh'-ret*	*yā ēh ohnd*

I am very sorry.

Jeg beklager det	Jeg er meget ked af det	Jag är mycket ledsen
yay beh-klāh'-ger deh	*yi air my'-et keth af deh*	*yā ēh mückĕ lĕssen*

I think so.

Jeg tror det	Jeg tror det	Jag tror det
yay trohr deh	*yi trohr deh*	*yā trohr dēh*

I don't think so.

Jeg tror ikke det	Jeg tror det ikke	Jag tror inte det
yay trohr ick'-kĕ deh	*yi trohr deh ick'-ke*	*yā trohr in'-tĕ dēh*

I know.

Jeg vet	Jeg ved	Jag vet
yay vēht	*yi veth*	*yā vēht*

Norwegian	Danish	Swedish

I don't know.

| Jeg vet ikke | Jeg ved det ikke | Jag vet inte |
| *yay vēht ick'-kĕ* | *yi veth deh ick'-ke* | *yā vēht in'-tĕ* |

I want.

| Jeg vil gjerne | Jeg vil gerne | Jag vill |
| *yay vill yair'-nĕ* | *yi vill gair'-ne* | *ya vill* |

I don't want.

| Jeg vil ikke | Jeg vil ikke | Jag vill inte |
| *yay vill ick'-kĕ* | *yi vill ick'-ke* | *yā vill in'-tĕ* |

I have lost.

| Jeg har mistet | Jeg har mistet | Jag har för-lorat |
| *yay hahr miss-tet* | *yi hahr miss'-tet* | *yā hār för-loh'-răt* |

I hope.

| Jeg håper | Jeg håber | Jag hoppas |
| *yay haw-per* | *yi haw'-ber* | *yā hop'-păs* |

I insist.

| Jeg insisterer | Jeg insisterer | Jag insisterar |
| *yay in-see-steh'-rer* | *yi in-see-steh'-rer* | *yā in-si-stēh'-răr* |

I promise you.

| Jeg lover Dem | Jeg lover Dem | Jag lovar er |
| *yay law-ver dem* | *yi law'-air dem* | *yā law-var ēhr* |

Is it not so?

| Er det ikke så? | Er det ikke sådan? | Är det inte så? |
| *air deh ick'-kĕ saw* | *air deh ick'-ke saw'-dähn* | *ēh dēh in'-tĕ saw* |

I will give you my address.

| Jeg vil gi Dem min adresse | Jeg vil give Dem min adresse | Jag ska ge er min adress |
| *yay vill yee dĕm meen ah-dres'-se* | *yi vil ghee'-ve dem meen äh-dres'-se* | *yā skä yēh ēhr min add-rĕss'* |

Let us go for a walk.

| La oss gå en tur | Lad os gå en tur | Låt oss ta en promenad |
| *lah oss gaw en toor* | *lath us gaw in toor* | *lawt oss tā en prom-me-näd'* |

| *Norwegian* | *Danish* | *Swedish* |

Listen.

Hør	Hør	Hör på
hör	*hör*	*hör paw*

Look out.

Pass på	Pas på	Se upp
păss paw	*pas paw*	*sēh oop*

More or less.

Mer eller mindre	Mere eller mindre	Mer eller mindre
mehr el-ler min'-drĕ	*mehr el-ler min'-dre*	*mēhr el-ler min'-drĕ*

Not so fast.

Ikke så hurtig	Ikke så hurtigt	Inte så fort
ick'-kĕ saw hoor'-tee	*ick'-ke saw hoor'-teet*	*in'-tĕ saw fohrt*

Please open the door.

Vær så vennlig å åpne døren	Vær venlig at åbne døren	Var snäll och öppna dörren
vair saw ven'-lee aw awpnĕ dö-ren	*vair ven'-lee at awpnĕ dö'-ren*	*vār snell ock öppnă dörrĕn*

Please shut the window.

Vær så vennlig å lukke vinduet	Vær venlig at lukke vinduet	Var snäll och stäng fönstret
vair saw ven'-lee aw lŏŏk-kĕ vin'-doo-ett	*vair ven'-lee at lŏŏk-kĕ vin'-doo-et*	*vār snell ock steng fön'-stret*

Please can you tell me.

Kan De være så vennlig å si meg	Vil De være venlig at sige mig	Vill ni vara snäll och säga mig
kan dee vair-ĕ saw ven'-lee aw see'may	*vil dee vai'-re ven'-lee at see'-ĕh my*	*vill nee vā-ră snell och sayă may*

Please repeat it.

Vær så vennlig å gjenta det	Vær venlig at gentage det	Var snäll och upprepa det
vair saw ven'-lee aw yen-tah deh	*vair ven'-lee at ghen'-tah deh*	*vār snell ock oop-rēh'-pă dēh*

Speak to him (her).

Snakk til ham (henne)	Tal til ham (hende)	Tala med honom (henne)
snăkk till hăm (hen'-nĕ)	*tahl til hahm (hin'-ne)*	*tālă mēd ho'-nom (hĕn'-nĕ)*

Norwegian	Danish	Swedish

Tell him to wait.

| Be ham vente | Bed ham om at vente | Be honom att vänta |
| beh hăm ven'-tĕ | beth hahm um at ven'-tĕ | bĕh ho'-nom att vĕn'-tă |

Wait a minute, please.

| Vær så vennlig å vente et øyeblikk | Vær venlig at vente et øjeblik | Var snäll och vänta ett ögonblick |
| vair saw ven'-lee aw ven'-tĕ ett öy-eh-blick | vair ven'-lee at ven-tĕ it oy'-ĕh-blick | văr snell ock vĕn'-tă ett ög'-on-blick |

Wait for us.

| Vent på oss | Vent på os | Vänta på oss |
| vent paw oss | vent paw us | vĕn'-tă paw oss |

We are very grateful.

| Vi er meget takknemmelige | Vi er meget taknemmelige | Vi är mycket tacksamma |
| vee air mĕh'-get tăkk-nem'-mĕ-lee-ĕ | vee air my'-et tăhk-nĕhm'-mĕ-lee-ĕ | vee ĕh mücke̊ tack'-săm-mă |

What?

| Hva? | Hvad? | Vad |
| vah | vath | văd |

What is it?

| Hva er det? | Hvad er der? | Vad är det? |
| vah air deh | vath air dair | văd ĕh dĕh |

What does that mean?

| Hva betyr det? | Hvad betyder det? | Vad betyder det? |
| vah beh-tür' deh | vath bĕh-tü'-ther deh | văd bĕh-tü'-dĕr dĕh |

What have I to pay?

| Hva skal jeg betale? | Hvad skal jeg betale? | Vad skall jag betala? |
| vah skăll yay beh-tah'-lĕ | vath skăl yi bĕh-tah'-lĕ | văd skăll yă bĕh-tă'-lă |

What is that for?

| Hva er det til? | Hvad er det til? | Vad är det till? |
| vah air deh till | vath air deh til | văd ĕh dĕh till |

| Norwegian | Danish | Swedish |

What is that in Norwegian, Danish, Swedish?

Hva er det på norsk, dansk, svensk?	Hvad hedder det på norsk, dansk, svensk?	Vad heter det på norska, danska, svenska?
vah air deh paw norsk, dahnsk, svensk	*vath heth'-ther deh paw norsk, dansk, svensk*	*vād hēh-tĕr dēh paw norskă, danskă, svĕhn'-skă*

What is the matter?

Hva er i veien?	Hvad er der i vejen?	Vad är det?
vah air ee vay-en	*vath air dair ee vy'-en*	*vād ĕh dēh*

What is your name?

Hva er Deres navn?	Hvad er Deres navn?	Vad heter ni?
vah air deh-res nahvn	*vath air deh'-res năhvn*	*vād hēh-tĕr nee*

What is your address?

Hva er Deres adresse?	Hvad er Deres adresse?	Vad är er adress?
vah air deh-res ah-dres'-sĕ	*vath air deh'-res ăh-dres'-sĕ*	*vād ĕh ēhr ădd-rĕss'*

Where.

Hvor	Hvor	Var
vohr	*vor*	*vār*

Where to?

Hvor hen?	Hvorhen?	Vart?
vohr hen	*vor-hen'*	*vărt*

Where are you going?

Hvor hen skal De gå?	Hvor går De hen?	Vart ska ni gå?
vohr hen skăll dee gaw	*vor gawr dee hen*	*vărt skă nee gaw*

Where do you live?

Hvor bor De?	Hvor bor De?	Var bor ni?
vohr bohr dee	*vor bohr dee*	*vār bohr nee*

Who, Who is it?

Hvem, Hvem er det?	Hvem, Hvem er det?	Vem, Vem är det?
vehm, vehm air deh	*vehm, vehm air deh*	*vĕm, vĕm ēh dēh*

Who is there?

Hvem der?	Hvem er der?	Vem är där?
vehm dair	*vehm air dair*	*vĕm ēh dair*

Norwegian	Danish	Swedish

Where can I wash my hands?

Hvor kan jeg vaske hendene?	Hvor kan jeg vaske mine hænder?	Var kan jag tvätta mig om händerna?
vohr kăn yay văs'-kĕ hen'-en-ĕ	*vor kan yi văhs'-ke mee'-ne hain'-ner*	*vär kăn yā tvĕt-tă may omm hĕn'-dĕr-nă*

Where is the lavatory?

Hvor er toalettet?	Hvor er toiletet?	Var är toiletten?
vohr air toh-ah-let'-tĕ	*vor air toh-ăh-let'-tet*	*văr ĕh to-ă-lĕt'-ten*

Where is the British Consulate?

Hvor er det Britiske Konsulatet?	Hvor er det Britiske Konsulat?	Var är brittiska konsulatet?
vohr air deh bree'-tis-ke kon-soo-lah'-tĕ	*vor air deh bree'-tis-ke kon-soo-laht'*	*văr ĕh britt-is-kă kon-soo-lă'-tet*

Why, Why not?

Hvorfor, Hvorfor ikke?	Hvorfor, Hvorfor ikke?	Varför, varför inte?
vohr-for, vohr-for ick' lĕ	*vor for', vor for' ick' ke*	*văr'-för, văr'-för in'-tĕ*

Will you come with me?

Vil De komme med meg?	Vil De komme med mig?	Vil ni komma med mig?
vill dee kom'-me meh may	*vil dee kom'-me meth my*	*vill nee komma mĕh may*

TELEPHONING

I want to telephone.

Jeg vil gjerne telefonere	Jeg ønsker at telefonere	Jag vill gärna telefonera
yay vill yair'-nĕ tele-foh-neh'-rĕ	*yi ŏn'-sker at tele-fŏh-nĕh'-rĕ*	*yā vill yair-nă tĕlĕ-fo-nĕh'-ră*

Telephone directory.

Telefonkatalog	Telefonbog	Telefonkatalog
tele-fohn'-kat-ah-lawg	*tele-fohn'-bow*	*tĕlĕ-fon'-kăt-tă-lawg'*

Hello.

Hallo	Hallo	Hallå
hah-loh	*hah-loh'*	*ha-law*

Norwegian	*Danish*	*Swedish*

Who is speaking?

Hvem taler jeg med?	Hvem taler jeg med?	Vem talar jag med?
vehm tah'-ter yay meh	*vehm tah'-ler yi meth*	*vēm tā-lär yā mēh*

This is ...

Dette er ...	De taler med ...	Detta är ...
det-tĕ air ...	*dee tah'-ler meth ...*	*dĕttä ēh ...*

May I speak to?

Kan jeg få tale med?	Må jeg få lov at tale med?	Kan jag få tala med?
kăn yay faw tah'-lĕ meh	*maw yi faw lohv at tah'-lĕ meth*	*kan yā faw tā-lä mēh*

A telephone call.

En telefonsamtale	En telefonsamtale	Ett telefonsamtal
ehn tele-fohn'-säm-tah-lĕ	*in tele-fohn'-sam-tāh-lĕ*	*ett tĕlĕ-fon'-sämm-tāl*

Telephone, Telephone box.

Telefon, Telefonkiosk	Telefon, Telefonboks	Telefon, Telefonkiosk
tele-fohn', tele-fohn'-kiosk	*tele-fohn', tele-fohn'-box*	*tĕlĕ-fon', tĕlĕ-fon'-kiosk*

Operator.

Frøken	Telefondame	Telefonfröken
frö-ken	*tele-fohn'-dah-me*	*tĕlĕ-fon'-frö'-kĕn*

Engaged.

Opptatt	Optaget	Upptaget
opp-tătt	*up'-tāh-et*	*opp'-tā-gĕt*

You're through.

De får	Klar	Ni får
dee fawr	*klahr*	*nee fawr*

You gave me the wrong number.

De ga meg feil nummer	De gav mig et forkert nummer	Ni gav mig fel nummer
dee gah may fayl nŏŏm'-mer	*dee gahv my it for-kchrt' nŏŏm'-mer*	*nee gäv may fēhl noom'-mer*

I shall ring later.

Jeg ringer senere	Jeg ringer senere	Jag ringer senare
yay ring-er seh'-ne-rĕ	*yi ring'-er seh'-ne-rĕ*	*yā ring-er sēh-nä-rĕ*

Norwegian	Danish	Swedish

Will you give me the number?

Vil de gi meg nummeret?	Vil De være venlig at give mig nummeret?	Vill ni ge mig numret?
vill dee yee may nōōm'-me-rĕ	*vil dee vaire ven'-lee at gee'-ve my nōōm'-me-ret*	*vill nee yĕh may nōōm'-ret*

Ring me up.

Ring meg	Ring mig op	Ring mig
ring may	*ring my up*	*ring may*

Telegrams.

Telegrammer	Telegrammer	Telegram
tele-grăm'-mer	*tele-gram'-mer*	*tele-gram'*

I want to send a telegram.

Jeg vil gjerne sende et telegram	Jeg vil gerne sende et telegram	Jag vill skicka ett telegram
yay vill yair'-nĕ sen'-nĕ ett tele-grăm'	*yi vill gair'-ne sen'-nĕ it tele-gram'*	*yă vill shĭck'-ka ett tele-gram'*

Trunk call.

Rikstelefon	Rigstelefon	Rikssamtal
ricks'-tele-fohn	*rees'-tele-fohn*	*riks-săm-tāl'*

TRAVELLING
ARRIVING

What station is this?

Hvilken stasjon er dette?	Hvilken station er dette?	Vilken station är detta?
vill-ken stah-shohn' air det-tĕ	*vil-ken stăh-shōhn' air det'-te*	*vil-kĕn stă-shohn' ĕh dĕttă*

How long does the train stop?

Hvor lenge stopper toget?	Hvor længe holder toget?	Hur länge står tåget?
vohr leng-ĕ stop-per taw-get	*vor laing'-ĕh hol'-ler toh-ĕt*	*hoor leng-ĕ stawr taw'-gĕt*

Norwegian	Danish	Swedish

B

Can I get out?

| Kan jeg gå ut? | Kan jeg stå ut? | Kan jag gå av? |
| *kăn yay gaw oot* | *kan yi staw ooth* | *kăn yā gaw āv* |

Have I time to go to the refreshment room?

| Har jeg tid til å gå til restauranten? | Har jeg tid til at gå hen til buffeten? | Hinner jag gå till restaurangen? |
| *hahr yay teed till aw gaw till res-too-rang'-ĕn* | *har yi teeth til at gaw hen til bü-feh'-en* | *hinner yā gaw till restau-rangen* |

Where is the refreshment room?

| Hvor er restauranten? | Hvor er buffeten? | Var är restaurangen? |
| *vohr air res-too-rang'-en* | *vor air bü-feh'-en* | *vär ēh restau-rangen* |

Two cups of coffee, please.

| To kopper kaffe, takk | Jeg vil gerne have to kopper kaffe | Två kaffe, tack |
| *toh kop-per kăf'-fĕ, tăkk* | *yi vill ger'-ne hah toh kup'-per kăhf'-fĕ* | *tvaw kăf-fĕ, tăck* |

Is the train late?

| Er toget forsinket? | Er toget forsinket? | Är tåget försenat? |
| *air taw-get for-sink-ĕt* | *air toh-et for-seen'-ket* | *ēh taw'-gĕt för-sēhn'-ăt* |

Tickets, please.

| Billetter, takk | Billetter, tak | Får jag be om biljetterna |
| *bil-let'-ter, tăkk* | *bil-let'-ter tăhk* | *fawr yā bēh om bill-yĕt'-tĕr-nă* |

I want a taxi.

| Jeg vil gjerne ha en drosje | Jeg vil gerne have en taxa | Jag vill gärna ha en taxi |
| *yay vill yair'-nĕ hah ehn drosh'-ĕ* | *yi vil ger'-ne hah in tăx'-ăh* | *yā vill yair-nă hā en tăxi* |

How far is it ...?

Hvor langt er det ...?	Hvor langt er det ...?	Hur långt är det ...?
vohr lahngt air deh ...	*vor langht air deh ...*	*hoor longt ēh dēh ...*
Norwegian	Danish	Swedish

CHANGING TRAINS

Must I change trains?

Behøver jeg bytte tog?	Behøver jeg at skifte tog?	Behöver jag byta tåg?
beh-hö'-ver yay büt-tĕ tawg	*beh-hö'-ver yi at skeef'-te toh*	*bĕh-hö'-vĕr yä bü-tä tawg*

Where must I change?

Hvor må jeg bytte tog?	Hvor skal jeg skifte?	Var ska jag byta?
vohr maw yay büt-tĕ tawg	*vor skal yi skeef'-te*	*vär skä yä bü'-tä*

Is there a good connection?

Er der en god forbindelse?	Er der en god forbindelse?	Finns det en bra förbindelse?
air dair ehn goh for-bin'-nel-sĕ	*air dair in goth for-bin'-nel-se*	*finns dēh en brä fŏr-bln'-dĕl-sĕ*

From the same station?

Fra den samme stasjon?	Fra den samme station?	Från samma station?
frah den säm'-mĕ stah-shohn'	*frah den sam'-me stäh-shōhn'*	*frawn säm-mä stä-shohn'*

How long have I to wait?

Hvor lenge må jeg vente?	Hvor længe skal jeg vente?	Hur länge behöver jag vänta?
vohr leng-ĕ maw yay ven'-tĕ	*vor laing'-eh skal yt ven'-te*	*hoor lenge bĕh-hö'-vĕr yä vĕn-tä*

Is there a through train to . . .?

Er der direkte tog til . . .?	Er der et gennem-gående tog til . . .?	Finns det ett direkt tåg till . . .?
air dair dee-rĕk'-tĕ tawg till	*air dair it gehn'-nem-gaw-ĕh-nĕ toh till*	*finns dēh ett dir-ekt' tawg till*

Does the train go to . . .?

Går toget til . . .?	Går toget til . . .?	Går tåget till . . .?
gawr taw-get till . . .	*gawr toh-ĕt till . . .*	*gawr taw'-gĕt till . . .*

Does it stop at . . .?

Stopper det på . . .?	Stopper det i . . .?	Stannar det vid . . .?
stop-per deh paw . . .	*stop'-per deh ee . . .*	*stän-när dēh veed . . .*

Norwegian	Danish	Swedish

Does the train pass through . . . ?

Går toget forbi . . . ?	Kører toget	Passerar tåget
gawr taw-get for-bee . . .	gennem . . . ?	genom . . . ?
	köʹ-rer tohʹ-ĕt	*păssēhʹ-rär tawʹ-gĕt*
	gehnʹ-nem . . .	*yēhʹ-nom . . .*

Is the train for . . . in?

Er toget til . . . inne?	Er toget til . . . inde?	Är tåget till . . . inne?
air taw-get till . . . in-ne	*air tohʹ-ĕt till . . . inʹ-ne*	*ēh tawʹ-gĕt till . . . in-ne*

Is there a dining-car?

Er der spisevogn?	Er der en spisevogn?	Finns det en
air dair speeʹ-se-vawgn	*air dair in speeʹ-se-vawn*	restaurangvagn?
		finns dēh en
		restau-rangʹ-vangn

DEPARTING

Which is the way to the station?

Hvordan kommer man til stasjonen?	Hvordan kommer man til stationen?	Hur kommer man till stationen?
vohr-dan komʹ-mer măn till stah-shohnʹ-ĕn	*vor-danʹ komʹ-mer man til stah-shōhʹ-nen*	*hoor komʹ-mer man till stă-shohʹ-nen*

When does the train for —— leave?

Når går toget til . . . ?	Hvornår går toget til . . . ?	När går tåget till . . . ?
nawr gawr taw-get till . . .	*vor-nawrʹ gawr tohʹ-ĕt til . . .*	*nair gawr tawʹ-gĕt till . . .*

From which platform does the train go?

Hvilken plattform går toget fra?	Hvilken perron går toget fra?	Från vilken plattform går tåget?
villʹ-ken plăttʹ-form gawr taw-get frah	*vilʹ-ken pair-rongʹ gawr tohʹ-ĕt frăh*	*frawn vil-ken platt-form gawr tawʹ-gĕt*

Which is the way to platform number . . . ?

Hvordan kommer man til plattform nummer . . . ?	Hvordan kommer man til perron nummer . . . ?	Hur kommer man till plattform nummer . . . ?
vohrʹ-dăn kom-mer măn till plăttʹ-form nŏŏmʹ-mer . . .	*vor-danʹ komʹ-mer man til pair-rongʹ nŏŏmʹ-mer . . .*	*hoor komʹ-mer man till plăttʹ-förm nŏŏmʹ-mer . . .*

Norwegian	Danish	Swedish

Where is the booking-office?

Hvor et billettkontoret?	Hvor er billet kontoret?	Var är biljettkontoret?
vohr air bil-let' *kon-toh'-rĕ*	*vor air bil-let'* *kon-tōh'-ret*	*vär ēh* *bill-yĕtt'-kŏn-toh'-ret*

Is it an express?

Er det et ekspress tog?	Er det et ekspres tog?	Är det ett expresståg (snälltag)?
air deh ett express tawg	*air deh it express toh*	*ēh dēh ett express-tawg (snell-tawg)*

Is there a supplementary charge?

Er der tilleggspris?	Er der et eksprestogs-tillæg?	Behövs det tilläggsbiljett?
air dair til'-legs-prees	*air dair it express'-tohs'-til-leg*	*beh-hövs' dēh till'-lĕggs-bill-yett*

Is this ticket valid for an express?

Gjelder denne billetten til et ekspresst og?	Er denne billet gyldig til et ekspres tog?	Gäller denna biljett till ett expresståg?
Yel-ler den'-nĕ bil-let'-ten till ett express tawg	*air den-ne bil-let' gül'-dee til it express'-toh*	*yĕl-lĕr dĕnnă bill-yett' till ett ĕxprĕss'-tawg*

Is there a first, second, third class?

Er der første, annen, tredje klasse?	Er der første, anden, tredie klasse?	Finns det första, andra, tredje klass?
air dair förs-tĕ, ähn'-nen, tray'-ĕ klas'-sĕ	*air dair för'-ste, ahn'-nen, tray'-the klas'-se*	*finns dēh för'-stă, än'-dră, trēhd-ye kläss*

Is there a dining-car, sleeping-car, on the train?

Er der spisevogn, sovevogn, på toget?	Er der en spisevogn, sovevogn, på toget?	Finns det en restaurangvagn, sovvagn, på tåget?
air dair spee'-se-vawgn, saw'-ve-vawgn, paw taw-get	*air dair in spee'-se-vawn, soh'-ve-vawn, paw toh'-ĕt*	*finns dēh en restaurang'-vängn, sawv-vängn, paw taw'-gĕt*

In the front, middle, rear of the train.

Foran, midt i, bak i toget	Forand, i midten, bagi toget	Framme i, mitt i, bak i tåget
for'-än, mit ee', bahk ee' taw-get	*for'-ahn, ee mit'-ten, bagh'-ee toh'-ĕt*	*fram-mĕ ee, mitt ee, bāk ee taw'-gĕt*

Norwegian	*Danish*	*Swedish*

Can I reserve a seat, sleeper?

Kan jeg få reservert en sitteplass, soveplass?
kăn yay faw reh-sair-vehrt' ehn sit'-tĕ-plass, saw'-ve-plass

Kan jeg reservere en plads, køje?
kan yi reh-sair-veh'-reh in plăhs, koy'-ĕh

Kan jag reservera en plats, sovplats?
kăn yă rĕ-sĕr-vēh'-ră en plats, sawv-plats

I want a smoking, non-smoking, compartment.

Jeg vil gjerne ha en røkekupé, ikke røkekupé.
Yay vill yair'-nĕ hah ehn rŏ'-kĕ-koo-pé, ick'-kĕ rŏ'-kĕ-koo-pé

Jeg vil gerne have en ryger, ikke-ryger
yi vil gair'-ne hah in rü'-air, ick'-ke-rü'-air

Jag vill gärna ha en rökkupé, icke rökkupé
yă vill yair-nă hă en rök-kŏo-pé, icke rök-kŏo-pé

Are there any seats left?

Er der noen ledige plasser?
air dair noh-en leh'-dee-ĕ plăs'-ser

Er der nogen pladser tilbage?
air dair noh'-en plăh'-ser til-bahg'-ĕh

Finns det några platser kvar?
finns dĕh naw'-gră plăt-sĕr kvăr

Facing, back to, the engine.

I kjøreretningen, mot kjøreretningen
ee chŏ'-rĕ-ret-ning-en, moht chŏ'-rĕ-ret-ning-en

I køreretningen, imod køreretningen
ee kŏ'-rĕ-ret-ning-en, ee-moth' kŏ'-rĕ-ret-ning-en

Framlänges, baklänges
frămm'-lĕng-ĕs, bak-lĕng-ĕs

A window seat.

En vindusplass
ehn vin'-doos-plăss

En vindus plads
in vin'-doos plăhss

En fönsterplats
en föns-ter-plăts

First, second, third class return to . . .

Første, annen, tredje, klasse tur retur til . . .
ŏrs'-tĕ ahn'-nen, tray'-ĕ, klăs-sĕ toor' reh-toor' till . . .

Første, anden, tredie klasse retur til . . .
fŏr'-ste, ahn'-nen, tray'-ye klăs'-sĕ reh-toor' til . . .

En första, andra, tredje klass tur och retur till . . .
en fŏr'-stă, an'-dră, trĕhd-yĕ, klăss toor ock rĕh-tōor till . . .

Single to, two singles to . . .

En billett, to billetter til . . .
ehn bil-let', toh bil-let'-ter till . . .

Enkelt, to enkelte, til . . .
in'-kelt, toh in'-kel-te, til . . .

Enkel till, Två enkla till . . .
ĕnkel till, tvaw ĕnklă till . . .

| Norwegian | Danish | Swedish |

Please write down the price.

Norwegian	Danish	Swedish
Vær så vennlig å skrive ned prisen	Vær venlig at skrive prisen ned	Var snäll och skriv priset
vair saw ven'-lee aw skree-vĕ nehd' pree'-sen	*vair ven'-lee at skree'-ve pree'-sen neth*	*vär snell ock skreev pree'-sĕt*

Where can I get a platform ticket?

Hvor kan jeg få en plattform billett?	Hvor kan jeg købe en perron billet?	Var kan jag få en perrongbiljett?
vohr kän jey faw ehn plätt'-form bil-let'	*vor kan jey kö'-be in pair-rong' bil-let'*	*vär kän yä faw en per-rong'-bill-yett'*

Where is the guard, attendant?

Hvor er konduktøren?	Hvor er konduktøren?	Var är konduktören?
vohr air kon-dŏŏk-tö'-ren	*vor air kon-dook-tö'-ren*	*vär ēh kon-dook-tö'-ren*

Can I have an upper, lower, berth?

Kan jeg få øverste, nederste, køye?	Jeg vil gerne have en over, under, køje	Kan jag få en överkoj, underkoj?
kän yay faw öv'-er-stĕ, neh'-der stĕ, köy-uh	*yi vil gair'-ne hah in oh'-er, ŏŏn' ner, koy oh*	*kän yä faw en ö'-ver-koy, oon-der-koy*

I should like a pillow, a rug.

Jeg vil gjerne ha en pute, et teppe	Jeg vil gerne have en pude, et tæppe	Jag skulle vilja ha en kudde, en filt
Yay vill yair'-nĕ hah ehn poo-tĕ, ett tep'-pĕ	*yi vil gair'-ne hah en poo'-the, it taip'-pe*	*yä skŏŏl'-lĕ vil-la hä ĕn kood-dĕ, ĕn filt*

What time is breakfast, lunch, tea, dinner?

Når er frokost, lunch, te, middag?	Hvornår serveres der morgenmad, frokost, the, middag?	Hur dags är det frukost, lunch, te, middag?
nawr air froh'-kost, loonsh, teh, mid'-dahg	*vor-nawr' sair-veh'-res dair mor'-en-math, froh'-kosst, teh, mee'-däh*	*hoor dägs ēh dēh froo'-kost, lunch, tēh, middä*

When do we arrive?

Når er vi fremme?	Hvornår ankommer vi?	När är vi framme?
nawr air vee frĕm'-mĕ	*vor-nawr' ahn'-kom-mer vee*	*nair eh vee fram-mĕ*

Norwegian	Danish	Swedish

Wake me at . . .

Vekk meg klokken . . .	Væk mig klokken . . .	Väck mig klockan . . .
vek may klock'-ken . .	*vaik my klock'-ken . . .*	*veck may klock'-ăn . .*

I should like tea, coffee, in the morning.

Jeg vil gjerne ha te, kaffe, i morgen tidlig	Jeg vil gerne have the, kaffe, om morgenen	Jag skulle vilja ha te, kaffe, på morgonen
yay vill yair'-ne hah teh, kaf'-fĕ, ee mor-en teed'-lee	*yi vil gair'-ne hah teh, kaffe, um mor'-nen*	*ya skŏol'-le vil-lă hā tĕh, kăf-fĕ, paw morr'-ŏ-nen*

LUGGAGE

Porter.

Baerer	Drager	Bärare
bair'-er	*drah'-er*	*bair'-ăr-ĕ*

Please take my luggage.

Vær så vennlig å ta min bagasje	Vær venlig at tage min bagage	Var snäll och tag mitt bagage
vair saw ven'-lee aw tah min bah-gah'-sheh	*vair ven'-lee at tah meen băh-gāh'-sheh*	*vār snell ock tăg mitt bă-gāsh'*

Be careful with this case.

Vær forsiktig med denne kofferten	Pas på denne koffert	Var försiktig om den här väskan
vair for-sick'-tee meh den-ne kohf'-fert-en	*pas paw den'-ne kohf'-fĕrt*	*vār för-sik'-tig omm dĕn hair vĕskan*

I have some heavy luggage too.

Jeg har noe tung bagasje også	Jeg har også noget tungt bagage	Jag har en del tungt bagage också
yay hahr noh-ĕ toong bah-gah'-sheh os-saw	*yi hahr aw'-saw noh'-et toonkt bah-gah'-sheh*	*yā hār en dĕhl toongt bă-gāsh' ock'-saw*

Four pieces.

Fire kolli	Fire stykker	Fyra kolli
fee'-rĕ kol'-lee	*fee'-re stück'-kĕr*	*fü'-ră kol'-lee*

Where is the left-luggage office?

Hvor er oppbevaringen?	Hvor er garderoben?	Var är resgodsinlämningen?
vohr air op'-beh-vahr-ing-en	*vor air gahr-dĕ-rōh'-ben*	*vār ĕh rĕhs'-goods-in-lemn'-ing-ĕn*

Norwegian	*Danish*	*Swedish*

Where can I register the luggage?

Hvor kan jeg registrere bagasjen?	Hvor kan jeg indskrive bagagen?	Var kan jag polletera bagaget?
vohr kăn yay reh-gee-streh'-rĕ bah-gah'-shehn	*vor kan yi in'-skree-vĕ băh-găh'-shen*	*văr kăn yă pol-le-tēh'-ră bă-gāsh'-ĕt*

Can I take these bags in the compartment with me?

Kan jeg ta disse reisevesker med meg i kupéen?	Kan jeg tage disse kofferter med mig i kupeen?	Kan jag ta de här väskorna med mig in i kupén?
kăn yay tah dis-sĕ ray'-sĕ-vehs-ker meh may ee koo-pe'-en	*kan yi tah dees'-se kohf'-fert-er meth my ee koo-pēh'-en*	*kan yă tă dēh hair ves'-ker-nă mēh may in ee koo-pĕn*

Put them here.

Sett dem her	Stil dem her	Ställ dem här
set dem hair	*still dem hear*	*stĕll dem hair*

Trunk, suitcase, briefcase, parcel.

Reisekoffert, koffert, mappe, pakke	Rejse-koffert, taske, mappe, pakke	Koffert, väska, portfölj, paket
ray'-se-kohf-fert, kohf'-fert, măhp-pĕ, păhk-kĕ	*ry'-se-kohf-fert, tahs'-kĕ, mahp'-pĕ, pahk'-kĕ*	*kof'-fert, ves'-kă, port-följ', pă-kēht'*

I want to insure my luggage.

Jeg vil gjerne assurere min bagasje	Jeg ønsker at forsikre min bagage	Jag vill försäkra mitt bagage
yay vill yair'-nĕ as-soo-re'-rĕ meen bah-gah'-sheh	*yi ön'-sker at for-sick'-rĕ meen bah-găh'-sheh*	*yă vill för-saik'-ră mitt bă-gāsh'*

I shall be back soon.

Jeg kommer snart tilbake	Jeg kommer snart tilbage	Jag kommer snart tillbaka
yay kom'-mer snahrt till-bah'-ke	*yi kom'-mĕr snahrt til-bahg'-ĕh*	*yă kom'-mer snărt till-bā'-kă*

What does it cost?

Hvor mye koster det?	Hvad koster det?	Vad kostar det?
vohr mü-ĕ kos'-ter deh	*vath kos'-ter deh*	*văd koss'-tar dēh*

Norwegian	Danish	Swedish

It is not worth while.

Det er ikke bryet verd	Det er det ikke værd	Det är det inte värt
deh air ick'-kĕ brü'-ett vaird	*deh air deh ick'-ke vair*	*dēh ēh dēh in'-tĕ vairt*

Here is the receipt.

Her er kvitteringen	Her er kviteringen	Här är kvittot
hair air kvit-teh'-ring-en	*hear air kvee-tēh'-ring-en*	*hair ēh kvit'-tot*

Where can I find you?

Hvor kan jeg finne Dem?	Hvor kan jeg finde Dem?	Var kan jag finna er?
vohr kăn yay fin'-nĕ dem	*vor kan yi fin'-ne dem*	*vār kan yā fin-nă ēhr*

Wait for me here.

Vent på meg her	Vent på mig her	Vänta på mig här
vent paw may hair	*vent paw my hear*	*ven'-tă paw may hair*

I am going to the buffet.

Jeg går til restauranten	Jeg går ind i buffeten	Jag går till restauranten
yay gawr till res-too-rang'-en	*yi gawr in ee bü-feh'-en*	*yā gawr till restau-rangen*

I shall wait for you on the platform, at the entrance.

Jeg venter på Dem på plattformen, ved inngangen	Jeg venter på Dem på perronen, ved indgangen	Jag väntar på er på perrongen, vid ingången
yay ven'-ter paw dem paw plătt'-form-en veh in'-găng-en	*yi ven'-ter paw dem paw pair-rong'-en, veth in'-gang-en*	*yā ven-tăr paw ēhr paw pĕr-rong'-en, veed in'-gŏng-en*

AT THE LEFT-LUGGAGE

I wish to leave these things here.

Jeg vil gjerne få disse tingene oppbevart her	Jeg ønsker at efterlade disse ting her	Jag skulle vilja lämna de här sakerna här
yay vill yair'-nĕ faw dis'-sĕ ting'-en-ĕ op'-beh-vährt hair	*yi ŏn'-sker at efter'-lăh-the dees'-se ting hear*	*ya skŏol'-lĕ vil-la lem'-nă dēh hair sā-ker-nă hair*

This is not mine.

Dette er ikke min	Dette er ikke min	Detta är inte min
det-tĕ air ick'-kĕ min	*det'-te air ick'-ke meen*	*detta ēh in'-tĕ min*

Norwegian	Danish	Swedish

Three cases, a raincoat.

Tre kofferter, en regnfrakke	Tre kofferter, en regnfrakke	Tre väskor, en regn-rock
treh kohf'-fer-ter, ehn rayn'-fråhk-kĕ	*tray kohf'-fer-ter, in ryn'-fråhk-kĕ*	*trēh ves-kor, en rengn-rock*

Those are my things over there.

De tingene der borte er mine	Det er mine ting derovre	Det är mina saker där borta
dee ting'-en-nĕ dair bohr-tĕ air mee'-nĕ	*deh air mee'-ne teeng dair'-oh-rĕ*	*dēh ēh mee'-nă sā-ker dair bor'-tă*

There is one suitcase missing.

Der mangler en koffert	Der mangler een koffert	Det fattas en väska
dair mahng'-ler ehn kohf'-fert	*dair mangh'-ler ayn kohf'-fert*	*dēh făt-tăs en ves-kă*

Where is my umbrella?

Hvor er paraplyen min?	Hvor er min paraply?	Var är min paraply?
vohr air pah-rah-plü'-en min	*vor air min påh-răh-plü'*	*văr ēh min păr-ră-plü'*

That is mine over there.

Den der borte er min	Det er min derovre	Den där borta är min
den dair bohr'-tĕ air min	*deh air meen dair'-oh-rĕ*	*dĕn dair bor'-tă ēh min*

I want to take out one suitcase.

Jeg vil gjerne ta ut en koffert	Jeg ønsker at tage een koffert væk	Jag vill ta ut en väska
yay vill yair'-nĕ tah oot ehn kohf'-ert	*yi ön'-sker at tah ayn kohf'-fert vaik*	*yā vill tā ōot en ves'-kă*

The remainder can stay.

Resten kan være	Resten kan blive	Resten kan stanna kvar
res'-ten kăn vai-rĕ	*rahs'-ten kan blee'-ve*	*res'-ten kăn stän-nă kvăr*

How much do you charge for each item?

Hvor mye koster det for hvert kolli?	Hvor meget tager De for hver ting?	Hur mycket tar ni per kolli?
vohr mü-eh kos-ter deh for vairt kol'-lee	*vor my'-et tahr dee for vair teeng*	*hōōr mückĕ tār nee pĕr kol'-lee*

Norwegian	Danish	Swedish

Do I pay now or when I collect the things?

Skal jeg betale nå eller når jeg henter tingene?	Betaler jeg nu eller når jeg henter tingene?	Betalar jag nu eller när jag hämtar sakerna?
skăl yay beh-tah'-lĕ naw' ell-er nawr yay hen'-ter ting-en-ĕh	*beh-tah'-ler yi noo ell'-er nawr yi hen'-ter teeng'-ĕh-nĕ*	*bĕh-tă'-lăr yă nöö ĕllĕr nair yă hem'-tăr să-ker-nă*

This case is not locked.

Denne kofferten er ikke låst	Denne taske er ikke låset	Den här väskan är inte låst
den-ne kohf'-er-ten air ick'-kĕ lawst	*den'-ne tah'-ske air ick'-ke law'-set*	*dĕn hair ves-kăn ĕh in'-tĕ lawst*

Please keep an eye on my things.

Vær så vennlig å holde et øye med tingene mine	Vær venlig at se efter mine ting	Var snäll och håll ett öga på mina saker
vair saw ven'-lee aw hol'-lĕ ett ö-yeh meh ting-en-ĕh mee'-nĕ	*vair ven'-lee at seh efter mee'-ne teeng*	*văr snĕll ock holl ett ö-gă paw mee-nă să-ker*

AT THE STATION, GENERAL

Enquiry office.

Informasjons kontor	Informations kontor	Upplysningsbyrå
in-for-mah-shohns' kon-tohr'	*in-for-măh-shohns' kon-tohr'*	*oŏp'-lüs-nings-bü'-raw*

Booking-office.

Billettkontor	Billet salg	Biljettkontor
bil-let'-kon-tohr'	*bil-let' salgh*	*bill-yett'-kon-tohr'*

Left-luggage.

Oppbevaring	Garderobe	Resgodsinlämning
op'-beh-vahr-ing	*găhr-de-röh'-bĕ*	*rēhs'-goods-in-lem'-ning*

Waiting-room.

Venteværelse	Venteværelse	Väntsal
ven'-te-vai-rel-sĕ	*ven'-te-vai-rel-sĕ*	*vĕnt-săl*

Lost Property Office.

Hittegodskontor	Hittegodskontor	Hittegodskontor
hit'-te-gohds-kon-tohr'	*hit'-te-gaws-kon-tohr'*	*hit'-tĕ-goods-kon-tohr'*

Norwegian	Danish	Swedish

Stationmaster.

Stasjonsmester	Stationsforstander	Stationsinspektor
stah-shohns'-mes-ter	*stah-shohns'-for-stahn'-ner*	*stä-shoons'-in-spek-tohr'*

Railway official.

Jernbanefunksjonær	Jernbanefunktionær	Järnvägstjänsteman
yairn'-bah-nĕ-foonk-shŏ-nair'	*yairn'-bah-nĕ-foonk-shŏ-nair'*	*yairn'-vaigs-chĕns-tĕ-män*

Ladies, Gentlemen.

Damer, Herrer	Damer, Herrer	Damer, Herrar
dah'-mer, hĕrr-ĕr	*dah'-mer, hair'-rĕ*	*dä'-mer, hĕr'-răr*

Bookstall.

Aviskiosk	Aviskiosk	Tidningskiosk
ah-vees'-kiosk	*ah-vees'-kee-osk*	*teed'-nings-kiosk*

Have you any English papers, books?

Har De noen engelske aviser,bøker?	Har De nogle engelske aviser, bøger?	Har ni några engelska tidningar, böcker?
hahr dee noh'-en ehng'-elsk-ĕ ah-vee'-ser, bŏ'-ker	*hahr dee noh'-le ehng'-el-ske äh-vee'-ser, bŏ'-ĕr*	*har nee naw-grä ehng'-el-skä teed'-ningar, böck'-ĕr*

These are old.

Disse er gamle	Disse er gamle	De här är gamla
dis'-sĕ air găhm-lĕ	*dees'-se air gahm'-lĕ*	*dĕh hair ĕh găm'-lä*

Where can I post a letter?

Hvor kan jeg poste et brev?	Hvor kan jeg poste et brev?	Var kan jag posta ett brev?
vohr kăn yay pos'-tĕ ett brehv	*vor kan yi poss'-te it brev*	*vär kăn yä poss'-tä ett brĕhv*

Have you any postcards?

Har De noen brevkort?	Har De postkort?	Har ni brevkort?
hahr dee noh-en brehv'-kort	*hahr dee posst'-kort*	*här nee brĕhv'-kort*

Where can I get stamps?

Hvor kan jeg kjøpe frimerker?	Hvor kan jeg købe frimærker?	Var kan jag få frimärken?
vohr kăn yay chö-pĕ free'-mehr-ker	*vor kan yi kŏ'-be free'-mair-ker*	*vär kăn yä faw free'-mĕr-kĕn*

Norwegian	Danish	Swedish

Where can I send a telegram?

Norwegian	Danish	Swedish
Hvor kan jeg sende et telegram?	Hvor kan jeg sende et telegram?	Var kan jag skicka ett telegram?
vohr kăn yay sen'-nĕ ett tele-grăhm'	*vor kan yi sen'-ne it tele-grăhm'*	*văr kăn yă shick'-kă ett tele-grăm'*

TIME-TABLES

Please can I have a time-table?

Norwegian	Danish	Swedish
Kan jeg få en togtabell?	Kan jeg få en togplan?	Skulle jag kunna få en tidtabell?
kăn yay faw ehn tawg'-tah-bell	*kan yi faw in toh'-plahn*	*skŏŏl'-lĕ yă kŏŏn'-nă faw en teed'-tă-bell*

Can you show me how to use this time-table?

Norwegian	Danish	Swedish
Kan De vise meg hvordan jeg skal bruke denne togtabellen?	Kan De vise mig hvordan jeg skal bruge denne togplan?	Kan ni visa mig hur man använder den här tidtabellen?
kăn dee vee-sĕ may vohr-dăn yay skăl broo'-kĕ den'-nĕ tawg'-tă-bell-ĕn	*kan dee vee'-sĕ my vor-dan' yi skal broo'-ĕh den'-nĕ toh'-plahn*	*kăn nee vee'-să may hŏŏr măn ăn'-ven-dĕr den hair teed'-tă-bell'-ĕn*

What does this mean?

Norwegian	Danish	Swedish
Hva betyr dette?	Hvad betyder dette?	Vad betyder detta?
vah beh-tür' det'-tĕ	*vath beh-tü'-ther det'-te*	*văd bĕh-tü'-dĕr dĕttă*

Weekdays only, Saturdays, Sundays, Holidays.

Norwegian	Danish	Swedish
Bare hverdager, lørdager, søndager, ferietiden	Kun hverdage, lørdag, søndag, ferier	Endast vardagar, lördagar, söndagar, helgdagar
bah-rĕ vair'-dah-ger, lör'-dah-ger, sön'-dah-ger, feh'-ree-ĕh-tee-den	*koon vair'-dăh-ĕh, lör'-dăh, sön'-dăh, feh'-ree-ĕr*	*ĕn-dăst văr'-dă-găr, lör-dă-găr, sön-dă-găr, hell'-dă-găr*

ON THE TRAIN

Is this seat free?

Norwegian	Danish	Swedish
Er denne plassen ledig?	Er denne plads ledig?	Är den här platsen ledig?
air den'-nĕ plăss'-en leh'-dee	*air den'-ne plăhs leh'-thee*	*ĕh dĕn hair plăt'-sĕn lĕh'-dig*

Norwegian	Danish	Swedish

That seat is taken.

Den plassen er opptatt *den' pläss'-en air op'-tätt*	Den plads er optaget *den plähs air up'-täh-et*	Den platsen är upptagen *den plät'-sĕn ĕh ōōp'-tä-gĕn*

Put my luggage on the rack, under the seat.

Legg bagasjen min i nettet, under setet *leg bah-gah'-shen min ee net'-ĕt, ōōn'-der sĕh-tĕ*	Vær venlig at putte min bagage, i nettet, under sædet *vair ven'-lee at put'-te meen bäh-gäh'-sheh ee net'-tet, ōōn'-ner sai-thet*	Sätt mitt bagage på hyllan, under bänken *sett mitt bä-gäsh' paw hül-län, ōōn'-dĕr bĕnk-ĕn*

Excuse me (may I pass).

Unnskyld, (kan jeg komme forbi?) *ōōn-shül, (kăn yay kom'-mĕ for-bee)*	Undskyld, (må jeg komme forbi?) *ōōn'-sküll, (maw yi kom'-me for-bee')*	Förlåt (får jag komma förbi) *för-lawt' (fawr yä kom-må för-bee')*

I am sorry to disturb you.

Unnskyld at jeg forstyrrer Dem *ōōn-shül' at yay for-stür'-er dem*	Undskyld jeg forstyrrer Dem *ōōn'-sküll yi for-stür'-re dem*	Förlåt att jag stör er *för-lawt att yä stör ĕhr*

Are these things in your way?

Er disse tingene i veien for Dem? *air dis'-sĕ ting'-en-ĕh ee vay'-ĕn for dem*	Er disse ting i vejen for Dem? *air dees'-se teeng ee vy'-en for dem*	Är de här sakerna i vägen för er? *ĕh dĕh hair sä-kĕr-nä ee vaig'-ĕn för ĕhr*

It's quite all right.

Det er helt i orden *deh air hĕhlt ee ŏr'-den*	Det er helt i orden *det air hehlt ee ŏhr'-den*	Det går utmärkt *dĕh gawr ōōt'-mĕrkt*

It is hot, cold.

Det er varmt, kaldt *deh air vahrmt, kält*	Det er varmt, koldt *deh air vahrmt, kolt*	Det är varmt, kallt *dĕh ĕh vărmt, källt*

Can you give me a light?

Kan De låne meg en fyrstikk? *kăn dee law'-nĕ may ehn für'-stick*	Kan De låne mig en tændstik? *kan dee law'-ne my in ten'-stick*	Skulle ni kunna ge mig en tändsticka? *skōōl'-lĕ nee kōōn'-nä yĕh may en tend'-stickă*

Norwegian	Danish	Swedish

May I borrow your newspaper?

Kan jeg få låne avisen Deres?	Må jeg låne Deres avis?	Får jag låna er tidning?
kăn yay faw law'-nĕ ah-vees'-en dēr-ĕs	*maw yi law'-ne deres äh-vees'*	*fawr yā law-nă ēhr teed'-ning*

Would you like to look at the paper?

Har De lyst å se avisen?	Vil De læse avisen?	Vill ni titta på tidningen?
hahr dee lüst aw seh ah-vees'-en	*vil dee laise äh-vee'-sen*	*vill nee tĭt-tă paw teed'-ning-ĕn*

May I open the window?

Får jeg åpne vinduet?	Må jeg åbne vinduet?	Får jag öppna fönstret?
fawr yay awp'-nĕ vin'-doo-ĕh	*maw yi awp'-ne vin'-doo-et*	*fawr yā öpp-nă fön'-strĕt*

Could you shut the window, please?

Vil De være så vennlig å lukke vinduet?	Vil De være venlig at lukke vinduet?	Skulle ni vilja stänga fönstret?
vill dee vai-rĕ saw ven'-lee aw lŏŏk-kĕ vin-doo-ĕh	*vil dee vaire ven'-lee at lŏŏk'-kĕ vin'-doo-ĕt*	*skŏŏl'-lĕ nee vil-lă stengă fön'-strĕt*

The window does not close, open.

Vinduet kan ikke lukkes, åpnes	Vinduet kan ikke lukkes, åbnes	Fönstret går inte att stänga, öppna
vin'-doo-ĕh kăn ick'-kĕ lŏŏk'-kĕs, awp'-nĕs	*vin'-doo-et kan ick'-ke lŏŏk'-kes, awp'-nes*	*fön'-strĕt gawr in'-tĕ att stengă, öpp'-nă*

The door is jammed.

Dören har satt seg fast	Døren er gået i baglås	Dörren har fastnat
dö'-ren hahr sătt say făst	*dö'-ren air gaw'-et ee bagh'-laws*	*dör'-rĕn hăr făst-năt*

Do you feel a draught?

Trekker det?	Trækker det?	Drar det?
trek'-ker deh	*traik'-ker deh*	*drăr dĕh*

Is the sun troubling you?

Sjenerer solen Dem?	Generer solen Dem?	Besvärar solen er?
sheh-nēr'-ĕr soh'-len dem	*shĕh-nĕh'-rer soh'-len dem*	*bĕh-svair'-răr soh-lĕn ēhr*

Norwegian	Danish	Swedish

Please pull down the blind.

Vær så vennlig å trekke for gardinet	Vær venlig at trække gardinet ned	Var snäll och drag ned gardinen
vair saw ven'-lee aw trĕk'-kĕ for gahr-dee'-nĕ	*vair ven'-lee at traik'-kĕ gåhr-dee'-net neth*	*vår snĕll ock drå nĕhd går-dee'-nĕn*

I should like something to drink, eat.

Jeg vil gjerne ha noe å drikke, spise	Jeg vil gerne have noget at drikke, spise	Jag skulle vilja ha något att dricka, äta
yay vil yair'-nĕ hah noh-ĕ aw drik'-kĕ, spee'-sĕ	*yi vil gair'-ne hah noh'-et at drik'-kĕ, spee'-sĕ*	*ya skōōl'-lĕ vil-lå ha naw'-got att drick'-kå, ait'-tå*

How much longer is it to . . . ?

Hvor mye lengere er det til . . . ?	Hvor meget længre er det til . . . ?	Hur långt är det kvar till . . . ?
vohr mü'-ĕ lehng'-ĕr-ĕ air deh till . . .	*vor my'-et laing'-rĕ air deh til . . .*	*hōōr longt ĕh dĕh kvär till . . .*

Are we nearly there?

Er vi der nesten?	Er vi der næsten?	Är vi nästan framme?
air vee dair nes'-ten	*air vee dair nes'-ten*	*ĕh vee nes'-tän frăm'-mĕ*

Are we very late?

Er vi mye forsinket?	Er vi meget forsinket?	Är vi mycket försenade?
air vee mü-ĕ for-sink'-ĕt	*air vee my'-et for-sink'-et*	*ĕh vee mück-ĕt för-sĕh'-nă-dĕ*

We are on time.

Vi er presis	Vi er præsis	Vi är punktliga
vee air prĕh-sees'	*vee air prĕh-sees'*	*vee ĕh pŏŏnkt'-lee-gå*

Where are we now?

Hvor er vi nå?	Hvor er vi nu?	Var är vi nu?
vohr air vee naw	*vor air vee nŏŏ*	*vär ĕh vee noo*

Here is my ticket.

Her er billetten min	Her er min billet	Här är min biljett
hair air bil-let'-ten min	*hear air meen bil-let'*	*hair ĕh min bill-yĕtt'*

Norwegian	Danish	Swedish

Somebody is sitting in my place.

Der sitter noen på min plass	Der sidder nogen på min plads	Någon sitter på min plats
dair sit'-ter noh-en paw min plåss	*dair seeth'-ther noh'-en paw meen plåhs*	*naw'-gon sit-tĕr paw min plåts*

Where is the communication cord?

Hvor er nödbremsen?	Hvor er nødbremsen?	Var är nödbromsen?
vohr air nöd'-brĕhm-sen	*vor air nöth'-brĕhm-sen*	*vär ĕh nöd'-brom-sĕn*

Please put on the light.

Vær så vennlig å tenne lyset	Vær venlig at tænde lyset	Var snäll och tänd ljuset
vair saw ven'-lee aw ten'-nĕ lü'-sĕ	*vair ven'-lee at tain'-nĕ lü'-set*	*vär snell ock tend yoo'-set*

TRAVELLING BY SEA

Shipping company, Agents.

Dampskipsselskap, Agenter	Rederi, Skibsmægler	Rederi, Skeppsmäklare
dămp'-sheeps-sel-skahp, ah-gen'-ter	*reh-ther-ree', skeebs'-maih-ler*	*rĕh-dĕ-ree', shepps-maik'-lărĕ*

Can I book a passage to . . . ?

Jeg vil gjerne bestille en plass til . . . ?	Kan jeg bestille plads til . . . ?	Kan jag få beställa en biljett till . . . ?
yay vill yair'-nĕ beh-stil'-lĕ ehn plåss till . . .	*kan yi beh-stil'-lĕ plåhs til . . .*	*kăn yă faw bĕh-stĕl'-lă en bill-yett' till . . .*

First, Second, Third, Tourist class.

Første, Annen, Tredje, Turist klasse	Første, Anden, Tredie, Tourist klasse	Första, Andra, Tredje, Turistklass
förs'-tĕ, ăhn'-nen, tray'-ĕ, too-rist' klås-sĕ	*för'-ste, ahn'-nen, tray'-the, tou-rist' klås'-sĕ*	*för'-stă, ăn'-dră, trĕhd-ye, too-rist'-klăss*

Sailing, Arrival date.

Avreise, Ankomst dato	Sejl, Ankomst dato	Avgångs-, Ankomstdatum
ahv'-ray-sĕ, ăhn'-komst dah'-toh	*sail, ăhn'-komst dah'-toh*	*ăv'-gongs-, ăn'-komst-dăh'-tŏŏm*

Norwegian	Danish	Swedish

From which dock?

| Fra hvilken kai? | Fra hvilken havn? | Från vilken kaj? |
| *frah vill'-ken kähy* | *fra vil'-ken hähvn* | *frawn vil-kĕn kähy* |

At what time do we embark?

| Når må vi være ombord? | Hvornår går vi ombord? | Hur dags ska vi gå ombord? |
| *nawr maw vee vai'-rĕ om-bohr'* | *vor-nawr' gawr vee um-bohr'* | *hōōr dägs skä vee gaw omm-boord,* |

When do we sail?

| Når går båten? | Hvornår sejler vi? | Hur dags går båten? |
| *nawr gawr baw'-ten* | *vor-nawr' sigh'-ler vee* | *hōōr dägs gawr baw'-ten* |

Where do I get the tickets?

| Hvor får jeg billettene? | Hvor får jeg billetterne? | Var köper jag biljetter? |
| *vohr fawr yay bil-let'-te-nĕ* | *vor fawr yi bil-let'-ter-nĕ* | *vär chö-per yä bill-yett'-ĕr* |

Will you show me my cabin?

| Vil De vise meg min lugar? | Vil De vise mig min kahyt? | Vill ni visa mig min hytt? |
| *vill dee vee'-sĕ may min loo-gahr'* | *vil dee vee'-sĕ my meen kah-hüt'* | *vill nee vee'-sä may min hütt* |

Can I change my berth?

| Kan jeg få bytte køye? | Kan jeg få en anden køje? | Kan jag få byta koj? |
| *kän yay faw büt'-tĕ köy-ĕ* | *kan yi faw in ahn'-nen koy'-ĕh* | *kän yä faw büt'-tä koy* |

Which is the way on deck, below?

| Hvordan kommer man opp på dekket, ned? | Hvordan kommer man på dækket, nedenunder? | Hur kommer man upp på däck, ner under däck? |
| *vohr-dän kom'-mer män ŏp paw deck'-kĕ, nêhd* | *vor-dan' kom'-mer man paw deck'-ket, neh'-then-n'-ŏŏner* | *hōōr kom'-mĕr män ōŏpp paw deck, nêhr oŏn-dĕr deck* |

Where is the purser's office?

| Hvor er purserens kontor? | Hvor er hovmesterens kontor? | Var är purserns kontor? |
| *vohr air purser-ĕns kon-tohr'* | *vor air haw'-mest-rens kon-tohr'* | *vär ĕh purserns kon-tohr'* |

| Norwegian | Danish | Swedish |

Where is the dining-room, lounge, bar?

Norwegian	Danish	Swedish
Hvor er spisesalen, salongen, baren?	Hvor er spisesalonen, rygesalonen, baren?	Var är matsalen, salongen, baren?
vohr air spee'-se-sah-len, sah-long'-en, bah'-ren	*vor air spee'-se-sah-long'-en, rü'-eh-sah-long'-en, bäh'-ren*	*vär ēh mät'-sä-lĕn, sä-long-ĕn, bä-rĕn*

When does it open?

Når åpner det?	Hvornår åbner det?	När öppnas det?
nawr awp'-ner deh	*vor-nawr' awp'-ner deh*	*nair öpp-nas dēh*

I can't find my luggage.

Jeg kan ikke finne bagasjen min	Jeg kan ikke finde min bagage	Jag kan inte finna mitt bagage
yay kăn ick'-kĕ fin'-nĕ bah-gah'-shen min	*yi kan ick'-ke fin'-nĕ meen băh-gäh'-shĕh*	*yă kăn in'-tĕ fin-nă mitt bă-gäsh'*

My luggage is not all here.

All bagasjen min er ikke her	Alt min bagage er her ikke	Allt mitt bagage är inte här
ăhl bah-gah'-shen min air ick'-kĕ hair	*ăhlt meen băh-gäh'-sheh air hear ick'-ke*	*ăllt mitt bă-gäsh' ēh in'-tĕ hair*

Will you close the porthole?

Vil De lukke ko-øyet?	Vil De være venlig at lukke koøyet?	Vill ni stänga hyttgluggen?
vill dee look'-kĕ koh-öy-ĕ	*vil dee vaire ven'-lee at lŏŏk'-ke koh'-öy-et*	*vill nee stēnga hütt'-glŏŏg-gen*

Is there a ventilator?

Er der en ventil?	Er der en ventilator?	Finns det en ventil?
air dair ehn ven-teel'	*air dair in ven-tee-lāh'-tor*	*finns dēh en ven-teel'*

The fan does not work.

Viften fungerer ikke	Viften virker ikke	Fläkten fungerar inte
vif'-ten foong-geh'-rer ick'-kĕ	*veef'-ten veer'-ker ick'-ke*	*flĕk-ten fŏŏng-gēh'-rär in'-tĕ*

I need another pillow, blanket.

Jeg trenger en pute, et ulltøppe, til	Jeg vil gerne have een pude, et tæppe, til	Jag behöver en kudde, en filt till
yay trehng'-ĕr ehn poo'-tĕ, ett ŏŏl'-tep'-pĕ till	*yi vil ger'-ne hah in poo'-the, it tep'-pe, till*	*yă bēh-hö'-vĕr en kŏŏd-dĕ, en filt till*

Norwegian	Danish	Swedish

I need a towel, soap.

Jeg har bruk for et håndkle, sepe	Jeg har brug for et handklæde, sæbe	Jag behöver en handduk, en tvål
yay hahr brōōk for ett hon-klēh, sēh'-pĕ	*yi hahr broo for it hawn'-klai-the, saï'-bĕ*	*yā bēh-hö'-vĕr en hănd'-dook, en tvawl*

I need some drinking water.

Jeg vil gjerne ha noe drikkevann	Jeg vil gerne have noget drikkevand	Jag vill gärna ha lite dricksvatten
yay vill yair'-nĕ hah noh-ĕ drik'-kĕ vănn	*yi vil gair'-ne hah noh'-et drik'-keh-văhn*	*yā vill yair-na hā lee-tĕ dricks-văt-ten*

I feel sick.

Jeg er kvalm	Jeg føler mig utilpads	Jag mår illa
yay air kvahlm	*yi fö'-ler my oo'-til-păs*	*yā mawr illă*

Bring a basin.

Hent et fat	Bring et vandfad	Ta hit ett handfat
hehnt ett faht	*bring it văhn'-fath*	*ta heet ett hănd'-făt*

Bring me a brandy.

Hent en konjakk	Bring mig en cognac	Ge mig en konjak
hehnt ehn kon'-yăck	*bring my in kon'-yăck*	*yeh may en kon'-yăck*

Bring me something to drink.

Bring meg noe å drikke	Bring mig noget at drikke	Ge mig något att dricka
bring may noh-ĕ aw drik'-kĕ	*bring my noh'-et at drik'-kĕh*	*yēh may naw'-got att drick'-kă*

I feel better.

Jeg føler meg bedre	Jeg har det bedre	Jag mår bättre
yay fö'-ler may beh'-drĕ	*yi hahr deh bēth'-rĕ*	*yā mawr bet'-trĕ*

I hope you feel better.

Jeg håper De føler Dem bedre	Jeg håber De føler Dem bedre tilpads	Jag hoppas ni mår bättre
yay haw'-per dee fö'-ler dem bēh-drĕ	*yi haw'-ber dee fö'-ler dem bēth'-re til-păs'*	*yā hop'-păs nee mawr bet'-trĕ*

What is the charge?

Hva koster det?	Hvad koster det?	Vad kostar det?
vah kos'-ter deh	*vath kos'-ter deh*	*văd koss'-tar dēh*

Norwegian	Danish	Swedish

I want a deck-chair.

Norwegian	Danish	Swedish
Jeg vil gjerne ha en dekkstol	Jeg vil gerne have en dækstol	Jag vill ha en däckstol
yay vill yair'-ně hah ehn deck-stohl	*yi vil gair'-ne hah in daik'-stohl*	*yā vill hā en deck'-stohl*

When does the ship reach . . .?

Når kommer skipet til . . .?	Hvornår kommer skibet til . . .?	Når kommer båten till . . .?
nawr kom'-mer shee'-pě till . . .	*vor-nawr' kom'-mer skee'-bet till . . .*	*nair kom-měr baw-ten till . . .*

Can we go ashore in . . .?

Kan vi gå på land i . . .?	Kan vi gå fra borde i . . .?	Kan vi gå i land i . . .?
kăn vee gaw paw lăn' ee . . .	*kan vee gaw fra boh'-rě ee . . .*	*kăn vee gaw ee länd ee . . .*

Must I get a landing ticket?

Må jeg ha et landgangskort?	Bliver jeg nødt til at få en landgangsbillet?	Måste jag ha ett landstigningskort?
maw yay hah ett lăn-găhngs-kort	*bleer yi nöt til at faw in lan'-găhngs-bil-let'*	*moss-tě yā hā ett länd'-steeg-nings-kohrt*

Do we need to take our passports?

Behøver vi å ta med oss passene?	Behøver vi at tage vores pas med?	Behöver vi ta våra pass?
beh-hö'-ver vee aw tah meh os păs'-se-ně	*be-hö'-ver vee at tah vo'-res pas meth*	*běh-hö'-ver vee ta vaw-ră păss*

Are the passports examined on board?

Blir passene kontrollert ombord?	Bliver passene kontroleret om bord?	Är det passkontroll ombord?
bleer păs'-se-ně kon-troh-lehrt om-bohr	*bleer pas'-sě-ne kon-tro-lěh'-ret om bohr*	*ěh děh păss-kon-troll' omm-bohrd'*

TRAVELLING BY AIR

Where is there a Travel Agency?

Hvor er der et reisebyrå?	Hvor er rejsebureauet?	Var är resebyran?
vohr air dair ett ray'-sě-bü-raw'	*vor air ry'-se-bü-rō'-et*	*var eh reh'-se-bü-rawn*

Norwegian	Danish	Swedish

Is there a plane from here to . . . ?

Er der et fly herfra til . . . ?	Er der en maskine herfra til . . . ?	Går det ett plan härifran till . . . ?
air dair ett flü hair'-frah till . . .	*air dair in mă-skee'-ne hehr'-fra till . . .*	*gawr dēh ett plän hair-ee-frawn till . . .*

When does the plane leave?

Når går flyet?	Hvornar går maskinen?	Hur dags går planet?
nawr gawr flü'-ĕ	*vor-nawr' gawr mă-skee'-nen*	*hōōr dags gawr plä'-net*

When do we reach . . . ?

Når kommer vi til . . . ?	Hvornår kommer vi til . . . ?	När kommer vi till . . . ?
nawr kom'-mer vee till	*vor-nawr' kom'-mer vee till*	*nair kom-mĕr vee till*

Can I go direct?

Kan jeg fly direkte?	Kan jeg flyve direkte dertil?	Kan jag fara direkt?
kăn yay flü dee-rek'-tĕ	*kan yi flü'-vĕ dee-rek'-te dair-til'*	*kăn ya fä-rä dee-rekt'*

Do we land anywhere before reaching . . . ?

Lander vi noen steder før vi kommer til . . . ?	Lander vi noget sted før vi når . . . ?	Landar vi någonstans innan vi kommer till . . . ?
län'-ner vee noh-en stēh'-der för vee kom'-mer till . . .	*lan'-ner vee noh'-et steth för vee nawr . . .*	*län-där vee naw-gon-stäns in-năn vee kom-mer till . . .*

What is the fare, single, return?

Kva koster billetten, enkel, retur?	Hvad koster billeten, enkelt, retur?	Vad koster biljetten, enkel, retur?
vah kos'-ter bil-let'-ten, ĕn-kel, rēh'-toor	*vath kos'-ter bil-let'-ten en'-kelt, reh-toor'*	*väd koss'-tär bill-yet'-ten, ēn-kĕl, rēh'-toor*

How do I get to the airport?

Hvorledes kommer jeg til flyplassen?	Hvordan kommer jeg til lufthavnen?	Hur kommer jag til flygplatsen?
vohr-leh'-des kom'-mer yay till flü'-plàs-sen	*vor-dan' kom'-mer yi til lōōft'-hähv-nen*	*hōōr kom-mer yä till flüg'-plăt-sen*

Norwegian	Danish	Swedish

I want to reserve a seat in the plane for ...

Jeg vil gjerne få reservert en plass i flyet til ...	Jeg ønsker at reservere en plads i maskinen til ...	Jag vill reservera en plats på planet till ...
yay vill yair'-ne faw reh-sair-vehrt' ehn pläss ee flü'-ĕ till ...	*yi ön'-sker at reh-sair-vēh'-rĕ in plähs ee ma-skee'-nen till ...*	*yā vill rĕ-sĕr-vēh'-rä en plats paw plä'-net till ...*

Is there transport?

Er der noe befordringsmiddel?	Er der transport?	Finns det transport?
air dair noh-ĕ beh-for'-drings-mid'-del	*air dair trans-port'*	*finns dēh träns-port'*

I must cancel my reservation.

Jeg må avbestille min plass	Jeg må afbestille min reservering	Jag måste avbeställa min reserverade plats
yay maw ahv'-beh-stil'-lĕ min pläss	*yi maw aw'-beh-stil-le meen reh-sair-vēh'-ring*	*yā moss-te äv'-beh-stel'-la min rĕ-sĕr-vēh'-rä-dĕ pläts*

How much luggage may I take?

Hvor mye bagasje kan jeg ta med?	Hvor meget bagage må jeg tage med?	Hur mycket bagage får jag ta?
vohr mü-ĕ bah-gah'-sheh kän yay tah meh	*vor myet bäh-gāh'-sheh maw yi tah meth*	*hōor mückĕ bä-gäsh' fawr yā tä*

Can I change my seat?

Kan jeg bytte plass?	Kan jeg bytte min plads?	Kan jag byta min plats?
kän yay büt-tĕ pläss	*kan yi büt'-te meen plähs*	*kän yā bü'-tä min pläts*

I suffer from air sickness.

Jeg plages av luftsyke	Jeg lider af luftsyge	Jag är luft-sjuk
yay plah'-ges ahv lōoft'-sü-kĕ	*yi lee'-ther aw lōoft'-sü-ĕh*	*yā ēh lōoft-shōok*

It is the first time I have travelled by air.

Det er første gang jeg har fløyet	Det er første gang jeg har fløjet	Det är första gången jag flyger
deh air för'-ste gahng yay hahr flöy'-et	*deh air för'-ste gahng yi hahr flöy'-et*	*dēh ēh för-stä gong-ĕn ya flü'-gĕr*

Norwegian	*Danish*	*Swedish*

Fasten safety-belts.

Fest sikkerhetsbeltene	Spænd sikkerheds-belterne	Sätt fast säkerhetsbältena
fest	*spen*	*sĕtt fässt*
sick'-ker-hehts-bel'-tĕ-nĕ	*sick'-ker-heths-bel'-ter-nĕ*	*saik'-er-hĕhts-bel'-tĕ-nă*

Emergency exit.

Nødutgang	Nødudgang	Reservutgång
nöd'-ōōt-gäng	*nöth'-ooth-gang*	*rĕ-serv'-oot-gong'*

CUSTOMS

Where is the customs?

Hvor er tollen?	Hvor er tolden?	Var är tullen?
vohr air tol'-len	*vor air tol'-len*	*vär ĕh tōōl'-len*

Where are the passports examined?

Hvor blir passene kontrollert?	Hvor bliver passene kontroleret?	Var är passkontrollen?
vohr bleer păs'-sĕ-nĕ kon-tro-lehrt'	*vor bleer pas'-sĕ-nĕ kon-tro-lēh'-ret*	*vär ĕh păss'-kōn-trol'-len*

Here is my passport.

Her er passet mitt	Her er mit pas	Här är mitt pass
hair air păs'-set mit	*hear air meet pas*	*hair ĕh mitt păss*

How much money have you?

Hvor mange penger har De?	Hvor mange penge har De?	Hur mycket pengar har ni?
vohr muhng'-ĕh pĕng'-ĕr hahr dee	*vor mung'-ĕh peng'-ĕh hahr dee*	*hūōr mŭckĕ pĕngär här nee*

I have ... pounds, kroner.

Jeg har ... pund, kroner	Jeg har ... pund, kroner	Jag har ... pund, kronor
yay hahr ... pōōn, kroh'-ner	*yi hahr ... poon, kroh'-ner*	*yă här ... poond, kroh-nor*

These are all mine.

Alle disse er mine	Disse er alle mine	Allt det här är mitt
ăl-lĕ dis'-sĕ air mee'-nĕ	*dees'-se air al'-lĕh mee'-nĕ*	*ăllt dĕh hair ĕh mitt*

Norwegian	Danish	Swedish

I have . . . in travellers' cheques.

Norwegian	Danish	Swedish
Jeg har . . . i reisesjekker	Jeg har . . . i rejsechecks	Jag har . . . i resechecker
yay hahr . . . ee ray-se-shek'-ker	*yi hahr . . . ee ry'-se-checks*	*yā hār . . . ee rēh'-sĕ-chĕck-ĕr*

This is my luggage.

Dette er min bagasje	Dette er min bagage	Det här är mitt bagage
det'-tĕ air min bah-gah'-sheh	*det'-te air meen băh-gāh'-sheh*	*dēh hair ēh mitt bă-gāsh'*

Have you anything to declare?

Har De noe å fortolle?	Har De noget at deklarere?	Har ni något att förtulla?
hahr dee noh-ĕ aw for-tol'-lĕ	*hahr dee noh'-et at deh-klāh-re'-rĕ*	*har nee naw-got att för-tööl-lă*

Please open your cases.

Vær så vennlig å åpne koffertene Deres	Vær venlig at åbne Deres kofferter	Var snäll och öppna era väskor
vair saw ven'-lee aw awp'-nĕ kohf'-fer-te-nĕ deh'-res	*vair ven'-lee at awpne daires kohf'-fer-ter*	*văr snell ock öpp-nă ĕhrä ves-kor*

For my personal use.

Til privat bruk	Til privat brug	För personligt bruk
till pree-vaht' brōōk	*till pree-vāht' broo*	*för pĕr-sohn'-lit brōōk*

I am a tourist.

Jeg er turist	Jeg er tourist	Jag är turist
yay air too-rist'	*yi air too-rist'*	*yā ēh too-rist'*

I am here on holiday.

Jeg er her på ferie	Jeg er her på ferie	Jag är här på semester
yay air hair paw feh'-ree-eh	*yi air hear paw feh'-ree-ĕh*	*yā ēh hair paw sĕh-mes'-ter*

It is a business visit.

Det er et forretningsbesøk	Det er et forretnings besøg	Det är ett affärsbesök
deh air ett for-ret'-nings-beh-sök'	*deh air it for-ret'-nings-beh-söh'*	*dēh ēh ett ăf-fairs'-bēh-sök'*

Norwegian	*Danish*	*Swedish*

I am staying here for a fortnight.

Jeg blir her i fjorten dager	Jeg bliver her i fjorten dage	Jag ska stanna här i fjorton dagar
yey bleer hair ee fyor'-ten dah'-ger	*yi bleer hear ee fyor'-ten dah'-ĕh*	*yā skā stăn-nă hair ee fyor'-ton där*

It has been used.

Det er brukt	Det har været brugt	Den är använd
deh air brōōkt	*deh hahr vair'-ret brōōgt*	*dĕn ēh ăn'-vend*

I have only bought a few things during my stay.

Jeg har bare kjøpt noen få ting under mitt opphold	Jeg har kun købt nogle få ting under mit besøg	Jag har bara köpt några få saker under mitt besök
yay hahr bah'-rĕ chöpt noh-ĕn faw ting ŏŏn'-der mit op'-hol	*yi hahr kŏŏn köbt noh'-le faw ting oon'-ner meet beh-söh'*	*yā hār bă'-rä chöpt naw'-grä faw säker oon'-der mitt bēh-sök'*

Is this dutiable?

Er dette tollpliktig?	Skal jeg betale told på dette?	Är detta tullpliktigt?
air det'-tĕ tol'-plick-tee	*skal yi be-tah'-le tol paw det'-te*	*ēh dettă tŏŏll'-plik-tit*

How much must I pay?

Hvor mye må jeg betale?	Hvor meget skal jeg betale?	Hur mycket behöver jag betala?
vohr mü-ĕ maw yay beh-tah'-lĕ	*vor my'-et skal yi be-tah'-lĕ*	*hōōr mück-ĕt bēh-hö'-ver yā bēh-tă'-lä*

Where do I pay?

Hvor betaler jeg?	Hvor betaler jeg?	Var betalar jag?
vohr beh-tah'-ler yay	*vor be-tah'-ler yi*	*vär bēh-tă'-lär yā*

Have you finished?

Er De ferdig?	Er De færdig?	Är ni färdig
air dee fair'-dee	*air dee fair'-dee*	*eh nee fair-dee*

I cannot close the case now.

Jeg kan ikke lukke kofferten nå	Jeg kan ikke lukke kofferten nu	Jag kan inte stänga väskan nu
yay kan ick'-kĕ lōōk'-kĕ kohf'-fer-ten naw	*yi kan ick'-ke lōōk'-ke kohf'-fĕr-ten nōō*	*yā kăn in'-tĕ stĕn-gă ves'-kăn noo*

Norwegian	*Danish*	*Swedish*

Have the cases been marked?

Er koffertene blitt merket?	Er kofferterne blevet markeret?	Har väskorna blivit märkta?
air kohf'-fer-ten-ně blit mehr'-ket	*air kohf'-fĕr-tĕr-ne bleh'-vet mar-kĕh'-ret*	*hăr ves-kor-nă blee-vit mĕrk'-tă*

My luggage has been examined.

Min bagasje er undersøkt	Min bagage er kontroleret	Mitt bagage är undersökt
min bah-gah'-sheh air ŏŏn'-der'sökt	*meen băh-găh'-sheh air kon-tro-lĕh'-ret*	*mitt bă-găsh' ĕh ŏŏn-der-sökt'*

AT THE HOTEL OR BOARDING HOUSE

The three National Travel Associations publish excellent particulars of hotels and boarding-houses in their respective countries.
It is advisable to book in advance in Oslo, Copenhagen and Stockholm during the months of July and August. Breakfast is not included in the price of the room. Rooms with private baths are considerably more expensive; a room with a shower, however, is not so expensive. Service charges are added to the bill. They average throughout Scandinavia 10% — 15%. The most expensive hotels may charge up to 25%.

Can you recommend a hotel, a boarding-house?

Kan De anbefale et hotell, et pensjonat?	Kan De anbefale et hotel, et pensionat?	Kan ni rekommendera et hotell, ett pensionat?
kän dee ăn'-beh-fa-lĕ ett ho-tel, ett pahng-shoh-naht'	*kan dee an'-beh-făh-lĕ it ho-tel', it păhn-shō-naht'*	*kän nee rĕ-kom-men-dĕh'-ră ett ho-tell', ett păn-sho-naht'*

I don't want to be in a noisy area.

Jeg vil ikke bo i et urolig strøk	Jeg vil ikke være i et larmende kvarter	Jag vill inte bo i ett bullersamt område
yay vill ick'-kě boh ee ett oo-roh'-lee strök	*yi vil ick'-ke vaire ee it lahr'-men-ne kvăhr-ter'*	*yă vill in-tě boh ee ett bull'-er-sämt omm'-raw-dě*

Norwegian	Danish	Swedish

I want to be near the centre of the town.

Jeg vil gjerne være nær byens centrum	Jeg ønsker at være nær byens centrum	Jag vill vara nära stadens centrum
yay vill yair'-ne vairĕ nair bü'-ens cen'-trōōm	*yi ŏn'-sker at vaire nair bü'-ens cen'-trōōm*	*yā vill vā-ră nairă stă'ns cen'-trōōm*

Where is the reception desk?

Hvor er resepsjonen?	Hvor er receptionen	Var är receptionen?
vohr air reh-cep-shohn'-en	*vor air re-cep-shōh'-nen*	*văr ĕh rĕ-cep-shohn'-ĕn*

Where is the porter?

Hvor er portieren?	Hvor er hotelkarlen?	Var är portiern?
vohr air por-tee'-ĕr-ĕn	*vor air hotel'-kāh-len*	*văr ĕh por-tee'-ĕrn*

Have you a room vacant?

Har De et ledig værelse?	Har De et værelse ledigt?	Har ni något rum ledigt?
hahr dee ett lĕh' dee vair-el-sĕ	*hahr dee it vair'-el-sĕ leh'-theet*	*hăr nee nuw'-got rōōm lĕh-dit*

I should like a single, double, room.

Jeg vil gjerne ha et enkelt-, dobbelt-, værelse	Jeg vil gerne have et enkelt, dobbelt, værelse	Jag skulle vilja ha ett enkelrum, ett dubbelrum
yay vill yair'-nĕ hah ett ĕhn'-kelt, dob'-belt, vair'-el-sĕ	*yi vil gair'-ne hah it en'-kelt, dob'-belt, vair'-rel-sĕ*	*yā skōōl'-lĕ vil-lă hā ett ĕn-kel-rōōm, ett dōōb-bel-rōōm*

A room for the children.

Et værelse til barnene	Et værelse til børnene	Ett rum för barnen
ett vair'-el-sĕ till băhr'-ne-nĕ	*it vair'-rel-sĕ til bör'-nĕ-nĕ*	*ett rōōm för bārn-ĕn*

A room with a bath.

Et værelse med bad	Et værelse med bad	Ett rum med bad
ett vair'-el-sĕ meh bahd	*it vair'-rel-sĕ meth băth*	*ett rōōm mēhd băd*

Full board.

Full pensjon	Fuld pension	Helpension
full pahng-shohn'	*full pahn-shohn'*	*hēhl-păn-shohn'*

Norwegian	Danish	Swedish

For one night only.

Bare for en natt	Kun for een nat	Bara för en natt
bah'-rĕ for ehn nätt	*koon for ayn nat*	*bā-rǎ för en nätt*

For a week, perhaps longer.

For en uke, kansje lengere	For en uge, måske længre	För en vecka, kanske längre
for ehn ŏŏk'-kĕ kăn'-sheh lehng'-er-rĕ	*for in oo'-eh, maw-skĕh' laing'-rĕ*	*för en vĕk'-kǎ, kăn'-shĕ lĕng-rĕ*

May I see the room?

Kan jeg få se værelset?	Må jeg få lov at se værelset?	Får jag se på rummet?
kän yay faw seh vair'-el-sĕ	*maw yi faw lov at seh vair'-rel-set*	*fawr yā sēh paw rŏŏm-met*

That is expensive.

Det er dyrt	Det er dyrt	Det är dyrt
deh air dürt	*deh air dürt*	*dēh ēh dürt*

Have you anything cheaper?

Har De noe billigere?	Har De noget billigere?	Har ni något billigare?
hahr dee noh-eh bil'-lee-ĕr-eh	*hahr dee noh'-et bil'-lee-rĕ*	*här nee naw'-got bil'-lee-gǎ-rĕ*

This is too small.

Dette er for lite	Dette er for lille	Detta är för litet
det'-tĕ air for lee'-tĕ	*det'-te air for lil'-lĕ*	*dettǎ ēh för leet-ĕt*

I will take this room.

Jeg tar dette værelset	Jeg tager dette værelse	Jag tar det här rummet
yay tahr det'-tĕ vair'-el-sĕ	*yi tahr det'-te vair'-rel-sĕ*	*yā tār dēh hair rŏŏm-met*

What is the number of the room?

Hva er værelsenummeret?	Hvad er værelsets nummer?	Vad är nummret på rummet?
vah air vair'-el-sĕ-nŏŏm'-mer-ĕh	*vath air vair'-rel-sets nŏŏm'-mer*	*vād ēh nŏŏm'-ret paw rŏŏm-met*

Have you got my key?

Har De nøkkelen min?	Har De min nøgle?	Har ni min nyckel?
hahr dee nŏk'-kel-en min	*hahr dee meen nöy'-lĕ*	*här nee min nück-kĕl*

Norwegian	Danish	Swedish

Is there a lift?

Er der heis?	Er der en elevator?	Finns det hiss?
air dair hays	*air dair in elĕh-vāh'-tŏr*	*finns dēh hiss*

Please send the luggage to our room.

Vær så vennlig å bringe bagasjen opp til værelset vårt	Vær venlig at sende bagagen op til vort værelse	Var snäll och skicka bagaget till vårt rum
vair saw ven'-lee aw bring-eh băh-găh'-shen op till vair'-el-sĕ vawrt	*vair ven'-lee at sen'-nĕ băh-găh'-shen up til vort vair'-rel-sĕ*	*văr snĕll ock shik'-kă bă-gāsh'-ĕt till vawrt rŏŏm*

The luggage is in the station, in the taxi.

Bagasjen er på stasjonen, i drosjen	Bagagen er på stationen, i taxaen	Bagaget är på station, i taxin
băh-găh'-shen air paw stăh-shŏh'-nen, ee drosh'-en	*băh-găh'-shen air paw stăh-shŏh'-nen, ee tax'-āh-ĕn*	*bă-gāsh'-ĕt ēh paw stă-shohn', ee taxin*

Can I have a meal in my room?

Kan jeg få mat opp på værelset?	Kan jeg spise på mit værelse?	Kan jag få mat på mitt rum?
kăn yay faw maht op paw vair'-el-sĕ	*kan yi spee'-se paw meet vair'-rel-sĕ*	*kăn yă faw măt paw mitt rŏŏm*

Please open the windows.

Vær så vennlig å åpne vinduene	Vær venlig at åbne vinduerne	Var snäll och öppna fönstren
vair saw ven'-lee aw awp'-nĕ vin'-doo-en-nĕ	*vair ven'-lee at awp'-nĕ veen'-doo-er-nĕ*	*văr snĕll ock öpp'-nă föns-trĕn*

Where have you put our things?

Hvor har De plasert tingene våre?	Hvor har De stillet vore ting?	Var har ni ställt våra saker?
vohr hahr dee plah-sert' ting'-en-nĕ vaw'-rĕ	*vor hahr dee stil'-let vore ting*	*văr har nee stĕllt vaw-ră să-kĕr*

Where is the bathroom, lavatory?

Hvor er badeværelset, toalettet?	Hvor er badeværelset, toilettet?	Var är badrummet, toiletten?
vohr air băh'-de-vair-el-sĕ, toh-āh-let'-tĕ	*vor air băh'-the-vair-rel-set, to-āh-let'-tet*	*văr ēh băd'-rŏŏm-met, toh-āh-let'-ten*

Norwegian	Danish	Swedish

Where is the bell?

Hvor er ringeapparatet?	Hvor er klokken?	Var är ringklockan?
vohr air ringë-ahp-pah-raht'-ëh	*vor air klock'-ken*	*vār ēh ring-klock-ăn*

I am going out now.

Jeg går ut nå	Jeg går ud nu	Jag går ut nu
yay gawr ōōt naw	*yi gawr ooth noo*	*yā gawr ōōt nōō*

I shall be back for lunch, for dinner.

Jeg kommer tilbake til lunsi, til middag	Jeg vil være tilbage til frokost, middag	Jag kommer tillbaka till lunch, till midda
yay kom'-mer till-bāh'-kĕ till loonsh, mid'-dahg	*yi vil vaire til-bāh'-ëh til froh'-kŏst, mee'-dăh*	*yā kom'-mer till-bā'-kă till lunch, till mid'-dăg*

Do you serve tea?

Serverer De te?	Serverer De the?	Serverar ni te?
ser-veh'-rer dee teh	*ser-vēh'-rĕ dee tēh*	*sĕr-vēh'-rär nee tēh*

Please bring me some soap, a towel, hot water.

Vær så vennlig å bringe et stykke såpe, et håndkle, varmt vann	Vær venlig at bringe noget sæbe, et håndklæde, varmt vand	Var snäll och ge mig en tvål, en handduk, varmt vatten
vair saw ven'-lee aw bring'-ëh ett stück'-kĕ saw'-pĕ, ett hawn'-kleh, vahrmt vănn	*vair ven'-lee at bringë noh'-et saibe, it hawn'-klai-the, vāhrmt văhn*	*vār snĕll ock yĕh may en tvawl, en hånd'-dōōk, vărmt văt-ten*

Can I have a bath?

Kan jeg ta et bad?	Kan jeg få et bad?	Kan jag få ett bad?
kăn yay tah ett bahd	*kan yi faw it bath*	*kän yā faw ett bād*

Call me at . . .

Vekk meg klokken . . .	Kald på mig klokken...	Väck mig klockan . . .
vĕk may klock'-ken . . .	*kal paw my klock'-ken...*	*veck may klock'-ăn . . .*

Who is there?

Hvem er det?	Hvem er der?	Vem är det?
vehm air deh	*vehm air dair*	*vĕm ēh dēh*

Norwegian	Danish	Swedish

Can I have my shoes cleaned?

Norwegian	Danish	Swedish
Kan jeg få skoene mine pusset?	Kan jeg få mine sko pudset?	Kan jag få mina skor borstade?
kăn yay faw skoh'-en-ně mee'-ně pŏŏs'-set	*kan yi faw mee'-ne skoh poos'-set*	*kăn yā faw mee'-nă skohr bŏr'-stă-dě*

I should like my clothes brushed, pressed.

Norwegian	Danish	Swedish
Jeg ville gjerne ha klærne mine børstet, presset	Jeg vil gerne have mit tøj børstet, presset	Jag skulle vilja ha mina kläder borstade och pressade
yay vil'-lě yair'-ně hah klair'-en-ně mee'-ně bŏrs'-tet, prěs'-set	*yi vil gair'-ne hah meet tøy bŏr'-stet, pres'-set*	*yā skŏŏl'-lě vil'-lă hā mee-nă klai'-děr bŏr'-stă-dě ock prěs'-să-dě*

Are there any letters for me?

Norwegian	Danish	Swedish
Er der noen brev til meg?	Er der nogen breve til mig?	Finns det några brev till mig?
air dair noh'-en brěhv till may	*air dair noh'-en breh'-ve till mv*	*finns děh naw'-grä brěhv till may*

Has anyone asked for me?

Norwegian	Danish	Swedish
Har noen spurt etter meg?	Er der nogen der har spurgt efter mig?	Har någon frågat efter mig?
hahr noh'-en spoort ět'-ter may	*air dair noh'-en dair hahr spŏŏrt ef'-ter my*	*har naw'-gon fraw'-găt ěf-ter may*

Did anyone telephone for me?

Norwegian	Danish	Swedish
Har noen telefonert til meg?	Er der nogen der har telefoneret til mig?	Har någon ringt till mig?
hahr noh'-en tele-foh-něrt' till may	*air dair noh'-en dair hahr tele-fo-ně'-ret till my*	*hăr naw'-gon ringt till may*

I want to post a letter.

Norwegian	Danish	Swedish
Jeg vil gjerne poste et brev	Jeg vil poste et brev	Jag vill posta ett brev
yay vill yair'-ně pos'-tě ett brěhv	*yi vill pos'-te it brehv*	*yā vill poss-tă ett brěhv*

Have you any stamps?

Norwegian	Danish	Swedish
Har De noen frimerker?	Har De nogle frimærker?	Har ni några frimärken?
hahr dee noh'-en free'-měr-ker	*hahr dee noh'-le, free'-mair-ker*	*hăr nee naw'-grä free-měrk'-ěn*

Norwegian	Danish	Swedish

C

Can I get something to eat, drink, when I return?

Kan jeg få noe å spise, drikke, når jeg kommer tilbake?	Kan jeg få noget at spise, drikke, når jeg kommer tilbage?	Kan jag få något att äta, dricka, när jag kommer tillbaka?
kǎn yay faw noh'-eh aw spee'-sě, drick'-kě, nawr yay kom'-mer till-bāh'-kě	*kan yi faw noh'-et at spee'-se, drik'-ke, nawr yi kom'-mer till-bāh'-ěh*	*kǎn yǎ faw naw'-got att aitǎ, drik'-kǎ, nair yǎ kom'-mer till-bā-kǎ*

Is there a night-porter on duty?

Er der nattevakt tilstede?	Er der en natportier på vagt?	Finns det någon natt-portier?
air dair nǎt-tě-vahkt till stēh'-dě	*air dair in naht'-por-tjeh paw vaght*	*finns dēh naw'-gon nǎtt'-por-tiěh*

Is ... still in his (her) room?

Er ... fremdeles på sitt værelse?	Er ... stadig på sit værelse?	Är ... fortfarande i sitt rum?
air ... frem-dēh'-lěs paw sit vair'-el-sě	*air ... stǎh'-thee paw seet vair'-rel-sě*	*eh ... fohrt'-fār-ǎn-dě ee sitt rōōm*

Will you send a message to him (her)?

Vil De gi ham (henne) en beskjed?	Vil De sende en besked til ham (hende)?	Vill ni skicka ett bud till honom (henne)?
vill dee yee hǎhm (hen'-ně) ehn beh-sheh'	*vil dee sen'-ně in beh-sketh' til hahm (hen'-ně)*	*vill nee shik'-kǎ ett bōōd till hon-om (hen'-ně)*

I should like some tickets for the cinema, theatre.

Jeg vil gjerne ha noen kinobilletter, teaterbilletter	Jeg vil gerne have nogle billetter til biografen, teateret	Jag skulle vilja ha några biobiljetter, teaterbiljetter
yay vill yair'-ně hah noh'-en chee'-noh-bil-let'-ter, teh-āht'-er-bil-let'-ter	*yi vil gair'-ne hah noh'-le bil-let'-ter til bio-grāh'-fen, teh-āh'-te-ret*	*yǎ skōōl'-lě vil'-lǎ hǎ naw'-grǎ beeð-bill-yet'-ter, tēh-āht'-ěr-bill-yet'-ter*

What time does it begin?

Når begynner det?	Hvad tid begynder det?	Hur dags börjar det?
nawr beh-yün'-ner deh	*vath teeth beh-gün'-ner deh*	*hōōr dǎgs bör'-yǎhr dě*

Norwegian	Danish	Swedish

Push, Pull, Press.

Skyv, Trekk, Trykk	Tryk, Træk, Tryk	Skjut, Drag, Tryck
shüv, trĕhck, trück	*trük, traik, trük*	*shoot, dräg, trück*

Maid.

Pike	Stuepige	Städerska
pee'-kĕ	*stōō'-ĕh-pee-ĕh*	*stai'-dĕr-skä*

LEAVING THE HOTEL

I wish to pay my bill.

Jeg vil gjerne betale regningen	Jeg vil gerne betale min regning	Jag vil gärna betala min räkning
yay vill yair'-nĕ beh-täh'-le	*yi vill gair-ne beh-täh'-lĕ meen*	*yä vill yair'-nä bĕh-tä'-lä min*
rayn'-ing-ĕn	*ry'-ning*	*raik-ning*

How much is it?

Hvor mye er det?	Hvor meget lyder den på?	Hur mycket är det?
vohr mü-ĕh air deh	*vor my'-et lü'-ther den paw*	*hŭŏr mŭcket ĕh dĕh*

What are these charges for?

Hva er disse beløpene for?	Hvad er disse poster for?	Vad är dessa avgifter för?
vah air dis'-sĕ beh-lö'-pe-nĕ for	*vath air dee'-se pos'-ter for*	*väd ĕh des-sä äv'-gift-ĕr för*

I did not have . . .

Jeg fikk ikke . . .	Jeg fik ikke . . .	Jag fick inte . . .
yay fick ick'-kĕ . . .	*yi fik ick'-ke . . .*	*yä fick in'-tĕ . . .*

You said the rooms cost . . .

De sa at værelsene kostet . . .	De sagde værelserne kostede . . .	Ni sade att rummen kostade . . .
dee säh at vair'-el-se-nĕ kos'-tet . . .	*dee säh vair'-rel-ser-nĕ kos'-te-the . . .*	*nee sä att rŏŏm-men koss'-tä-dĕ*

May I have the receipt?

Kan jeg få kvitteringen?	Må jeg få kviteringen?	Kan jag få kvittot?
kän yay faw kvee-tĕh'-ring-ĕn	*maw yi faw kvee-tĕh'-ring-ĕn*	*kän yä faw kvitt'-ŏt*

Norwegian	Danish	Swedish

I think there is a mistake here.

Jeg tror det er en feil her	Jeg tror der er en fejl her	Jag tror det är ett misstag här
yay trohr deh air ehn fayl hair	*yi trohr dair air in fyl hear*	*yā trohr dēh ēh ett miss'-täg hair*

Do I tip, or is there a charge for service in the bill?

Skal jeg gi drikkepenger, eller er de inkludert i regningen?	Skal jeg give drikkepenge, eller er service inkluderet i regningen?	Ska jag betala dricks eller är det inkluderat i räkningen?
skal yay yee drick'-kĕ-pehng-ĕr, ĕl'-ler air de in-cloo-dēhrt ee rayn'-ing-en	*skal yi ghee drek-ke'-peng-ĕh, el'-ler air sair-vee'-sĕh in-cloo-dēh'-ret ee ry'-ning-ĕn*	*skä yā bēh-täl'-lǎ dricks ĕl-ler ēh dēh in-clōō-dēh-rät ee raik'-ning-ĕn*

I am leaving tomorrow, tonight, this afternoon.

Jeg reiser i morgen, i kveld, i ettermiddag	Jeg rejser i morgen, i aften, i eftermiddag	Jag reser i morgon, i kväll, i eftermiddag
yay ray'-ser ee mor'-en, ee kvĕl, ee ĕtt'-er-mid-dahg	*yi ry'-ser ee mor'-en, ee ähf'-ten, ee ef'-ter-mee-dāh*	*yā rēh-sĕr ee mor'-ron, ee kvell, ee ĕf-ter-mid-däh*

Have my luggage brought down.

Vær så vennlig å få bagasjen båret ned	Vær venlig at få min bagage bragt ned	Var snäll och låt bära ner mitt bagage
vair saw ven'-lee aw faw băh-gāh'-shen baw-ret nēhd	*vair ven'-lee at faw meen băh-gāh'-sheh brahgt neth*	*vār snell ock lawt bai'-rä nēhr mitt bä-gäsh'*

Send the luggage to the station.

Send bagasjen til stasjonen	Send bagagen til stationen	Skicka bagaget till stationen
sĕn băh-gäh'-shen till stäh-shōh'-nen	*sehn băh-gāh'-shen til stäh-shōh'-nen*	*shik'-kǎ bä-gäsh'-ĕt till stä-shohn'-ĕn*

How soon should I leave?

Når bør jeg gå?	Hvornår behøver jeg at tage afsted?	När bör jag ge mig av?
nawr bör yay gaw	*vor-nawr' beh-hö'-ver yi at tah ăh-steth'*	*nair bör yā yĕh may äv*

Norwegian	*Danish*	*Swedish*

How long does it take to the station, the dock, the airport?

Hvor lang tid tar det til stasjonen, kaien, flyplassen?	Hvor lang tid tager det til stationen, havnen, lufthavnen?	Hur lång tid tar det till stationen, till kajen, till flygplatsen?
vohr lahng teed tahr deh till stäh-shōh'-nen, kähy-en, flü'-plås-sen	*vor lang teeth tähr deh til stäh-shōh'-nen, häwn'-nen, looft'-häwn-nen*	*hōōr long teed tär dēh till stä-shohn'-en, till kähy-ĕn, till flüg'-plăt-sen*

Can I walk?

Kan jeg gå dit?	Kan jeg spadsere?	Kan jag gå till fots?
kän yay gaw deet	*kan yi späh-sēh'-rĕ*	*kän yå gaw till fŏhts*

Please get a taxi.

Vær så vennlig å få fatt i en drosje	Vær venlig at få en taxa	Var snäll och skaffa en taxi
vair saw ven'-lee aw faw fätt ee ehn drosh'-ĕh	*vair ven'-lee at faw in taxa*	*vär snĕll ock skäf'-fä en tăxi*

Have you any labels?

Har De noen merkelapper?	Har De nogle sedler?	Har ni några adresslappar?
hahr dee noh'-ĕn mĕhr'-ke-lähp-per	*hahr dee noh'-le saith'-ler*	*här nee naw'-grä äh-dress'-läp-pär*

I should like some food for the journey.

Jeg vil gjerne ha noe niste med på reisen	Jeg vil gerne have noget mad med på rejsen	Jag skulle vilja ha lite matsäck på resan
yay vill yair'-nĕ ha noh'-ĕh nis'-tĕ meh paw ray'-sen	*yi vil gair'-ne häh noh'-et math meth paw ry'-sen*	*yå skōōl'-lĕ vil'-lä hä lee-tĕ măt-seck paw rēh-sän*

When must I leave my room?

Når må jeg forlate værelset?	Hvornar skal jeg gå fra mit værelse?	Hur dags behöver jag vara ur mitt rum?
nawr maw yay for-lah'-tĕ vair'-el-sĕ	*vor-nawr' skal yi gaw fra meet vair'-rel-sĕ*	*hōōr dägs bēh-hö'-vĕr yå vä-rä oor mitt rōōm*

I have been very comfortable.

Jeg har vært meget komfortabel	Jeg har været godt tilpads	Jag har trivts utmärkt
yay hahr vairt mēh'-get kom-for-täh'-bel	*yi hahr vai'-ret got til-pas'*	*yå här treevts oot'-mĕrkt*

Norwegian	Danish	Swedish

Can I leave my luggage here?

Norwegian	Danish	Swedish
Kan jeg la bagasjen stå her?	Kan jeg efterlade min bagage her?	Kan jag lämna mitt bagage här?
kăn yay lah băh-gäh'-shen staw hair	*kan yi efter'-läh-the meen băh-gäh'-sheh hear*	*kăn yä lem-nă mitt bă-gäsh' hair*

If any letters come for me, please send them to this address.

Norwegian	Danish	Swedish
Hvis der kommer noen brev til meg, vær vennlig å sende dem til denne adresse	Hvis der kommer nogle breve til mig, vær venlig at sende dem til denne adresse	Om det kommer några brev till mig, vill ni skicka dem till den här adressen
viss dair kom'-mer noh'-ĕn brēhv till may, vair saw ven'-lee aw sen'-nĕ dem till den'-nĕ ah-dres'-sĕ	*vis dair kom'-mer noh'-le breh'-vĕ til my, vair ven'-lee at sen'-ne dem til den'-ne ăh'-dres'-sĕ*	*omm dēh kom'-mer naw'-gră brēhv till may, vill nee shik'-kă dom till den hair ah-dres'-sen*

LAUNDRY

I have some things to be washed.

Norwegian	Danish	Swedish
Jeg har noen ting som skal vaskes	Jeg har noget der skal vaskes	Jag har en del saker som behöver tvättas
yay hahr noh'-ĕn ting som skal văhs'-kes	*yi hahr noh'-et dair skal vahs'-kes*	*yä här en dēhl să-'ker som bēh-hö'-ver tvet-tăs*

When will they be ready?

Norwegian	Danish	Swedish
Når blir de ferdige?	Hvornår er de færdige?	När blir de färdiga?
nawr bleer dee fair'-dee-ĕh	*vor-nawr' air dee fair'-dee*	*nair bleer dēh fair'-dee-gă*

Can they be ready tomorrow, in two days?

Norwegian	Danish	Swedish
Kan de være ferdige i morgen, i overmorgen?	Kan de være færdige i morgen, om to dage?	Kan det bli färdigt i morgon, om två dagar?
kăn dee vairĕ fair'-dee-ĕh ee mor'-ĕn, ee aw'-ver-mor-ĕn	*kan dee vaire fair'-dee ee mor'-en, om toh dāh-ĕh*	*kăn dēh blee fair'-digt ee mor'-ron, omm tvaw dă̄r*

I leave on . . .

Norwegian	Danish	Swedish
Jeg reiser på . . .	Jeg rejser på . . .	Jag far på . . .
yay ray'-ser paw . . .	*yi ry'-ser paw . . .*	*yä fär paw . . .*

I should like these things back as soon as possible.

Jeg vil gjerne ha disse tingene tilbake snarest mulig	Jeg vil gerne have disse ting tilbage snarest muligt	Jag skulle vilja ha de här sakerna tillbaka så snart som möjligt
yay vill yair'-ně hah dis'-sě ting'-en-ěh till-bāh'-kě snahr'-rest moo'-lee	*yi vil gair'-ne hah dees'-se ting til-bāh'-ěh snåhr'-rest moo'-lit*	*yå skōōl'-lě vil'-lå hå děh hair sā'-ker-nǎ till-bǎ'-kǎ saw snahrt som möy-lit*

Be very careful with these things.

Vær meget forsiktig med disse tingene	Vær meget forsigtig med disse ting	Var mycket försiktig om de här sakerna
vair měh'-get for-sick'-tee meh dis'-sě ting'-en-ěh	*vair my'-et for-sick'-tee meth dees'-sě ting*	*vår mücket för-siktig omm děh hair sā'-ker-nǎ*

Don't starch the collars.

Ikke stiv snippene	Flipperne skal ikke stives	Stärk inte kragarna
ick'-kě steev snip'-pě-ně	*flip'-per-ne skal ick'-ke stee'-ves*	*stairk in'-tě krå'-går-nǎ*

Some of the things need mending.

Noen av tingene trenger reparasjon	Nogle af tingene trænger til at blive repareret	En del saker behöver lagas
noh'-ěn ahv ting'-en-ěh trehng'-ěr rěh-påh-råh-shohn'	*noh'-le af ting'-ēně train'-er til at blee'-ve rěh-påh-rěh'-ret*	*en děhl sā'-ker běh-hö'-ver lå'-gäs*

Can you send my laundry to this address if it isn't ready in time?

Kan De sende vasketøyet mitt til denne adresse hvis det ikke er ferdig tidsnok?	Kan De sende mit vasketøj til denne adresse hvis det ikke er færdig i tide?	Kan ni skicka tvätten till den här adressen om den inte är färdig i tid?
kǎn dee sen'-ně vahs'-ke-töy-et mit till den'-ně ah-dres'-sen viss deh ick'-kě air fair'-dee tis'-nok	*kan dee sen'-ně meet vahs'-ke-töy til den'-ně ah-dres'-sě vis deh ick'-ke air fair'-dee ee tee'-the*	*kän nee shik'-kǎ tvet'-ten till děn hair ah-dres'-sen om den in'-te ěh fair'-dee ee teed*

Norwegian	Danish	Swedish

Can you arrange to have them mended for me?

Kan De få dem reparert for meg?	Kan De få dem repareret for mig?	Kan ni få dem lagade för mig?
kăn dee faw dem rēh-păh-rēhrt' for may	kan dee faw dem rēh-păh-rēh'-ret for my	kăn nee faw dom lā-gă-dĕ för may

There are . . . missing.

Der mangler . . .	Der mangler . . .	Det saknas . . .
dair mahng'-ler . . .	dair mangh'-ler . . .	dēh săk'-năs . . .

LOCAL TOURS, EXCURSIONS

FINDING THE WAY

I want a guide book, a map of the city.

Jeg vil gjerne ha en reisehåndbok, et kart av byen	Jeg vil gerne have en vejviser, et kort af byen	Jag vill ha en resehandbok, en karta över staden
yay vill yair'-nĕ hah ehn ray'-sĕ-hon-bohk, ett kahrt ahv bü'-en	yi vil gair'-ne hah in vy'-vee-ser, it kort aw bü'-en	yă vill hā en rēh'-sĕ-hand-bohk, en kăr-tă ö-ver stā-dĕn

Have you one in English?

Har De en på engelsk?	Har De en på engelsk?	Har ni någon på engelska?
hahr dee ehn paw ehng'-elsk	hahr dee in paw ehng'-elsk	hăr nee naw'-gon paw ehng'-elskă

Could you tell me the way to . . . ?

Kan De vise meg veien til . . . ?	Vil De være venlig at vise mig vejen til . . . ?	Kan ni visa mig vägen till . . . ?
kăn dee vee'-sĕ may vay'-en till . . .	vil dee vaire ven'-lee at vee'-se my vy'-en till . . .	kăn nee vee-să may vaig'-ĕn till . . .

Is this the right way to . . . ?

Er dette rette veien til . . . ?	Er dette den rigtige vej til . . . ?	Är detta rätt väg till . . . ?
air det'-tĕ ret'-tĕ vay'-ĕn till . . .	air det'-te den reeg'-tee-ĕh vy till . . .	ēh det'-tă rĕtt vaig till . . .

Norwegian	Danish	Swedish

How do I get from here to . . . ?

Hvorledes kommer jeg herfra til . . . ?	Hvordan kommer jeg herfra til . . . ?	Hur kommer man härifrån till . . . ?
vohr-lēh'-des kom'-mer yay hair'-frah till . . .	*vor-dan' kom'-mer yi hear'-fra till . . .*	*hōōr kom'-mer män hair-ee-frawn till . . .*

I want to go to . . .

Jeg skal til . . .	Jeg vil til . . .	Jag vill komma till . . .
yay skäl till . . .	*yi vil till . . .*	*yä vill kom'-mä till . . .*

I am looking for . . .

Jeg leter etter . . .	Jeg leder efter . . .	Jag letar efter . . .
yay lēh'-ter ĕt'-ter . . .	*yi leh'-ther ef'-ter . . .*	*yä lēh-tär ĕf-ter . . .*

Is it far?

Er det langt?	Er det langt?	Är det långt?
air deh lahngt	*air deh lahngt*	*ēh dēh longt*

What distance is it?

Hvor lang vei er det?	Hvor lang vej er det?	Hur långt är det?
vohr lahng vay air deh	*vor lahng vy air deh*	*hōōr longt ēh dēh*

How long does it take?

Hvor lang tid tar det?	Hvor lang tid tager det?	Hur lång tid tar det?
vohr lahng teed' tahr deh	*vor lahng teeth tahr deh*	*hōōr long teed tär dēh*

Is it better to go by taxi, tram, bus?

Er det bedre å ta drosje, trikk, buss?	Er det bedre at tage med taxa, sporvogn, bus?	Är det bättre att ta en taxi, spårvagn, buss?
air deh bēh'-dre aw tah drosh'-ĕh, trick, bōōs	*air deh beth'-rĕ at täh meth taxa, spohr'-vown, bōōs*	*ēh dēh bet-trĕ ätt tä en täxi, spawr-vangn, bōōs*

Where is the tram stop, bus stop?

Hvor er trikkeholde-plassen, bussholdeplassen?	Hvor er sporvognstoppestedet, busstoppestedet?	Var är spårvagnshåll-platsen, busshållplatsen?
vohr air trick'-ĕh-hol-lĕ-plås-sen, bōōs'-hol-lĕ-plås-sen	*vor air spohr'-vowns-stop-pĕ-stēh'-thet, bōōs'-stop-pe-steh'-thet*	*vär ēh spawr'-vangns-holl-plät'-sen, bōōs'-holl-plät'-sen*

Norwegian	Danish	Swedish

Does this bus, train, go to . . . ?

Går denne bussen, dette toget, til . . . ?	Går denne bus, dette tog, til . . . ?	Går den här bussen, det här tåget, till . . . ?
gawr den'-nĕ bŏŏs'-sen, det'-tĕ taw'-get, till . . .	*gawr den'-ne bŏŏs, det'-te toe, till . . .*	*gawr dĕn hair bŏŏs-sen, dĕh hair taw'-get, till . . .*

Is this the terminus?

Er dette endestasjonen?	Er dette endestationen?	Är detta ändstationen?
air det'-tĕ ĕhn-dĕh-stah-shōh'-nen	*air det'-te en'-ne-stäh-shōh'-nen*	*ĕh det'-tă ĕnd'-stā-shoh'-nen*

Do I have to change?

Behøver jeg bytte?	Behøver jeg at skifte?	Behöver jag byta?
beh-hö'-ver yay büt-tĕ	*be-hö'-ver yi at skeef'-tĕ*	*bĕh-hö'-ver yä bü'-tă*

Straight ahead.

Rett fram	Lige ud	Rakt fram
rĕt främ	*lee'-eh tŏŏh*	*rākt främm*

To the right, left.

Til høyre, venstre	Til højre, venstre	Till höger, till vänster
till höy'-rĕ, ven'-strĕ	*till hoy'-rĕ, ven'-strĕ*	*till hö'-ger, ven'-ster*

First turning on the right.

Første gate til høyre	Første gade på højre hånd	Första avtagsvägen till höger
för'-stĕ gah'-tĕ till höy'-rĕ	*för'-ste gah'-the paw hoy'-re hawn*	*för'-stă āv-tāgs-vaig-ĕn till hö'-ger*

Second turning on the left.

Annen gate til venstre	Anden gade på venstre hånd	Andra avtagsvägen till vänster
ahn'-nen gah'-tĕ till ven'-strĕ	*ahn'-nen gah'-the paw ven'-strĕ hawn*	*ăndră āv-tăgs-vaig-ĕn till ven'-stĕr*

Norwegian	Danish	Swedish

GOING BY CAR

I want to hire a car.

Jeg vil gjerne leie en bil
*yay vill yair'-në lay'-ëh
ehn beel*

Jeg vil gerne leje en bil
*yi vil gair'-ne lie'-ëh in
beēl*

Jag vill gärna hyra en bil
*yä vill yair'-nä hürä en
beel*

I want to go by car.

Jeg vil gjerne bile
yay vill yair'-në bee-lë

Jeg vil køre i bil
yi vil kö'-re ee beēl

Jag vill fara med bil
yä vill färä mëh beel

Is there a driver who speaks English?

Er der en sjafør som
snakker engelsk?
*air dair ehn shah'-för
som snak'-kër
ehng'-elsk*

Er der en chauffeur
som taler engelsk?
*air dair in chau-för'
sum tah'-ler ehng'-elsk*

Finns det en chaufför
som talar engelska?
*finns dëh en shaw-för'
som tä-lär ehng-elskä*

How many kilometres is it?

Hvor mange kilometer
er det?
*vohr mahng'-ëh
kilo-moh' ter air deh*

Hvor mange kilometer
er det?
*vor mang'-ëh
kilo-meh'-ter air deh*

Hur många kilometer
är det?
*hōōr mongä
kilo-meh'-ter ëh dëh*

I must be back by . . .

Jeg må være tilbake
klokken . . .
*yay maw vairë
till-bāh'-kë
klock'-ken . . .*

Jeg skal være tilbage
inden . . .
*yi skal vaire til-bah'-ëh
in'-nen . . .*

Jag måste vara tillbaka
klockan . . .
*yä moss-të vä-rä
till-bäh'-ka
klock'-än . . .*

SIGHT-SEEING

Is there an English-speaking guide?

Er der en guide som
snakker engelsk?
*air dair ehn guide som
snäk'-ker ehng'-elsk*

Er der en rejsefører
der taler engelsk?
*air dair in ry'-se-fö-rër
dair tāh'-ler ehng'-elsk*

Finns det en guide
som talar engelska?
*finns dëh en guide som
tä-lär ehng'-ëlskä*

Have we time to see . . . ?

Har vi tid å se . . . ?
hahr vee teed aw sēh . . .

Har vi tid til at se . . . ?
*hahr vee teeth til at
sēh . . .*

Har vi tid att se . . . ?
här vee teed ätt sēh . . .

| Norwegian | Danish | Swedish |

I want to see all that is worth seeing.

Jeg ønsker å se alt som
er verdt å se

*yay öns'-ker aw sēh
ahlt' som air vairt'
aw sēh*

Jeg ønsker at se alt
hvad der er værd at se

*yi ön'-sker at sēh ahlt
vath dair air vair at sēh*

Jag vill se allt som är
värt att se

*yā vill sēh ållt som ēh
vairt' ätt sēh*

At what time does the excursion start (end)?

Når begynner (slutter)
turen?

*nawr beh-yün'-ner
(slōōt'-ter) tōō'-ren*

Hvornår begynder
(ender) turen?

*vor-nawr' be-gün'-ner
(en'-ner) tōō'-ren*

Hur dags startar
(slutar) utfärden?

*hōōr dågs stär'-tär
(slōōt'-är) oot'-fair-dēn*

I have only two hours to spare.

Jeg har bare to timer
å avse

*yay hahr bah'-rĕ toh
tee'-mer aw ahv-seh*

Jeg har kun to timer
til min rådighed

*yi hahr koon toh
tee'-mer til meen
raw'-thee-heth*

Jag är bara ledig två
timmar

*yā ēh bā-rä leh'-dig
tvaw' tim'-mär*

What street (church) is this?

Hvilken gate (kirke)
er dette?

*vill'-ken gah'-tĕ
(cheer'-kĕ) air det'-tĕ*

Hvilken gade (kirke)
er dette?

*vill'-ken gah'-the
(keer'-ke) air det'-te*

Vad är detta för en
gata (kyrka)?

*väd ēh det'-tä för en
gā-tä (chür'-kä)*

What building is that?

Hvilken bygning er
det?

*vill'-ken büg'-ning air
deh*

Hvad er det for en
bygning?

*vath air deh for in
büg'-ning*

Vad är det för en
byggnad?

*väd ēh dēh för en
büg'-näd*

I am interested in art galleries, museums.

Jeg er interessert i
kunstgallerier, museer

*yay air in-ter-re-sēhrt'
ee kōōnst-gal-le-ree'-er,
moo-seh'-ĕr*

Jeg er interesseret i
kunst gallerier,
museer

*yi air in-tĕ-rĕ-sēh'-ret
ee kōōnst gal-lē-ree'-er,
moo-say'-ĕr*

Jag är intresserad av
konstmuseer, museer

*yā ēh in-tres-seh'-rad
av konst-moo-seh'-er,
moo-seh'-er*

Is it worth getting out?

Er det umaken verdt
å gå ut?

*air deh ōō'-mah-ken
vairt aw gaw ōōt*

Er det værd at stå ud?

air deh vair at staw ōōth

Är det mödan värt
att gå ut?

*ēh dēh mö'-dän vairt
ätt gaw ōōt*

| Norwegian | Danish | Swedish |

**I want to see the church, cathedral, the town hall, the
university.**

Jeg ønsker å se kirken, domkirken, rådhuset, universitetet	Jeg vil gerne se kirken, domkirken, rådhuset, universitetet	Jag vill see kyrkan, domkyrkan, stadshuset, universitetet
yay öns'-ker aw sëh cheer'-ken, dom'-cheer-ken, rawd'-hoos-eh, oo-nee-vair-see-teh-të	*yi vil gair'-ne sëh keer'-ken, dom'-keer-ken, rawth'-hoos-et, öö-nee-vair-see-teh'-tët*	*yä vill sëh chürk'-än, dom'-chürk-än, städs'-hoos-ët, oo-nee-ver-see-tëh'-tet*

I should like to visit the botanical gardens, the zoo.

Jeg vil gjerne se den botaniske hage, den zologiske hage	Jeg vil gerne se den botaniske have, zoologiske have	Jag skulle gärna vilja besöka botaniska trädgården, zoologiska trädgården
yay vill yair'-në sëh den bo-tah'-nee-skë hah-gë, den zo-lohg'-iske hah'-gë	*yi vil gair'-ne seh den bo-täh'-nee-ske häh'-vë, zo-lõhg'-iske häh'-vë*	*yä sköōl'-lë yair'-nä vil'-lä beh-sö'-kä bo-tän'-iskä trëd'-gawr-den, zoolog-iskä trëd'-gawr-den*

Wait here.

Vent her	Vent her	Vänta här
vent hair	*vent hear*	*ven'-tä hair*

Is it open?

Er det åpent?	Er det åbent?	Är det öppet?
air deh aw'-pent	*air deh aw'-pent*	*ëh dëh öp'-pet*

When does it open (close)?

Når åpner (lukker) det?	Hvornår åbner (lukker) det?	Når öppnar (stänger) det?
nawr awp'-ner (look'-ker) deh	*vor-nawr' awp'-ner (luk'-ker) deh*	*nair öpp'-när (stëng'-ër) dëh*

To whom does one apply for permission to enter?

Hvem må man spørre om tillatelse til å gå inn?	Hvem henvender man sig til for at få lov til at komme ind?	Vem vänder man sig till för att få lov att gå in?
vehm maw män spör'-rë om til-lah'-tel-së till aw gaw in	*vehm hen'-ven-ner man sigh til for at faw law til at kom'-me in*	*vëm ven'-dër män say till för ätt faw lawv ätt gaw in*

Norwegian	*Danish*	*Swedish*

Can one see over the church, the castle?

Norwegian	Danish	Swedish
Kan man få se seg om i kirken, på slottet?	Kan man kikke på kirken, på slottet?	Kan man bese kyrkan, slottet?
kăn măn faw sēh say om ee cheer'-ken, paw slot'-tĕ	*kan man keek'-keh paw keer'-ken, paw slot'-tet*	*kăn măn bēh-sēh' chür'-kăn, slot'-tĕt*

Can we go round alone?

Kan vi gå rundt alene?	Kan vi gå rundt alene?	Kan vi gå omkring ensamma?
kăn vee gaw rŏōnt ah-le'-nĕ	*kan vee gaw rŏōnt al-le'-ne*	*kăn vee gaw omm-kring' ĕn'-săm-mă*

Do we need a guide?

Behøver vi en guide?	Behøver vi en fører?	Behöver vi en guide?
beh-hö'-ver vee ehn guide	*beh-hö'-ver vee in fö'-re*	*bēh-hö'-ver vee en guide*

When does the next tour start?

Når begynner neste omvisning?	Hvornår begynder den næste omvisning?	När börjar nästa visning?
nawr beh-yün'-ner nes'-tĕ om'-vees-ning	*vor-nawr' be-gün'-ner den neste om'-vēēs-ning*	*nair bör'-yăr nĕstă vees'-ning*

How long must we wait?

Hvor lenge må vi vente?	Hvor længe skal vi vente?	Hur länge behöver vi vänta?
vohr lehn-gĕ maw vee ven'-tĕ	*vor laing'-eh skal vee ven'-te*	*hōōr lĕngĕ bēh-hö'-ver vee ven'-tă*

I am not interested in that.

Jeg er ikke interesert i det	Jeg er ikke interesseret i det	Jag är inte intresserad av det
yay air ick'-kĕ in-teh-reh-sehrt' ee deh	*yi air ick'-ke in-te-re-seh'-ret ee deh*	*yă ēh in'-tĕ in-trĕs-seh'-răd ăv dēh*

How much farther have we to go?

Hvor meget lengere er det å gå?	Hvor langt har vi endnu at gå?	Hur långt har vi kvar att gå?
vohr mēh'-get lehng'-er-ĕh air deh aw gaw	*vor lahngt hahr vee en'-noo at gaw*	*hōōr longt hăr vee kvăr att gaw*

How many rooms, steps, are there?

Hvor mange rom, trin, er der?	Hvor mange værelser, trin, er der?	Hur många rum, trapsteg, är det?
vohr mahng-ĕh rohm, trin air dair	*vor mangh'-eh vair'-rel-ser, treen, air dair*	*hōōr mongă rōōm, trăp-stĕg ēh dēh*

Norwegian	Danish	Swedish

Is there a good view?

Er der god utsikt?	Er der en god udsigt?	Är det bra utsikt?
air dair goh oot'-sickt	*air dair in goth ōōth'-sickt*	*ēh dēh brä oot'-sikt*

May I take a photograph here?

Kan jeg fotografere her?	Må jeg fotografere her?	Får jag fotografera här?
kăn yay fo-to-grăh-feh'-rě hair	*maw yi fo-to-grăh-fē'-rě hehr*	*fawr yă fo-to-grăh-feh'-ră hair*

Please stop a moment.

Vær så vennlig å stoppe et øyeblik	Vent et øjeblik	Var snäll och stanna ett ögonblick
vair saw ven'-lee aw stop'-pě ett öy'-eh-blick	*vent it öy'-eh-blick*	*vär snĕll ock stăn-nă ett ög'-on-blick*

Is this the . . . memorial?

Er dette . . . minnesmerket?	Er dette . . . mindesmærket?	Är detta . . . minnesmärket över . . . ?
air det'-tě . . . min'-nes-mair-kě	*air det'-te . . . meen'-nes-mair-ket*	*ēh det'-tă min'-nes-mĕr'-ket ö'-ver . . .*

Where is . . . buried?

Hvor er . . . gravlagt?	Hvor er . . . begravet?	Var ligger . . . begravd?
vohr air . . . grahv'-lahgt	*vor air . . . beh-grăh'-vet*	*vär lig-ger . . . bēh-grävd,*

Where did . . . live?

Hvor bodde . . . ?	Hvor boede . . . ?	Var bodde . . . ?
vohr bohd-dě . . .	*vor bo'-the . . .*	*var bohd'-dě . . .*

What is the name of that?

Hva heter det?	Hvad hedder det?	Vad heter det?
vah hēh'-ter deh	*vath heth'-er deh*	*văd hēh'-ter dēh*

How much is the catalogue?

Hvor mye koster katalogen?	Hvad koster kataloget?	Vad kostar katalogen?
vohr mü-ĕh kos'-ter kăh-tăh-law'-gen	*vath kos'-ter kăh-tă-lōh'-ĕt*	*văd koss'-tăr kăh-tăh-log'-ĕn*

Norwegian	Danish	Swedish

Can I buy any picture-postcards?

Kan jeg få kjøpe noen prospektkort?	Kan jeg købe nogle prospektkort?	Kan man köpa vy-kort?
kăn yay faw chöpĕ noh-en proh-spĕhkt'-kort	*kan yi kö'-be noh'-le pro-spekt'-kort*	*kăn măn chö'-pă vü'-kohrt*

Have you a book about ...?

Har De en bok om ...?	Har De en bog om ...?	Har ni någon bok om ...?
hahr dee ehn bohk om ...	*hahr dee in bow om ...*	*hār nee naw'-gon bohk omm ...*

Does one have to walk?

Blir en nødt til å spasere?	Behøver man at gå?	Måste man gå till fots?
bleer ehn nut till aw spah-sēh'-rĕ	*be-hö'-ver man at gaw*	*moss'-tĕ măn gaw till föhts*

Is it close by?

Er det i nærheten?	Er det nær ved?	Är det nära?
air deh ee nair'-heh-ten	*air deh nair veth*	*ēh dĕh nairă*

Let us go.

La oss gå	Lad os gå	Låt oss gå
lah os gaw	*lath us gaw*	*lawt oss gaw*

Let us rest a bit.

La oss hvile en liten stund	Lad os hvile os et øjeblik	Låt oss vila oss ett tag
lah os vee'-lĕ ehn lee-ten stöön	*lath us vee'-le us it oy'-eh-blick*	*lawt oss vee'-lă oss ĕtt tāg*

It is too hot.

Det er for varmt	Det er for varmt	Det är för varmt
deh air for vahrmt	*deh air for vahrmt*	*dēh ēh för vahrmt*

Where can I get some refreshments?

Hvor kan jeg få noen forfriskninger?	Hvor kan jeg få lidt forfriskninger?	Var kan man få förfriskningar?
vohr kăn yay faw noh'-ĕn for-frisk'-ning-ĕr	*vor kan yi faw leet for-frisk'-ning-ĕr*	*văr kăn măn faw för-frisk'-ning-ăr*

Norwegian	Danish	Swedish

I have seen enough for today.

Jeg har sett nok i dag	Jeg har set nok i dag	Jag har sett nog för i
yay hahr set nok	*yi hahr seht nok ee day*	dag
ee dahg		*yā hār set nohg för ee*
		dāg

It is going to rain.

Det blir regn	Det bliver regnvejr	Det blir regn
deh bleer rayn	*deh bleer ryn'-vair*	*dēh bleer rĕngn*

Where can we shelter?

Hvor kan vi søke ly?	Hvor kan vi søge ly?	Var kan vi söka skydd?
vohr kăn vee sö'-kĕ lü	*vor kan vee sö'-ĕh lü*	*var kăn vee sö'-kă*
		shüdd

Can we get a taxi?

Kan vi få fatt i en	Kan vi få en taxa?	Kan vi få en taxi?
drosje?	*kan vee faw in taxa*	*kăn vee faw en tăxi*
kăn vee faw fătt ee		
ehn drosje'-ĕh		

Which is the best way back?

Hva er den beste vei	Hvad er den bedste vej	Vad är bästa vägen
tilbake?	tilbage?	tillbaka?
vah air den bes'-tĕ vay	*vath air den bes'-te vy*	*vād ĕh bes'-tă vaigĕn*
till-bah'-kĕ	*til-bāhg'-ĕh*	*till-bah'-kă*

Drive through . . .

Kjør gjennom . . .	Kør gennem . . .	Kör genom . . .
chör yen'-om . . .	*kör gen'-nem . . .*	*chör yĕh'-nom . . .*

Drive back as quickly as possible.

Kjør tilbake så hurtig	Kør tilbage så hurtigt	Kör tillbaka så fort
som mulig	som muligt	som möjligt
chör till-bah'-kĕ saw	*kör til-bāhg'-ĕh saw*	*chör till-bah'-kă saw*
hōōr'-tee som	*hōōr'-teet som*	*fohrt som möy-lit*
moo'-lee	*moo'-leet*	

How much ought I to give the guide?

Hvor mye bør jeg gi	Hvor meget bør jeg	Hur mycket bör jag
guiden?	give føreren?	ge guiden?
vohr mü-ĕh bör yay	*vor my'-et bör yi ghee*	*hōōr mücket bör yā*
yee guiden	*fö'-rĕ-ren*	*yĕh guiden*

Norwegian	*Danish*	*Swedish*

Are you free tomorrow?

Er De ledig i morgen?	Er De fri i morgen?	Är ni ledig i morgon?
air dee lēh'-dee ee mor'-en	*air dee free ee mor'-en*	*ēh nee lēh-dee ee mor'-ron*

Can you come at ten?

Kan De komme klokken ti?	Kan De komme klokken ti?	Kan ni komma klockan tio?
kän dee kom'-mĕ klock'-ken tee	*kan dee kom'-me klok'-ken tee*	*kän nee kom'-mă kloek'-än tee'-ŏh*

VISITING FRIENDS

I am looking for number . . .

Jeg leter etter nummer . . .	Jeg er ved at finde nummer . . .	Jag letar efter nummer . . .
yay lēh'-ter ĕt-ter nōōm'-mer . . .	*yi air veth at fin'-nĕ nōōm'-mer . . .*	*yā leh'-tar ĕf-ter nōōm'-mer . . .*

Does Mr. . . . live here?

Bor herr . . . her?	Bor herr . . . her?	Bor herr . . . här?
bohr hĕrr . . . hair	*bohr hair . . . hear*	*bohr hĕrr . . . hair*

Is he at home?

Er han hjemme?	Er han hjemme?	Är han hemma?
air hăhn yem'-mĕ	*air han yem'-me*	*ēh hăn hĕm'-mă*

I am . . .

Jeg er . . .	Jeg er . . .	Jag är . . .
yay air . . .	*yi air . . .*	*yā ēh . . .*

Tell him it is . . .

Kan De si ham at det er . . .	Sig til ham det er . . .	Säg honom att det är . . .
kän dee see hăm at deh air . . .	*see til ham deh air . . .*	*say hon'-om att dēh ēh . . .*

Here is my card.

Her er visittkortet mitt	Her er mit visitkort	Här är mitt visitkort
hair air vee-sit'-kort-tĕ mit	*hear air mit vee-sit'-kort*	*hair ēh mitt vee-seet'-kort*

Norwegian	Danish	Swedish

Please come in.

Værsågod kom inn	Vær så venlig at komme ind	Var så god och stig in
vair'-saw-goh kom' in	*vair saw ven'-lee at kom'-me in*	*vär saw gohd' ock steeg' in*

He will be in at . . .

Han vil være tilstede klokken . . .	Han vil være hjemme klokken . . .	Han är inne klockan . . .
hähn vill vairĕ till-stěh'-dĕ klock-ken . . .	*han vil vaire yem'-me klok'-ken . . .*	*hän ēh in-nĕ klock'-än . . .*

He won't be long.

Han blir ikke lenge	Han kommer snart	Han kommer inte att dröja länge
hähn bleer ick'-kĕ lehng-ĕh	*han kom'-mer snahrt*	*hän kom'-mer in'-tĕ att dröyä lĕngĕ*

Can you come at . . . ?

Kan De komme klokken . . . ?	Kan De komme klokken . . . ?	Kan ni komma klockan . . . ?
kän dee kom'-mĕ klock'-ken . . .	*kan dee kom'-me klok'-ken . . .*	*kän nee kom'-mä klock'-än . . .*

Please tell him I called.

Vær så vennlig å si at jeg har vært her	Vær venlig at fortælle ham jeg har været her	Var snäll och säg honom att jag har varit här
vair saw ven'-lee aw see at yay hahr vairt' hair	*vair ven'-lee at for-tĕl'-lĕ hahm yi hahr vairet hear*	*vär snĕll ock say hon'-om att yä här vuh'-rit hair*

Mr. . . . asked me to call on you.

Herr . . . ba meg om å besøke Dem	Hr. . . . bad mig indfinde mig her	Herr . . . bad mig besöka er
hĕrr . . . bah may om aw beh-sö'-kĕ dĕm	*hair . . . bā-th my in'-fin-ne my hear*	*hĕrr . . . bahd may bēh-sö'-kä ēhr*

I speak very little Norwegian, Danish, Swedish.

Jeg snakker svært lite norsk, dansk, svensk	Jeg taler meget lidt norsk, dansk, svensk	Jag talar mycket lite norska, danska, svenska
yay snak'-ker svairt lee'-tĕ norsk, dähnsk, svĕnsk	*yi täh'-ler my'-et lit norsk, dansk, svensk*	*ya tä'-lar mückĕ lee'-tĕ norskä, danskä, svenskä*

Norwegian	Danish	Swedish

How do you do.

Goddag	God dag	Goddag
goh-dahg'	*goh day*	*goh-dåg'*

Do you speak English, French, German?

Snakker De engelsk, fransk, tysk?	Taler De engelsk, fransk, tysk?	Talar ni engelska, franska, tyska?
snåk'-ker dee ehng'-elsk, frahnsk, tüsk	*tåh'-ler dee ehng'-elsk, fransk, tüsk*	*tå'-lar nee ehng'-elskå, franskå, tüskå*

I believe . . . has mentioned my name to you.

Jeg tror . . . har nevnt mitt navn for Dem	Jeg mener . . . har omtalt mig til Dem	Jag tror att . . . har nämnt mitt namn för er
yay trohr . . . hahr nehvnt mit nahvn for dem	*yi meh'-ner . . . hahr um'-tahlt my til dem*	*yå trohr att . . . hår nåmt mitt nåmn för åhr*

I have a letter of introduction.

Jeg har et introduksjonsbrev	Jeg har et anbefalingsbrev	Jag har ett introduktionsbrev
yay hahr ětt in-tro-dŏŏk-shohns'-brēhv	*yi hahr it ahn'-beh-fāh-lings-brehv*	*yå hår ětt intrŏ-dook-shohns'-brēhv*

He is a great friend of mine.

Han er en god venn av meg	Han er en god ven af mig	Han är en mycket god vän till mig
håhn air ehn goh věn ahv may	*han air in goth ven åh my*	*han ēh en mücket gohd ven till may*

I have known him for a long time.

Jeg har kjent ham lenge	Jeg har kendt ham længe	Jag har känt honom länge
yay hahr chěnt håm lehng'-ěh	*yi hahr kent hahm laing'-ěh*	*yå hår chěnt hon'-om lěngě*

I knew him in . . .

Jeg kjente ham i . . .	Jeg kendte ham i . . .	Jag kände honom i . . .
yay chen'-tě håm ee . . .	*yi ken'-te hahm ee . . .*	*ya chěn-dě hon'-om ee*

May I introduce . . . ?

Får jeg presentere . . . ?	Må jeg forestille . . . ?	Får jag presentera . . . ?
fawr yay preh-sen-te'-rě . . .	*maw yi fohr'-rě-still-lě . . .*	*fawr jag prě-sěn-tēh'-rǎ . . .*

Norwegian	Danish	Swedish

He sends you his greetings.

Han sender Dem sin hilsen	Han sender sine hilsner til Dem	Han hälsar er
hăhn sen'-ner dem sin hill'-sen	*hahn sen'-ner see'-ne hill'-sner till dem*	*hăn hĕl-sär ĕhr*

My wife, my husband, my son, my daughter, my friend.

Min frue, min mann, min søn, min datter, min venn	Min kone, min mand, min søn, min datter, min ven	Min hustru, min man, min son, min dotter, min vän
min froo'-ĕh, min mănn, min sön, min dăt'-ter, min ven	*meen koh'-nĕ, meen man, meen sön, meen dat'-ter, meen ven*	*min hŏŏs-trŏŏ, min mănn, min sawn, min dot-ter, min ven*

My uncle, aunt.

Min onkel, tante	Min onkel, tante	Min farbror, min tant
min ohnk'-ĕl, tăhn'-tĕ	*meen oon'-kel, tan'-tĕ*	*min făr-brohr, min tănt*

My nephew, niece.

Min nevø, niese	Min nevø, niece	Min brorson, min brorsdotter
min nĕh'-vö, nee-ēh'-sĕ	*meen neh-vö', nee-ais'-sĕh*	*min brohr-sawn, min brohrs-dŏt-ter*

My cousin (male, female).

Min fetter, kusine	Min fætter, kusine	Min kusin
min fet'-ter, kŏŏ-see'-nĕ	*meen fait'-ter, kŏŏ-see'-nĕ*	*min kŏŏ'-seen'*

My brother-in-law, sister-in-law.

Min svoger, svigerinne	Min svoger, svigerinde	Min svåger, svägerska
min svaw'-ger, svee-ger-in'-nĕ	*meen svoh'-ĕr, sveer-rin'-nĕ*	*min svaw-gĕr, svaig'-ĕr-skă*

I shall come to the hotel, boarding-house.

Jeg kommer til hotellet, pensjonatet	Jeg kommer til hotellet, pensionatet	Jag kommer till hotellet, pensionatet
yay kom'-mer till hoh-tel'-let, pahng-shoh-nah'-tĕ	*yi kom'-mer till hotel'-let, păhn-shoh-nāh'-tet*	*yă kom-mer till hotĕl-let, păn-shŏ-nah'-tet*

Here is the address.

Her er adressen	Her er adressen	Här är adressen
Hair air ăh-dres'-sen	*Hear air ăh-dres'-sen*	*Hair ĕh ad-dres'-sĕn*

Norwegian	Danish	Swedish

Please do not go to any trouble.

Ikke gjør noe ekstra bryderi	Lad være med at gøre for meget ud af det	Gör er inte något besvär
ick'-kĕ yŏr noh'-ĕh ĕks-trăh brüd'-dĕ-ree	*lath vaire meth at gŏ'-rĕ for my'-et ooth ăh deh*	*yŏr ēhr in'-tĕ naw'-got bĕh-svair'*

I hope it is not inconvenient.

Jeg håper det ikke er ubeleilig	Jeg håber det passer Dem	Jag hoppas det inte är besvärligt
yay haw'-per deh ick'-kĕ air oo-beh-lay'-lee	*yi haw'-per deh pas'-ser dem*	*yā hop'-păs dēh in-tĕ ĕh bĕh-svair'-lit*

I shall be glad to help you, accompany you, invite you.

Jeg vil gjerne hjelpe Dem, følge Dem, invitere Dem	Jeg vil gerne hjælpe Dem, tage med Dem, invitere Dem	Jag vill gärna hjälpa er, följa er, bjuda er
yay vill yair'-nĕ yel'-pĕ dem, fŏl'-lĕ dem, in-vee-te'-rĕ dem	*yi vill gair'-ne yel'-pe dem, tah meth dem, in-vee-tĕ'-rĕ dem*	*yā vill yair'-nă yel-pă ēhr, fŏl'-yă ēhr, bew-dă ēhr*

Until we meet again.

På gjensyn	På gensyn	På återseende
paw yen'-sün	*paw ghen'-sün*	*paw aw-tĕr-sĕh'-ĕn-dĕ*

Norwegian	Danish	Swedish

SHOPPING

Shops are generally open from 9 a.m. to 5 p.m., though many stay open until 6 p.m. On Saturdays the practice varies, some shops closing at 2 p.m., but others (including many food shops) staying open until 5 p.m. The Scandinavian countries use the metric system. 1 inch is rather less than 2½ centimetres; 1 metre is just under 40 inches; a kilogram is about 2¼ lb. (Some equivalent figures in the metric system are given on page 183.) In shoes a size 39 is a British size 6; 37 is a British size 5.

TOBACCONIST

British and American brands are plentiful but more expensive than in Britain. Swedish brands are cheaper than the medium-priced British cigarettes in Britain. Cigars (Dutch usually) are much cheaper than in Britain.

I want some cigarettes.

Jeg vil gjerne ha noen cigaretter *yay vill yair'-nĕ hah noh'-ĕn cig-ah-ret'-ter*	Jeg vil gerne have nogle cigaretter *yi vill gair'-ne hah noh'-le see-gah-ret'-ter*	Jag vill ha några cigarretter *yā vill hā naw'-grā cigarret'-ter*

A packet of cigarettes.

En pakke sigaretter *ehn păk'-kĕ sig-ah-ret'-ter*	En pakke cigaretter *in pak'-ke see-gah-ret'-ter*	Ett paket cigarretter *ĕtt păk-ĕht cigarret'-ter*

Cigars, pipe tobacco.

Sigarer, pipetobakk *see-gahr'-ĕr, pee'-peh-toh-băkk'*	Cigarer, pibe tobak *see-găhr'-ĕr, pee'-bĕ toh-băhk'*	Cigarrer, piptobak *see-gărr'-ĕr, peep-toh'-băhk*

Have you British, American cigarettes?

Har De engelske, amerikanske sigaretter? *hahr dee ehng'-elsk-ĕh, ăm-eh-ree-kahn'-skĕh cig-ah-ret'-ter*	Har De engelske, amerikanske cigaretter? *hahr dee ehng'-elske, ame-ree-kan'-skĕh see-gah-ret'-ter*	Har ni engelska, amerikanska cigarretter? *hăr nee ehng'-elskă, amri-kān-skă cigarret'-ter*

Have you a cheaper brand?

Har De et billigere merke? *hahr dee ett bil'-lee-ĕh-rĕ mair'-kĕ*	Har De et billigere mærke? *hahr dee it bil'-lee-re muir'-ke*	Har ni en billigare sort? *hăr nee en bil'-lee-gă-rĕ sort*

I shall take these.

Jeg tar disse *yay tahr dis'-sĕ*	Jeg tager disse *yi tar dees'-se*	Jag tar de här *yā tār dēh hair*

Have you any matches?

Har De fyrstikker? *hahr dee für'-stick-ker*	Har De tændstikker? *hahr dee ten'-stick-ker*	Har ni tändstickor? *hăr nee tĕnd'-stickor*

Cigarette case.

Sigarettetui *cig-ah-ret'-eh-too-ee*	Cigaretetui *see-gah-ret'- eh-too-ee*	Cigarrettetui *cigarrett'-ĕh-too-ee'*

| *Norwegian* | *Danish* | *Swedish* |

Cigarette-holder.

Sigarettmunnstykke	Cigaretrør	Cigarrettmunstycke
cig-ah-ret'-mōōn-	*see-gah-ret'-rŏr*	*cigarrett'-mōōn-*
stük'-kĕ		*stück'-kĕ*

Lighter, fuel.

Sigarettenner, bensin	Fyrtøj (lighter),	Cigarrettändare,
cig-ah-ret'-ten'-ner,	lightervædske	bensin
ben'-seen	*für'-toy, lighter'-vais-ke*	*cigarett'-ten-dă-rĕ,*
		ben'-seen

Flint, wick.

Flint, veke	Sten, væge	Flinta, veke
flint, vēh'-kĕ	*stehn, vai'-eh*	*flintă, vēh'-kĕ*

Pipe, pipe-cleaner.

Pipe, piperenser	Pibe, piberenser	Pipa, piprensare
pee'-pĕ, pee'-pĕ-ren-ser	*pee'-be, pee'-be-ren-ser*	*pee'-pă, peep'-rĕhn-sărĕ*

THE POST OFFICE

Where is the main post office?

Hvor er	Hvor er	Var är
hovedpostkontoret?	hovedpostkontoret?	huvudpostkontoret?
vohr air	*vor air*	*văr ēh*
hoh'-ved-post-kon-	*hoveth'-posst-kon-*	*hoo'-vod-posst-kon-*
toh'-rĕ	*toh'-ret*	*toh'-ret*

I want to send this letter by air mail.

Jeg vil gjerne sende	Jeg ønsker at sende	Jag vill skicka detta
dette brevet som	dette brev som	brevet som flygpost
flypost	luftpost	*yă vill shick'-kă det'-tă*
yay vill yair'-nĕ sen'-nĕ	*yi ön'-sker at sen'-ne*	*brēh'-vet som*
det'-tĕ brēh'-vĕ	*det-te brehv som*	*flüg'-posst*
som flü'-post	*lōōft-posst*	

What stamp is needed for this letter, this post card?

Hva blir portoen på	Hvilket frimærke skal	Vad är portot på det
dette brevet,	bruges til dette brev,	här brevet, kortet?
brevkortet?	dette kort?	*văh ēh portot paw dēh*
vah bleer pohr-'-toh-en	*vil-ket free'-mairke skal*	*hair brēh-vĕt, kohrt'-ĕt*
paw det'-tĕ brēh'-vĕ,	*broo'-es til det-te*	
brēhv'-kort-ĕh	*brehv, det-te kort*	

Norwegian	Danish	Swedish

By ordinary mail.

Som alminnelig post	Som admindelig	Med vanlig post
som ăl-min'-nĕ-lee post	postforsendelse	*mēh văn'-lee posst*
	som al-meen'-ne-lee	
	posst'-for-sen'-nel-se	

I want to send this parcel.

Jeg vil gjerne sende	Jeg vil gerne sende	Jag vill skicka det
denne pakken	denne pakke	här paketet
yay vill yair'-nĕ sen'-nĕ	*yi vil gair-ne sen'-ne*	*ya vill shick'-kă dēh*
den'-nĕ păk'-ken	*den'-ne pak'-ke*	*hair pah-keht'-ĕt*

This parcel is fragile.

Denne pakken er	Denne pakke er	Det här paketet är
knuselig	skrøbelig	ömtåligt
den'-nĕ păk'-ken air	*den'-ne pak'-ke air*	*deh hair pah-keht'-ĕt*
knŏŏ'-seh-lee	*skrö'-be-lee*	*ēh ŏmm'-taw-lit*

Which section do I go to?

Hvilken avdeling må	Hvilken afdeling skal	Vilken lucka ska jag
jeg gå til?	jeg gå til?	gå till?
vill'-ken ahv-dēhl'-ing	*vil'-ken aw'-deh-ling*	*vil'-ken look'-kă skă*
maw yay gaw till	*skal yi gaw till*	*yă gaw till*

I want to register this letter, parcel.

Jeg vil gjerne	Jeg ønsker at anbefale	Jag vill rekommendera
rekommandere dette	dette brev, pakke	det här brevet, paketet
brevet, denne pakken	*yi ŏn'-sker at*	*ya vill*
yay vill yair'-nĕ	*ahn'-beh-fah-le*	*re-kom-mĕn-deh'-ră*
reh-kom-măn-dĕh'-rĕ	*det-te brehv, pak'-ke*	*dēh hair brēh'-vet,*
det'-tĕ brēh'-vĕ,		*pah-keht'-ĕt*
den'-nĕ păk'-ken		

There is nothing dutiable in this package.

Der er ingenting	Der er intet	Det är inget
tollpliktig i denne	toldpligtigt i denne	tullpliktigt i paketet
pakken	pakke	*dēh ēh ingĕt*
dair air ing'-ehn-ting	*dair air in'-tet*	*tŏŏll-pliktit ee*
tol'-plick-tee ee	*tol'-plik-tit ee*	*pah-keht'-ĕt*
den'-nĕ păk'-ken	*den-ne pak'-ke*	

Air-mail.

Flypost	Luftpost	Flygpost
flü'-post	*lŏŏft'-posst*	*flüg'-posst*

Norwegian	*Danish*	*Swedish*

Letter-box, post-box.

Brevkasse, postkasse	Brevkasse, postkasse	Brevlåda
brēhv'-kăs-sĕ, *post'-kăs-sĕ*	*brehv'-kas-se,* *posst'-kas-se*	*brēhv-law-dă*

Inland mail, foreign mail.

Innenrikspost, utenrikspost	Indenlands post, udenlandsk post	Inrikes post, post till utlandet
in'-nen-ricks-post, *ōō'-ten-ricks-post*	*in'-nen-lansk posst,* *oothen'-lansk posst*	*in-reekĕs posst, posst* *till oot'-lăndĕt*

Where are the telegram forms?

Hvor er telegramblankettene?	Hvor er telegramblanketterne?	Var är telegramblanketterna?
vohr air *tele-grăm'-blahn-* *ket'-te-ne*	*vor air* *teh-leh-grăm'-blahn-* *ket'-ter-ne*	*văr ēh* *tele-gramm'-blăn-* *kett-ĕr-nă*

Where is the Poste Restante?

Hvor er poste restante?	Hvor er Post Restanten?	Var är poste restante?
vohr air poste restante	*vor air posst restan'-ten*	*văr ēh posste restante*

My name is ...

Mitt navn er ...	Mit navn er ...	Mitt namn är ...
mit nahvn air ...	*mit nahvn air ...*	*mitt nămn ēh ...*

I am expecting a letter, parcel, from ...

Jeg venter et brev, en pakke, fra ...	Jeg venter et brev, en pakke, fra ...	Jag väntar ett brev, paket, från ...
yay ven'-ter ett brēhv, *ehn păk'-kĕ, frah ...*	*yi ven'-ter it brehv, in* *pak-ke, fra ...*	*yă ven'-tar ett brēhv,* *pah-keht' frawn ...*

When does the last post go?

Når går siste post?	Hvornår er den sidste postgang?	När går sista posten?
nawr gawr sis'-tĕ post	*vor-nawr' air den* *sees'-te posst'-gang*	*nair gawr sis'-tă* *poss'-ten*

How much did it cost?

Hvor mye kostet det?	Hvor meget kostede det?	Hur mycket kostade det?
vohr mü-ĕh kos'-tet deh	*vor my'-et kos'-te-the* *deh*	*hōōr mücket koss'-tă-,* *dĕ dēh*

Norwegian	Danish	Swedish

Can you please post this letter for me?

Vil De være så vennlig å poste dette brevet for meg?	Vil De være venlig at poste dette brev for mig?	Skulle ni vilja posta det här brevet åt mig?
vill dee vairĕ saw ven'-lee aw post'-tĕ det'-tĕ brĕh'-vĕ for may	*vil dee vaire ven'-lee at poss'-te det-te brehv for my*	*skool'-lĕ nee vil'-lă poss'-tă dĕh hair brĕh-vet awt may*

THE CHEMIST

Is there a chemist near here?

Er der et apotek i nærheten?	Er der et apotek nær ved?	Finns det ett apotek i närheten?
air dair ett ăp-poh-tĕhk' ee nair'-heh-ten	*air dair et ah-poh-tek' nair veth*	*finns dĕh ett ap-poh-tehk' ee nair'-hĕh-ten*

Can you make up this prescription for me?

Kan De lage denne medisinen til meg?	Kan De lave denne medicin til mig?	Kan ni göra i ordning det här receptet till mig?
kăn dee lah-gĕ den'-nĕ meh-dee-seen'-en till may	*kan dee lah'-ve den-ne meh-dee-seen' til my*	*kan nee yŏră ee ord'-ning dĕh hair reh-cep'-tet till may*

I got this prescription in England.

Jeg fikk denne resepten i England	Jeg fik denne recept i England	Jag fick det här receptet i England
yay fick den'-nĕ reh-sĕpt'-en ee Ehng'-lăhn	*yi fik den-ne reh-cept' ee Ehng'-lahn*	*yā fick dĕh hair reh-cep'-tet ee Ehng'-land*

When will it be ready?

Når blir den ferdig?	Hvornår vil det være færdig?	När är det färdigt?
nawr bleer den fair'-dee	*vor-nawr' vil deh vaire fair'-dee*	*nair ĕh dĕh fair'-dit*

Can you give me something for ...?

Kan De gi meg noe for ...?	Kan De give mig noget til ...?	Kan ni ge mig något för ...?
kăn dee yee may noh'-ĕh for ...	*kan dee gee my noh'-et till ...*	*kăn nee yĕh may naw'-got för ...*

Norwegian	Danish	Swedish

A chill, cold, sunburn, headache.

Norwegian	Danish	Swedish
Forkjølelse, snue, solbrenthet, hodepine	En forkølelse, snue, solbrand, hovedpine	Förkylning, snuva, solbränna, huvudvärk
for-chöl'-ĕl-sĕ, snoo'-ĕh, sohl'-brĕnt-hĕht, hoh'-dĕ-pee-nĕ	*in for-köh'-lel-se, snoo'-eh, sol'-brahn, hoveth'-pee-nĕ*	*för-chül'-ning, snoová, sohl'-brĕnnă, hoov'-od-vĕrk*

Constipation, diarrhoea, insect bites, indigestion.

Norwegian	Danish	Swedish
Forstoppelse, diarre, insektstikk, dårlig fordøyelse	Forstoppelse, diarre, insektbid, mavepine (dårlig fordøjelse)	Förstoppning, diarre, insektsbett, dålig matsmältning
for-stop'-pel-sĕ, dee-ah-rēh', insect-stick, dawr-lee for-döy'-ĕl-sĕ	*for-stop'-pel-se, dee-ah-rēh', insekt'-beeth, mah'-ve-pee-ne (dawr'-lee for-doy'-el-se)*	*för-stopp'-ning, dee-ah-rēh', in'-sĕkts-bet, daw-lee mät'-smĕltning*

I want some antiseptic, aspirin.

Norwegian	Danish	Swedish
Jeg vil gjerne ha et antiseptisk middel, aspirin	Jeg vil gerne have et antiseptisk middel, nogle aspiriner	Jag vill ha något antiseptiskt medel, aspirin
yay vill yair'-nĕ hah ett anti-sep'-tisk middel, ahs-pee-reen'	*yi vil gair'-ne hah it ahn-tee-sep'-tisk mee'-thel, noh'-le aspee-ree'-ner*	*yă vill hā naw'-got ănti-sep'-tiskt mĕh'-dĕl, äspi-reen'*

Cotton wool, adhesive tape, bandages.

Norwegian	Danish	Swedish
Bomull, plaster, bandasjer	Vat, hæfteplaster, bandager	Bomull, häftplåster, gasbinda
bom'-ööl, pläss'-ter, bahn-dah'-shĕr	*vaht, hef'-te-plās-ter, ban-dā'-sher*	*bom'-ööll, heft'-plosstĕr, găs'-bindă*

I have something in my eye.

Norwegian	Danish	Swedish
Jeg har noe i øyet	Jeg har noget i øjet	Jag har något i ögat
yay hahr noh'-ĕh ee öy'-ĕh	*yi hahr noh'-et ee öy'-et*	*yă hār naw'-got ee ö'-găt*

I want some eye lotion.

Norwegian	Danish	Swedish
Jeg vil gjerne ha noe øyen-vann	Jeg vil gerne have noget øjenvand	Jag vill ha lite ögonvatten
yay vill yair'-nĕ hah noh'-ĕh öy'-ĕn-vănn	*yi vil ger'-ne hah noh'-et oy'-en-vahn*	*yă vill hā leetĕ ö-gon-văt'-ten*

Norwegian	Danish	Swedish

I feel sick, feverish.

Jeg føler meg kvalm, feberhet	Jeg føler mig dårlig, jeg har feber	Jag mår illa, jag känner mig febrig
yay fö'-ler may kvahlm, fēh'-ber-hēht	*yi föh'-ler my dawr'-lee, yi hahr feh'-ber*	*yā mawr illă, yā chĕn-ner may fēh'-brig*

I feel faint, giddy.

Jeg føler meg matt, svimmel	Jeg føler mig udmattet, svimmel	Jag känner mig matt jag känner mig yr
yay fö'-ler may mǎt, svim'-mel	*yi föh'-ler my ooth'-mat-tet, svim'-mel*	*yā chen'-ner may mǎtt yā chen'-ner may ŭr*

I don't feel well.

Jeg føler meg ikke bra	Jeg føler mig utilpads	Jag känner mig inte bra
yay fö'-ler may ick'-kě brah	*yi föh'-ler my oo'-til-pass*	*yā chen'-ner may in-tě brah*

Can I speak to you privately?

Kan jeg få snakke mød Dem privat?	Kan jeg tale med Dem allene?	Får jag tala med er i enrum?
kǎn yay faw snak'-kě mēh dem pree'-vaht	*kan yi tah'-le meth dem al-leh'-ne*	*fawr yā tā-lǎ mēh ēhr ee ēhn'-rōŏm*

May I speak to a male, female, assistant?

Kan jeg få snakke med en ekspeditør, ekspeditrise?	Kan jeg få lov at tale med en mandlig, kvindelig, assistent?	Får jag tala med en manlig, kvinnlig, expedit?
kǎn yay faw snak'-kě mēh en ex-peh-dee-tör, ex-peh-dee-tree'-sě	*kan yi faw law at tah'-le meth in mahn'-lee, kvin'-lee, as-see-stent'*	*fawr yā tā-lǎ mēh en mǎn'-lee, kvinn'-lee, expě-deet'*

I am being served.

Jeg blir ekspedert	Jeg bliver expederet	Jag är expedierad
yay bleer ex-peh-dehrt'	*yi bleer ex-peh-deh'-ret*	*yā ēh ex-pě-yeh'-rǎd*

I am waiting to speak to that lady, that gentleman.

Jeg venter på å få tale med den damen, den herren	Jeg venter på at tale med den dame, den herre	Jag väntar paw att få tala med den damen, den herrn
yay ven'-ter paw aw faw tah'-lě mēh den dah'-měn, den hěr'-ren	*yi ven'-ter paw at tah'-le meth den dah'-me, den hair'-re*	*yā ven'-tar paw ǎtt faw tā-lǎ meh den dā-men, den hěrrn*

Norwegian	*Danish*	*Swedish*

Can you recommend a doctor?

Kan De anbefale en doktor?	Kan De anbefale en læge?	Kan ni rekommendera en doktor?
kän dee än'-beh-fah-lĕ ehn doctor	*kan dee an'-beh-fah-le in laï'-ĕh*	*kän nee rēh-kom-mĕn-deh'-rǎ en doktor*

I want something for my feet.

Jeg vil gjerne ha noe for føttene mine	Jeg vil gerne have nogct til mine fødder	Jag vill ha något för mina fötter
yay vill yair'-nĕ hah noh'-ĕh for föt'-tĕ-nĕ mee'-nĕ	*yi vil gair'-ne hah noh'-et til meene föth'-er*	*yǎ vill hǎ naw'-got för meenǎ föt'-ter*

Blisters, corns.

Blemmer, liktorn	Vabler, ligtorne	Blåsor, liktornar
blĕm-mer, leek'-torn	*vahb'-ler, lee'-torne*	*blaw'-sor,leek'-tohr-nǎr*

Bath salts.

Badesalt	Badesalte	Badsalt
bah'-dĕ-sahlt	*bäh-the-sal'-te*	*bāhd'-sahlt*

Comb.

Kam	Kam	kamm
käm	*käm*	*käm*

Face cream, face cloth.

Ansiktskrem, vaskeklut	Ansigtscreme, vaskeklud	Ansiktskräm, tvättlapp
än'-sickts-krehm, väs'-kĕ-kloot	*ahn'-sigts-krehm, vahs'-ke-klooth*	*än'-sikts-kraim, tvĕtt-läpp*

Face powder.

Pudder	Ansigtspudder	(Ansikts)puder
pŏŏd'-der	*ahn'-sigts-pooth-er*	*(än'-sikts-)pŏŏd'-der*

Fruit salt.

Fruktsalt	Frugtsalt	Fruktsalt
frŏŏkt-sahlt	*frookt'-sahlt*	*frookt'-sǎllt*

Gargle.

Munnvann	Gurglevand	Gurgelvatten
mŏŏn-vänn	*gŏŏr'-le-vahn*	*gŏŏr'-gel-vat-ten*

Norwegian	Danish	Swedish

Hair cream, hair oil.

Hårkrem, brilliantine	Hårkrem, hårolie	Briljantin, hårolja
hawr-krehm,	*hawr'-krehm,*	*brill-yän-teen',*
bril-lee-an-tee'-në	*hawr'-oh-lee-eh*	*hawr'-oll-yä*

Inhaler.

Inhalator	Indhalerer	Inhalator
in-hah-lah'-tohr	*in'-hah-le-rer*	*in-hah-lah'-tohr*

Lipstick, mirror.

Lebestift, speil	Læbestift, spejl	Läppstift, spegel
lëh'-beh-stift, spale	*lai'-he-stift, spayl*	*lëpp'-stift, spëh-gël*

Medicine.

Medisin	Medicin	Medicin
meh-dee-seen'	*meh-dee-seen'*	*medi-ceen*

Nail brush, file, varnish.

Neglebørste, fil, lakk	Neglebørste, fil, lak	Nagelborste, fil, lack
nayl'-ëh-börs'-të,	*neg'-le-bör-ste, feel, lak*	*nä'-gël-, borstë, -feel,*
feel, läkk		*-läck*

Nail varnish remover.

Neglelakkfjerner	Neglelak fjerner	Aceton
nayl'-ëh-läkk-fyair'-ner	*neg'-le-lak fyair'-ner*	*ah-seh-tawn*

Ointment.

Salve	Salve	Salva
säl'-vë	*säl'-ve*	*säl'-vä*

Paper handkerchiefs.

Papirlommetørklær	Papirlommetørklæder	Pappersnäsdukar
pah-peer'-lom-më-tör-	*pah-peer'-lom-me-tör-*	*päp-përs-nais-dookär*
klair	*klai'-ther*	

Pills, plaster.

Piller, plaster	Piller, plaster	Piller, plåster
piller, pläss'-ter	*piller, pläss'-ter*	*piller, ploss'-ter*

Razor, blade.

Barbarhøvel,	Barbermaskine,	Rakhyvel, rakblad
barberblad	barberblad	*räk'-hü-vël, räk'-bläd*
bar-bëhr'-höv'-ël,	*barbehr'-maskine,*	
bar-bëhr'-blahd	*barbehr'-blath*	

Norwegian	*Danish*	*Swedish*

Sanitary towels.

Damebind	Damebind	Sanitetsbindor
dah-mĕ-bin′	dah′-me-bin	sänni-tehts′-bindor

Scissors.

Saks	Saks	Sax
săks	saks	sax

Shaving brush, stick, cream.

Barberkost, såpe, krem	Barberkost, sæbe; creme	Rakborste, raktvål, rakkrem
bar-bĕhr′-kohst, saw′-pĕ, krehm	barbehr′-kost, saibe; kreme	rāk′-borstĕ, rāk′-tvawl, rāk′-kraim

Sleeping tablets.

Sovetabletter	Sovetabeletter	Sömntabletter
saw′-vĕ-tah-blet′-ter	sow′-eh-tah-beh-let′-ter	sömn′-tă-blet′-ter

Sponge.

Svamp	Svamp	Svamp
svahmp	svahmp	svähmp

Sunburn ointment.

Salve mot solbrenthet	Solbrand salve	Brännsalva
sahl′-vĕ moht sohl′-brĕnt-hēht	sol′-brahn salve	brĕnn-săl-vă

Sunglasses.

Solbriller	Solbriller	Solglasögon
sohl′-bril-ler	sol′-bril-ler	sohl′-glahs-ö-gon

Suntan lotion.

Solbadolje	Solbrand vædske	Sololja
sohl′-bahd-ohl-yĕ	sol′-brahn vais′-ke	sohl′-ol-yă

Tooth brush, paste, powder.

Tannbørste, krem, pulver	Tandbørste, pasta, pulver	Tandborste, kräm, pulver
tănn′-börs-tĕ, krehm, pōōl′-ver	tan′-bör-ste, pahs′-tah, pol′-ver	tănd′-borstĕ, -kraim, -pōōl-ver

Tube (of paste, etc.).

Tube	Tube	Tub
too′-bĕ	too′-bĕ	toob

Norwegian	Danish	Swedish

THE HAIRDRESSER

Can you recommend a hairdresser?

Kan De anbefale en frisør?	Kan De anbefale en frisør?	Kan ni rekommendera en hårfrisörska?
kăn dee ăn'-beh-fāh lĕ en free'-sör	*kan dee ahn'-beh-fāh-le in free-sör'*	*kăn nee reh-kom-men-deh'-rä en hawr-free-sör'-skä*

Can I make an appointment?

Kan jeg få bestille time?	Kan jeg bestille (en) tid?	Kan jag beställa en tid?
kăn yay faw beh-stil'-lĕ tee-mĕ	*kan yi beh-stil'-le teeth*	*kăn yă beh-stĕl'-lă en teed*

When can I come?

Når kan jeg komme?	Hvornår kan jeg komme?	När kan jag komma?
nawr kăn yay kom'-mĕ	*vor-nawr' kan yi kom'-me*	*nair kăn yă kom'-mă*

I want a haircut, a trim.

Jeg vil gjerne klippes, trimmes	Jeg vil gerne klippes, studses	Jag vill ha klippning, putsning
yay vill yair'-nĕ klip'-pes, trim'-mes	*yi vil gair'-ne klip'-pes, stoos'-ses*	*yă vill hā klipp'-ning, pŏŏts'-ning*

Not too short.

Ikke for kort	Ikke for kort	Inte för kort
ick'-kĕ for kort	*ick'-ke for kort*	*in'-tĕ jör kort*

Fairly short.

Nokså kort	Temmeligt kort	Ganska kort
nok'-saw kort	*tem'-me-lit kort*	*găn-skă kort*

Don't use the razor on the neck.

Bruk ikke barberhøvelen i nakken	Lad være med at bruge kniven i nakken	Raka mig inte i nacken
brŏŏk ick'-kĕ bar-bēhr'-hö-vel-ĕn ee năk'-ken	*lath vaire meth at broo'-ĕh knee'-ven ee nak'-ken*	*rä-kă may in'-tĕ ee năhk'-ken*

Norwegian	Danish	Swedish

D

Don't take too much off the top.

Ikke for mye av på toppen	Ikke for meget af på toppen	Tag inte för mycket framtill
ick'-kĕ for mü-ĕh ahv paw top'-pen	*ick'-ke for my'-et af paw top'-pen*	*tā in'-te för mückĕ främ'-till*

At the back and sides.

I nakken og på sidene	Bagpå og på siderne	Där bak och på sidorna
ee näk'-ken aw paw see'-dĕ-nĕ	*bah'-paw aw paw see'-ther-ne*	*dair bāhk ock paw seed'-or-nä*

I want a shave.

Jeg vil gjerne barberes	Jeg vil gerne barberes	Jag vill bli rakad
yay vill yair'-nĕ bar-bēh'-res	*yi vil gair'-ne bahr-beh'-res*	*yā vill blee rä'-käd*

The water is too hot, cold.

Vannet er for varmt, koldt	Vandet er for varmt, koldt	Vattnet är för varmt, kallt
vän-net air for vahrmt, kolt	*vahn'-et air for vahrmt, kolt*	*vätt'-net ēh för vahrmt, källt*

Shampoo and set.

Vask og legg	Vask og opsætning	Tvättning och läggning
vahsk aw leg	*vahsk aw up'-said-ning*	*tvĕtt'-ning ock leg'-ning*

I want my hair washed.

Jeg vil gjerne ha håret vasket	Jeg vil gerne have mit hår vasket	Jag vill ha håret tvättat
yay vill yair'-nĕ hah haw'-ret vahs'-ket	*yi vil gair'-ne hah meet hawr vahs'-ket*	*yā vill hā haw'-ret tvĕt'-tät*

I want a permanent wave.

Jeg vil gjerne ha en permanent	Jeg vil gerne have mit hår permanentet	Jag vill ha en permanent
yay vill yair'-nĕ hah ehn pĕhr-mäh-nent'	*yi vil gair'-ne hah meet hawr per-mä-nen'-tet*	*yā vill hā en pĕr-mä-nent'*

I part my hair on this side, in the middle.

Jeg har skillen på denne siden, i midten	Jeg har skildning i denne side, i midten	Jag har benan på den här sidan, i mitten
yay hahr shil'-len paw den'-nĕ see'-den, ee mit'-ten	*yi hahr skil'-ning ee denne see-the, ee mit'-ten*	*yā hār bĕh'-nän paw dĕn hair see'-dän, ee mit'-ten*

Norwegian	Danish	Swedish

I brush my hair straight back.

Norwegian	Danish	Swedish
Jeg børster håret rett tilbake	Jeg børster mit hår lige tilbage	Jag borstar håret rakt bakåt
yay börs'-ter haw'-ret ret till-bah'-kĕ	*yi-bör'-ster meet hawr lee'-eh til-bāhg'-ĕh*	*yå bor'-stär haw'-ret råkt bāk'-awt*

Don't put anything on.

Jeg vil ikke ha noe i håret	Lad være med at putte noget på	Jag vill inte ha något i håret
yay vill ick'-kĕ hah noh'-ĕh ee haw'-ret	*lath vaire meth at put'-te noh'-et paw*	*yå vill in-tĕ ha naw'-got ee haw'-ret*

A little spray, cream.

Litt hårvann, krem	En lille smule hårvand, creme	Lite spray, fett
lit hawr'-vänn, krehm	*in lille smoo'-le hawr'-vähn, krĕhm*	*leetĕ spray, fĕtt*

Can I have a manicure?

Kan jeg bli manikyrert?	Kan jeg få en manicure?	Kan jag få en manikur?
kän yay blee mani-kü-rĕrt'	*kan yi faw in manicure*	*kän yå faw en mani-kür*

Face massage.

Ansikts massasje	Ansigtsmassage	Ansiktsbehandling
än-sickts-mah-sähs'-yĕ	*ahn'-sigts-mä-sähs-ye*	*änsikts-bĕh-hand'-ling*

Hairpins, slide.

Hårnåler, hårspenne	Hårklips, spænde	Hårnålar, spänne
hawr'-naw-ler, hawr'-spen-nä	*hawr'-klips, spen'-ne*	*hawr'-naw-lär, -spen'-nĕ*

Hair net.

Hårnett	Hårnet	Hårnät
hawr'-net	*hawr'-net*	*hawr'-nĕht*

Dryer.

Tørker	Tørremaskine	Torkhuv
tör'-ker	*tör'-re-mä-skee'-ne*	*tork'-hoov*

It is too hot.

Det er for varmt	Det er for varmt	Det är för varmt
deh air for vahrmt	*deh air for vahrmt*	*dĕh ĕh för värmt*

Norwegian	Danish	Swedish

PHOTOGRAPHY

Photography, photograph.

Fotografering, fotografi	Fotografering, fotografere	Fotografering, fotografi
foto-grǎ-fēh'-ring, foto-grǎh-fee'	*foto-grǎ-fēh'-ring, foto-grǎ-fee'*	*foto-grǎ-fēh'-ring, foto-grǎ-fee'*

Photographer.

Fotograf	Fotograf	Fotograf
foto-grǎhf'	*foto-grǎhf'*	*foto-grǎf'*

I want some films for my camera.

Jeg vil gjerne ha noen filmer til fotografiapparatet mitt	Jeg vil gerne have nogle film til mit kamera	Jag vill ha några filmer till min kamera
yay vill yair'-nĕ hah noh'-ĕn film-er till foto-grǎh-fee'-ǎp-pǎh-rǎht'-ĕh mit	*yi vil gair'-ne hah noh'-le film til meet kamē'-ra*	*yǎ vill hā naw'-gra film'-ĕr till min kah'-mĕ-rǎh*

Have you colour films?

Har De fargefilm?	Har De farve film?	Har ni färgfilm?
hahr dee far'-gĕ-film	*hahr dee far'-ve film*	*hǎr nee fair'-film*

Can you develop these films?

Kan De fremkalle disse filmene?	Kan De fremstille disse film?	Kan ni framkalla de här filmerna?
kǎn dee frĕm'-kǎl'-lĕ dis'-sĕ film-ĕn-ĕh	*kan dee frem'-stil-le dees'-se film*	*kǎn nee frǎm-kǎl-lǎ deh hair film'-ĕr-nǎ*

One print of each.

En kopi av hvert	Een kopi af hvert	En kopia av varje
ehn kŏh-pee' ahv vehrt	*ayn ko-pee' af vairt*	*en kŏ-pee'-ǎ ǎv vǎr-yĕ*

As soon as possible.

Så snart som mulig	Så hurtig som muligt	Så snart som möjligt
saw snahrt som moo'-lee	*saw hoor'-tit som moo'-lit*	*saw snǎrt sǫm möy'-lit*

About this size.

Omtrent denne størrelse	Som denne størrelse	Ungefär den här storleken
om-trent' den'-nĕ stŏr'-ĕl-seh	*som den'-ne stŏr'-rel-se*	*ŏŏn-yĕ-fair' dĕn hair stohr'-lēh-ken*

Norwegian	Danish	Swedish

Can you enlarge these snaps?

Kan De forstørre disse billedene?	Kan De forstørre disse optagelser?	Kan ni förstora de här fotografierna?
kän dee for-stör'-rĕ dis'-sĕ bill'-dĕ-nĕ	*kan dee for-stör'-re dees'-se up'-täh-el-ser*	*kän nee för-stoh'-rä dĕh hair foto-grä-fee'-ĕr-nä*

My camera is broken.

Fotografiapparatet mitt er i stykker	Mit fotografiapparat er gået i stykker	Min kamera är sönder
foto-gräh-fee'-äp-päh-räht'-ĕh mit air ee stück'-ĕr	*meet foto-grä-fee'-äp-päh-rät air gaw'-et ee stilk'-ker*	*min käh'-mĕ-räh eh sön-der*

Can you adjust this camera?

Kan De justere dette fotografiapparatet?	Kan De regulere dette apparat?	Kan ni justera den här kameran?
kän dee yoo-stēh'-rĕ det'-tĕ foto-gräh-fee'-äp-päh-räht'-ĕh	*kan dee rĕ-goo-lēre' dette äp-päh-rät'*	*kän nee shü-stēh'-rä dĕn hair käh'-mĕ-rähn*

This does not work properly.

Dette virker ikke ordentlig	Dette virker ikke rigtigt	Den här fungerar inte ordentligt
det'-tĕ veer-ker ick'-kĕ ornt'-lee	*dette veer'-ker ick'-ke rick'-tit*	*dĕn hair fŭŏng-gēh'-rär in-tĕ or-dent'-lit*

BOOKSHOP AND STATIONER

I want to go to a bookshop, stationer's.

Jeg vil gjerne gå til en bokhandler, papir-handler	Jeg ønsker at gå til en boghandler, papir-handler	Jag vill gå till en bokhandel, pappershandel
yay vill yair'-nĕ gaw till ehn bohk'-händ-ler, päh-peer-händ-ler	*yi ön'-sker at gaw til in bow'-han-ler, päh-peer-han-ler*	*yä vill gaw till en bohk'-händel, päp'-pĕrs-händel*

Have you any English books?

Har De noen engelske bøker?	Har De nogle engelske bøger?	Har ni några engelska böcker?
hahr dee noh'-ĕn ehng'-elsk-ĕh bö'-ker	*hahr dee noh'-le ehng'-elske bö'-er*	*här nee naw'-grä ehng'-elskä böckĕr*

Norwegian	Danish	Swedish

Have you any books by . . . in English?

Har De noen bøker	Har De nogle bøger	Har ni några böcker
av . . . på engelsk?	af . . . på engelsk?	av . . . på engelska?
hahr dee noh'-ĕn	*hahr dee noh'-le bö'-er*	*hār nee naw'-grä*
bö'-ker ahv . . . paw	*aw . . . paw ehng'-elsk*	*böckĕr äv . . . paw*
ehng'-elsk		*ehng'-elskă*

I want an English–Norwegian–Danish,–Swedish dictionary.

Jeg vil gjerne ha en	Jeg vil gerne have en	Jag vill ha ett
engelsk-norsk ordbok	engelsk-dansk ordbog	engelsk-svenskt
yay vill yair'-nĕ hah ehn	*yi vil gair'-ne hah in*	lexikon
ehng'-elsk-norsk	*ehng'-elsk-dansk*	*yä vill hä ĕtt*
ohr'-bohk	*ohr'-bow*	*ehng'-elsk-svĕnskt*
		lexi'-kon

Have you a book in very simple Norwegian (Danish, Swedish)?

Har De en bok på	Har De en bog på	Har vi någon bok på
meget enkelt norsk?	meget let dansk?	mycket lätt svenska
hahr dee ehn bohk paw	*hahr dee in bow paw*	*hār nee naw'-gon bohk*
mēh'-get ehnk'-ĕlt	*my'-et let dansk*	*paw myckĕ let*
norsk		*svĕnskă*

Have you a map of the city, region?

Har De et kart av byen,	Har De et kort af	Har ni en karta över
distriktet?	byen, distriktet?	staden, distriktet?
hahr dee ett kahrt ahv	*hahr dee et kort af*	*hār nee en kär'-tä övĕr*
bü'-ĕn, dee-strikt'-tĕ	*bü'-en, dee-strick'-tet*	*stä'-den, dee-strikt'-ett*

I want some ink.

Jeg vil gjerne ha noe	Jeg vil gerne have	Jag vill ha lite bläck
blekk	noget blæk	*yä vill hä lee'-tĕ blĕck*
yay vill yair'-nĕ hah	*yi vil gair'-ne hah*	
noh'-ĕh blĕck	*noh'-et blaik*	

Writing paper, envelopes.

Skrivepapir,	Skrivepapir,	Brevpapper, kuvert
konvolutter	konvolutter	*brēhv'-pặp-pĕr,*
skree'-vĕ-pă-peer',	*skree'-vĕ-pă-peer,*	*koo-vair'*
kon-voh-lut'-ter	*kon-vo-lut'-tĕr*	

Ball-point pen.

| Kulepenn | Kuglepen | Kulspetspenna |
| *koo'-lĕ-pen* | *koo'-lĕ-pen* | *kool'-spĕts-pĕn-nă* |

| Norwegian | Danish | Swedish |

Blotting paper.

| Trekkpapir | Trækpapir | Läskpapper |
| treck'-pă-peer | trek'-pă-peer | lĕsk'-păp'-ĕr |

Paper.

| Innpakningspapir | Brunt papir | Omslagspapper |
| in'-păk-nings-pă-peer | broont pă-peer' | ŏmm'-slăgs-păp'-ĕr |

Brush.

| Pensel | Pensel | Pensel |
| pen'-sel | pen'-sel | pen'-sel |

Fountain pen.

| Fyllepenn | Fyldepen | Reservoarpenna |
| fül'-lĕ-pen | fül'-le-pen | rĕsĕr-văr'-pĕn-nă |

Pen, nib.

| Penn, pennespiss | Pen, pennespis | Bläckpenna, stift |
| pen, pen'-nĕ-spiss | pen, pen'-ne-spis | bleck'-pĕn-nă, stift |

Pencil, propelling pencil.

Blyant, skrublyant	Blyant, skrueblyant	Blyertspenna,
blü'-ănt, skroo'-blü-ănt	blü'-ant,	skruvpenna
	skroov'-ĕh-blü'-ant	blü'-ĕrts-pĕn'-nă,
		skrōōv'-pĕn-nă

Paper clips.

| Binders | Papir clips | Pappersklämmor |
| bin'-dĕrs | pă-peer' clips | păp'-pĕrs-klĕm-mor |

Refill, rubber.

Refill, viskelær	Refill, viskelæder	Refill or reservstift
refill, vis'-kĕ-lair	refill, viss'-ke-lai-ther	gummi
		refill, rĕ-sĕrv'-stift,
		gŏŏm-mee

Sealing wax.

| Lakk | Forseglingslak | Lack |
| lăck | for-sigh'-lings-lak | lăck |

| _Norwegian_ | _Danish_ | _Swedish_ |

THE BANK

*Banks in all three countries are generally open from 10 a.m. until 3 p.m.
on weekdays, and 10 a.m. until 12 midday on Saturdays.*

Which is the way to the . . . Bank?

Hvordan finner jeg . . . banken?	Hvordan finder jeg . . . banken?	Hur kommer man till . . . banken?
vohr-dăn fin'-ner yay . . . bănken	*vor-dan' fin'-ner yi . . . banken*	*hōōr kom'-mer măn till . . . bănken*

When do they open, close?

Når åpner, lukker de?	Hvornår åbner, lukker de?	När öppnar, stänger de?
nawr awp'-ner, lŏŏk'-ker dee	*vor-nawr' awp'-ner, lŏŏk'-ker de*	*nair öppnăr, stěngĕr deh*

I want to cash some travellers' cheques.

Jeg vil gjerne heve noen reisesjekker	Jeg vil gerne hæve nogle rejsechecks	Jag vill växla några resechecker
yay vill yair'-ně hěh'-vě noh'-ěn ray'-sě-shěck-ker	*yi vil gair'-ne hai'-vě noh'-le ry'-sě-checks*	*yā vill vexlă naw'-gră rěh'-sě-chěckĕr*

Can you change this money, this note, for me?

Kan De veksle disse pengene, denne seddelen, for meg?	Kan De veksle disse penge, denne seddel, for mig?	Kan ni växla de här pengarna, den här sedeln, åt mig?
kăn dee veks'-lě dis'-sě pěng'-ěn-ně, den'-ně sed-del-ěn for may	*kan dee veks'-le dees'-se peng'-eh, den'-ne seth'-el, for my*	*kăn nee vexlă děh hair pěng'-ăr-nă, děn hair sēh'-děln, awt may*

What is the rate of exchange?

Hva er kursen?	Hvad er kursen?	Vad är växelkursen?
vah air koor'-sen	*vath air koor'-sen*	*văd ēh vex-ěl-kŏŏr-sen*

I have a letter of credit.

Jeg har et kreditiv	Jeg har et kreditbrev	Jag har ett resekreditiv
yay hahr ett credit-eev'	*yi hahr it credit'-brehv*	*yā hār ětt rēh'-sě-krě-dit-eev'*

I want to draw . . .

Jeg ønsker å heve . . .	Jeg ønsker at hæve . . .	Jag vill ta ut . . .
yay ön'-skěr aw hěh'-vě . . .	*yi ön'-sker at hai'-vě . . .*	*yā vill tā oot . . .*

Norwegian	*Danish*	*Swedish*

What is your address?

Hva er Deres adresse?	Hvad er Deres adresse?	Vad är er adress?
vah air deh'-res	*vath air dair'-es*	*vād ēh ēhr ăh-drĕss'*
ăh-drĕs'-sĕ	*ăh-dres'-se*	

Do I sign here?

Skal jeg undertegne	Skriver jeg under her?	Ska jag skriva under
her?	*skree'-ver yi ŏŏn'-ner*	här?
skăl yay	*hear*	*skā yā skree'-vă*
ŏŏn'-der-tay'-nĕ hair		*oon-dĕr hair*

May I see the manager?

Kan jeg få tale med	Må jeg tale med	Kan jag få tala med
direktøren?	direktøren?	direktören?
kăn yay faw tăh'-lĕ	*maw yi tah'-le meth*	*kăn yā faw tā-lă mēhd*
meh dee-rĕk-tö'-ren	*dee-rĕk-tö'-ren*	*dee-rĕk-tö'-ren*

When shall I come back?

Når skal jeg komme	Hvornår skal jeg	När ska jag komma
tilbake?	komme tilbage?	tillbaka?
nawr skăl yay kom'-mĕ	*vor-nawr' skal yi*	*nair skā yā kom'-mă*
till-bah'-kĕ	*kom'-me til-bāhg'-ĕh*	*till-bă'-kă*

I cannot wait so long.

Jeg kan ikke vente så	Jeg kan ikke vente så	Jag kan inte vänta så
lenge	længe	länge
yay kăn ick'-kĕ	*yi kan ick'-ke ven'-te*	*yă kăn in'-tĕ ven'-tă*
ven'-tĕ saw lehng-ĕh	*saw laing-ĕh*	*saw lĕngĕ*

GENERAL SHOPPING VOCABULARY

Alarm clock.

Vekkerklokke	Vækkeur	Väckarklocka
vĕck'-ker-klock'-kĕ	*vaik'-kĕ-ur*	*vĕck'-ăr-klock'-kă*

Bathing cap, bathing costume.

Badehette, badedrakt	Badehætte, badedragt	Badmössa, baddräkt
bah'-dĕ-het-tĕ,	*bah'-the-hait-te,*	*bād'-mössă, băd'-drĕkt*
bah'-dĕ-drăckt	*bah'-the-drahkt*	

Belt.

Belte	Bælte	Skärp, bälte (for men)
bell'-tĕ	*bell'-te*	*shĕhrp, bell'-tĕ*

Norwegian	*Danish*	*Swedish*

Blouse.

Bluse	Bluse	Blus
bloo'-sĕ	*blue'-sĕ*	*blōōs*

Bow-tie.

Sløyfe	Butterfly	Fluga
slöy'-fĕ	*butterfly*	*floogă*

Braces.

Seler	Seler	Hängslen
sēh'-ler	*sēh'-ler*	*hĕngs'-len*

Button.

Knapp	Knap	Knapp
knăpp	*knăp*	*knăpp*

Camera.

Fotografiapparat	Fotografiapparat	Kamera
foto-gräh-fee'-ăp-päh-räht	*foto-grä-fee'-ăp-päh-räht*	*käh'-mĕ-ră*

Cardigan.

Strikkejakke	Cardigan	Cardigan, kofta
strick'-kĕ-yăck-kĕ	*cardigan*	*cardigan, koff'-tă*

Carpet.

Gulv-teppe	Gulvtæppe	Matta
gŏŏlv'-tep-pĕ	*gŏŏlv'-taip-pĕ*	*măt'-tă*

Clothes brush.

Klesbørste	Børste	Klädesborste
klēhs-börs'-tĕ	*bör'-ste*	*klaid'-ĕs-borstĕ*

Coat.

Kåpe (ladies), frakk (gentlemen)	Frakke	Kappa (ladies), rock (gentlemen)
kaw'-pĕ, frăk	*frăk'-kĕ*	*kăp'-pă, rock*

Coat-hanger.

Kleshenger	Bøjle	Klädhängare
klēhs-henger	*boy'-le*	*klaid'-hengăr-rĕ*

Norwegian	Danish	Swedish

Collar.

Krave, snipp (men's)	Krave, flip	Krage
krah-vĕ, snip	*krăh'-ve, flip*	*krä'-gĕ*

Cork.

Kork	Prop	Kork
cork	*prop*	*korrk*

Cotton.

Bomull	Bomuld	Bomull
bom'-ŏŏl	*bohm'-ŏŏl*	*bom'-ŏŏll*

Cotton reel.

Trådsnelle	Garntrisse	Trådrulle
traw'-snĕl-lĕ	*găhrn'-tris-se*	*trawd'-rŏŏll-lĕ*

Cotton thread.

Bomullstråd	Bomuldsgarn	Tråd
bom'-ŏŏls-traw	*bohm'-ools-gåhrn*	*trawd*

Cuff-links.

Mansjettknapper	Manchetknapper	Manschettknappar
măn-shĕtt'-knăp-per	*mang-shet'-knăhp-per*	*mănn-shĕtt'-knăp-păr*

Dress.

Kjole	Kjole	Klänning
cho'-lĕ	*kyoh'-lĕ*	*klĕn'-ning*

Dressing gown.

Morgenkåpe	Slåbrok	Morgonrock
mor'-ĕn-kaw-pĕ	*slaw'-brock*	*mor'-ron-rock*

Dress material.

Kjolestoff	Kjolestof	Klänningstyg
cho'-lĕ-stof	*kyoh'-le-stof*	*klĕn'-nings-tüg*

Embroidery work.

Broderiarbeid	Broderiarbejde	Broderiarbete
broh-dĕr-ree'-ăr-bayd	*broh-der-ree'-ar-by-deh*	*broh-der-ree'-ăr-bē-tĕ*

Evening dress (male—dinner jacket).

Smoking	Smoking	Smoking
smoking	*smoking*	*smoking*

Norwegian	Danish	Swedish

Evening dress (female).

| Aftenkjole | Lang kjole | Aftonklänning |
| *äf'-ten-cho'-lě* | *lang kyoh'-le* | *äf'-ton-klěn-ning* |

Filigree work.

| Filigranarbeid | Filigranarbejde | Filigranarbete |
| *fili-grän'-är-bayd* | *fili-grän'-ar-by-deh* | *filli-grän'-är-bē-tě* |

Garters.

| Strømpebånd | Sokkeholdere | Strumpeband |
| *ström'-pě-bon* | *suck'-ke-hol-lě'-rě* | *stroom'-pě-bǎnd* |

Gloves.

| Hansker | Handsker | Handskar |
| *häns'-ker* | *hähn'-sker* | *händ'-skǎr* |

Gramophone record.

| Grammofonplate | Grammofonplade | Grammofonskiva |
| *grǎm-mo-fohn'-plah-tě* | *gram-mo-fohn'-pläh-the* | *grǎm-mǒ-fawn'-sheevǎ* |

Hair brush.

| Hårbørste | Hårbørste | Hårborste |
| *hawr'-börs-tě* | *hawr'-bör-ste* | *hawr'-bors-tě* |

Handbag.

| Håndveske | Taske | Handväska |
| *hon'-ves-kě* | *tas'-ke* | *händ'-ves-kǎ* |

Handkerchief.

| Lommetørkle | Lommetørklæde | Näsduk |
| *lom'-mě-tör-klěh* | *lom'-me-tör-ĸlai'-the* | *nais'-dook* |

Hat.

| Hatt | Hat | Hatt |
| *hätt* | *hät* | *hätt* |

Head scarf.

| Hodetørkle | Hovedtørklæde | Scarf, schalett |
| *hoh'-dě-tör-klěh* | *hoveth'-tör-klai'-the* | *scärf, shä-lett* |

Jacket.

| Jakke | Jakke | Jacka |
| *yäk'-kě* | *yahk'-kě* | *yäk'-kǎ* |

| *Norwegian* | *Danish* | *Swedish* |

Jumper.

Genser	Jumper	Jumper
gen'-ser	*jumper*	*jumper*

Lipstick.

Lebestift	Læbestift	Läppstift
lĕh'-bĕ-stift	*lat'-be-stift*	*lĕpp'-stift*

Magazine.

Blad	Magazine	Tidskrift
blahd	*magă-zin'*	*teed'-skrift*

Mat.

Matte	Måtte	Matta
măt'-tĕ	*mawt'-te*	*măt'-tă*

Mirror.

Speil	Spejl	Spegel
spale	*speil*	*spēh'-gĕl*

Needle.

Nål	Nål	Nål
nawl	*nawl*	*nawl*

Newspaper.

Avis	Avis	Tidning
ăh-vees'	*ăh-vees'*	*teed'-ning*

Nightdress.

Nattkjole	Natkjole	Nattlinne
nătt'-cho-lă	*nat'-kyoh-lo*	*nătt'-lin-nĕ*

Pants.

Underbukser	Underbukser	Underbyxor
ŏŏn'-der-book-ser	*ŏŏn'-ner-book-ser*	*ŏŏn'-dĕr-büxor*

Pins.

Knappenåler	Knappenåle	Knappnålar
knăp'-pĕ-naw-ler	*knăhp'-pe-naw-le*	*knăpp'-nawl-ar*

Pottery.

Fajanse	Lertøj	Lergods
fah-yan'-sĕ	*lear'-toy*	*lĕhr-gohds*

Norwegian	Danish	Swedish

Pullover.

Pullover	Pullover	Pullover
pull-aw'-ver	*pull-over'*	*pull-aw'-ver*

Purse.

Pengepung	Pung	Portmonnä
pĕng'-ĕh-pŏng	*pŏŏng*	*port-mon-naï'*

Pyjamas.

Pyjamas	Pyjamas	Pyjamas
pü-yah'-măhs	*pü-yah'-măhs*	*pü-yah'-măhs*

Raincoat.

Regnfrakk	Regnfrakke	Regnrock
rayn'-frăk	*rayn'-frăk-kĕ*	*rĕngn'-rock*

Rug (travelling).

Reisepledd	Plaid	Filt
ray'-sĕ-plĕdd	*plait*	*filt*

Rug (floor).

Teppe	Tæppe	Matta
tep'-pĕ	*taip'-pe*	*măt'-tă*

Safety-pins.

Sikkerhetsnåler	Sikkerhedsnåle	Säkerhetsnålar
sick'-ker-hehts-naw-ler	*sik'-ker-heths-naw-le*	*saik'-ĕr-hĕhts-naw-lar*

Scarf.

Sjal	Tørklæde	Scarf
shahl	*tör'-klai-the*	*scarf*

Shirt.

Skjorte	Skjorte	Skjorta
shohr'-tĕ	*skyor'-te*	*shohr'-tă*

Shoes.

Sko	Sko	Skor
skoh	*skoh*	*skohr*

Shoe brush.

Skobørste	Skobørste	Skoborste
skoh'-börs-tĕ	*skoh'-börs-te*	*skoh'-bors-tĕ*

Norwegian	*Danish*	*Swedish*

Shoe laces.

Skolisser	Snørrebånd	Skosnören
skoh'-lis-ser	*snö'-rĕ-băwn*	*skoh'-snö-ren*

Shoe polish.

Skosverte	Skosværte	Skokräm
skoh'-svehr-tĕ	*skoh'-svair-tĕ*	*skoh'-kralm*

Shop.

Butikk	Butik	Affär
boo-tick'	*boo-tik'*	*ăf-fair'*

Silk.

Silke	Silke	Silke, siden
sil'-kĕ	*sil'-kĕ*	*sil'-kĕ, see'-dĕn*

Skirt.

Skjørt	Nederdel	Kjol
shört	*nether'-dēhl*	*chohl*

Slippers.

Tøfler	Morgensko	Tofflor'
töf'-lĕr	*mor'-ĕn-skoh*	*toff'-lor*

Socks.

Sokker	Sokker	Sockor
sock'-ker	*sock'-ker*	*sock'-or*

Souvenir.

Souvenir	Souvenir	Souvenir
souvenir	*souvenir*	*souvenir*

Stamps.

Frimerker	Frimærker	Frimärken
free'-mĕr-ker	*free'-mair-ker*	*free'-mair-kĕn*

Stockings.

Strømper	Strømper	Strumpor
ström'-per	*ström'-per*	*stroom'-pŏr*

Studs.

Skjorteknapper	Skjorteknapper	Kragknappar
shohr'-tĕ-knăp-pĕr	*skyor'-te-knăhp-pĕr*	*krăg'-knăp-păr*

Norwegian	Danish	Swedish

Suit.

Norwegian	Danish	Swedish
Dress (men), drakt (women) *drĕss, drăhkt*	Sæt tøj *said toy*	Kostym (men), dräkt (women) *kos-stüm', drĕkt*

Suit case.

Koffert *kohf'-fert*	Koffert *kohf'-fert*	Väska *ves'-kă*

Suspenders.

Stropper *strŏp'-per*	Strømpeholdere *strŏm'-pĕ-hol-lĕ-rĕ*	Strumpeband *stroom'-pĕ-bănd*

Swim suit.

Badedrakt *bah'-dĕ-drăhkt*	Badedragt *bah'-the-drahkt·*	Baddräkt, simbyxor (men) *bād'-drĕkt, simm'-büx-ŏr*

Tie.

Slips *slips*	Slips *slips*	Slips *slips*

Towel.

Håndkle *hon'-kleh*	Håndklæde *hawn'-klai-the*	Handduk *hănd'-dook*

Toys.

Leker *lēh'-ker*	Lejetøj *lie'-ĕh-toy*	Leksaker *lēhk'-sā-kĕr*

Trousers.

Bukser *bŏŏk'-ser*	Bukser *bok'-ser*	Byxor *büx-or*

Umbrella.

Paraply *păh-ră-plü'*	Paraply *păh-ră-plü'*	Paraply *păh-ră-plü'*

Underclothes.

Undertøy *ŏŏn'-der-tŏy*	Undertøj *ŏŏn'-ner-toy*	Underkläder *ŏŏn'-dĕr-klaidĕr*

Norwegian	Danish	Swedish

Waistcoat.

Vest	Vest	Väst
vest	*vest*	*vest*

Walking stick.

Spaserstokk	Spadserestok	Spatserkäpp
spåh-sehr'-stok	*spåh-sěh'-re-stok*	*spåt-sehr'-chěpp*

Wallet.

Lommebok	Lommebog	Plånbok
lom'-mě-bohk	*lom'-me-bow*	*plawn'-bohk*

Watch.

Ur	Ur	Klocka
oor	*oor*	*klock-kå*

Zip fastener.

Lynlås	Lynlås	Blixtlås
lün'-laws	*lün'-lawo*	*blixt'-lawo*

This is not my size.

Dette er ikke min størrelse	Dette er ikke min størrelse	Det här är inte min storlek
det'-tě air ick'-kě min stör'-ěl-sě	*det'-te air ick'-ke meen stör'-rěl-sě*	*děh hair ěh in-tě min stohr'-lěhk*

It is too big, small.

Den er for stor, liten	Den er for stor, for lille	Den är för stor, liten
den air for stohr', lee'-ten	*den air for stor, for lil'-lo*	*děn ěh för stuhr, lee'-ten*

It is too wide, narrow, tight.

Den er for vid, smal, trang	Den er for bred, smald, snæver	Den är för vid, smal, trång
den air for vee', småhl, tråhng	*den air for breth, småhl, snai'-ver*	*děn ěh för veed, småhl, trong*

It is too long, short.

Den er for lang, kort	Den er for lang, kort	Den är för lång, kort
den air for låhng, kort	*den air for langh, kort*	*děn ěh för long, kort*

Norwegian	Danish	Swedish

This is not what I want.

Norwegian	Danish	Swedish
Dette er ikke hva jeg vil ha	Dette er ikke hvad jeg vil have	Detta är inte vad jag vill ha
det'-tĕ air ick'-kĕ vah yay vill hah	*det'-te air ick'-ke vath yi vil hah*	*det'-tă eh in'-tĕ väd yä vill hä*

I do not like this.

Jeg liker ikke denne	Jeg bryder mig ikke om denne	Jag tycker inte om den här
yay lee'-ker ick'-kĕ den'-nĕ	*yi brüh'-ther my ick'-ke om den'-ne*	*yä tückĕr in'-tĕ omm den hair*

I can't see the colour clearly here.

Jeg kan ikke se fargen skikkelig her	Jeg kan ikke se farven tydeligt her	Jag kan inte se färgen riktigt här
yay kăn ick'-kĕ sēh far'-gĕn shick'-ĕh-lee hair	*yi kan ick'-ke seh far'-ven tü'-the-lith hear*	*yä kăn in'-tĕ sēh fair'-yen rik'-tit hair*

I do not like the colour, pattern.

Jeg liker ikke fargen, mønsteret	Jeg bryder mig ikke om farven, mynsteret	Jag tycker inte om färgen, mönsteret
yay lee'-ker ick'-kĕ far'-gĕn, mŏns'-tĕr-rĕ	*yi brüh'-ther my ick'-ke om far'-ven, mün'-stret*	*yä tückĕr in'-tĕ omm fair'-yen, mŏns-ter'-ret*

It is too dark, light.

Den er for mørk, lys	Den er for mørk, lys	Den är för mörk, ljus
den air for mörk, lüs	*den air for mörk, lüs*	*dĕn ĕh för mörk, yoos*

Colour.

Farge	Farve	Färg
far'-gĕ	*far'-ve*	*fair*

Black, white, red.

Sort, hvit, rød	Sort, hvid, rød	Svart, vit, röd
sohrt, veet, rö	*sort, veeth, röth*	*svärt, veet, röd*

Blue, light blue, dark blue.

Blå, lyseblå, mørkeblå	Blå, lysseblå, mørkeblå	Blå, ljusblå, mörkblå
blaw, lüs'-sĕ-blaw, mör'-kĕ-blaw	*blaw, lüs'-sĕ-blaw, mör'-kĕ-blaw*	*blaw, yoos'-blaw, mörk'-blaw*

Norwegian	Danish	Swedish

Green, grey, brown.

Norwegian	Danish	Swedish
Grønn, grå, brun	Grøn, grå, brun	Grön, grå, brun
grönn, graw, broon	*grön, graw, broon*	*grön, graw, broon*

Yellow, pink.

Gul, lyserød	Gul, lysserød	Gul, skär
gool, lüs'-sĕ-rŏ	*gool, lüs'-sĕ-rŏth*	*gool, shair*

I want a better quality.

Jeg vil gjerne ha en bedre kvalitet	Jeg vil have en bedre kvalitet	Jag vill ha en bättre kvalitet
yay vill yair'-nĕ hah ehn bēh'-drĕ kvah-lee-tēht'	*yi vil hah in beth'-re kvàh-lee-tet'*	*ya vıll ha en bet'-rĕ kvàh-lee-tēh'*

I want something simple, self-coloured.

Jeg vil gjerne ha noe enkelt, ensfarget	Jeg vil have noget enkelt, ensfarvet	Jag vill ha något enkelt, enfärgat
yay vill yair'-nĕ hah noh'-ĕh ĕnk'-ĕlt, ĕhns'-far-get	*yi vil hah noh'-et eng'-kelt, ehns'-fähr-vet*	*yā vill hā naw'-got ĕnk-ĕlt, ĕhn'-fair-yăt*

I want something cheaper, dearer.

Jeg vil gjerne ha noe billigere, dyrere	Jeg vil have noget der er billigere, dyre	Jag vill ha något billigare, dyrare
yay vill yair'-nĕ hah noh'-ĕh bil'-lee-ĕr-ĕh, dür-ĕr-ĕh	*yi vil hah noh'-et dair air bil'-lee-reh, dü'-rĕh*	*yā vill hā naw'-got bil'-lig-gă-rĕ, dü'-ră-rĕ*

Does this material shrink?

Krymper dette stoffet?	Kryber dette stof?	Krymper det här tyget?
krüm'-per det'-tĕ stof'-fĕ	*krü'-ber det'-tĕ stof*	*krüm'-pĕr dĕh hair tü'-get*

May I try this on?

Kan jeg få prøve denne?	Må jeg prøve dette?	Får jag prova den här?
kăn yay faw prŏ'-vĕ den'-nĕ	*maw yi prŏ'-vĕ det'-tĕ*	*fawr yā proh-vă dĕn hair*

It does not fit me.

Den passer meg ikke	Det passer mig ikke	Den passar mig inte
den păs'-ser may ick'-kĕ	*deh pas'-ser my ick'-ke*	*dĕn păs'-săr may in'-tĕ*

Norwegian	Danish	Swedish

May I see how it looks in the mirror.

Norwegian	Danish	Swedish
Kan jeg få se hvordan det tar seg ut i speilet?	Må jeg se hvordan det ser ud i spejlet?	Får jag se hur det ser ut i spegeln?
kăn yay faw sēh vohr-dan den tahr say oot ee spale'-ĕh	*maw yi seh vor-dan' deh sehr ooth ee spei'-let*	*fawr yă sēh hoor dĕh sēhr oot ee spĕh'-gĕln*

It does not fit here.

Den passer ikke her	Det passer ikke her	Det sitter inte bra här
den păs'-ser ick'-kĕ hair	*deh pas'-ser ick'-ke hear*	*dĕh sit'-ter in'-tĕ brä hair*

It does not suit me.

Den klær meg ikke	Det passer ikke til mig	Den passar mig inte
den klair may ick'-kĕ	*deh pas'-ser ick'-ke til my*	*dĕn păs'-săr may in'-tĕ*

Have you nothing else, nothing better?

Har De ikke noe annet, ikke noe bedre?	Har De ikke noget andet, noget bedre?	Har ni inget annat, inget bättre?
hahr dee ick'-kĕ noh'-ĕh ăn'-net, ick'-kĕ noh'-ĕh bēh'-drĕ	*hahr dee ick'-ke noh'-et ăhn'-net, noh'-et beth'-re*	*hār nee ing-ĕt ăn'-nat, ing-ĕt bĕt-trĕ*

What is the charge for making one?

Hva koster det å få en sydd?	Hvad koster det for at få en lavet?	Vad kostar det att låta göra en?
vah kos'-ter deh aw faw ehn süd	*vath kos'-ter deh for at faw in lăh'-vet*	*vād kos'-tăr dēh ătt law'-tă yörä ĕn*

When could it be ready?

Når kunne den være ferdig?	Hvornår kunne den være færdig?	När kunde den vara färdig?
nawr kŏŏ n'-nĕ den vairĕ fair'-dee	*vor-nawr' kŏŏn'-ne den vaire fair'-dee*	*nair kŏŏn-dĕ dĕn vā-rä fair'-dee*

Please send it.

Vær så vennlig å sende den	Vær venlig at sende den	Var snäll och skicka den
vair saw ven'-lee aw sen'-nĕ den	*vair ven'-lee at sen'-ne den*	*văr snĕll ock shick'-kă dĕn*

Norwegian	Danish	Swedish

I will take it with me.

Jeg tar den med meg	Jeg tager den med mig	Jag tar den med mig
yay tahr den měh' may	*yi tahr den meth my*	*yā tăr děn měh may*

I shall pay on delivery.

Jeg betaler ved levering	Jeg betaler når den	Jag betalar när ni
yay beh-tăh'-ler	bliver bragt ud	levererar den
leh-věhr'-ing	*yi beh-tăh'-ler nawr*	*yā běh-tăh'-lăr nair nee*
	den bleer braght ooth	*lě-vě-rěhr'-ăr děn*

I have not enough money with me.

Jeg har ikke nok	Jeg har ikke nok	Jag har inte tillräckligt
penger med meg	penge med mig	med pengar med mig
yay hahr ick'-kě nok	*yi hahr ick'-ke nok*	*yā hăr in-tě till-rěck'-lit*
pěng'-ěr měh may	*peng'-eh meth my*	*měh pěng-ăr měh*
		may

I shall come back for it.

Jeg kommer tilbake	Jeg vil komme tilbage	Jag kommer tillbaka
og henter den	efter det	och hämtar det
yay kom'-mer	*yi vil kom'-me*	*yā kom'-mer*
till-bah'-kě aw	*til-băhg'-ěh efter deh*	*till-bă'-kă ock*
hen'-ter den		*hěmtăr děh*

Please reserve it.

Vær så vennlig å	Vær venlig at holde	Var snäll och
reservere det	det tilbage	reservera det
vair saw ven'-lee aw	*vair ven-'lee at hol'-le*	*văr sněll ock*
reh-sehr-veh'-rě deh	*deh til-băhg'-ěh*	*rěh-sěr-věh'-ră děh*

I must have it before . . .

Jeg må ha den før . . .	Jeg skal have det	Jag måste ha det
yay maw hah den	inden . . .	före . . .
för . . .	*yi skahl hah deh*	*yā moss-tě hā děh*
	in'-nen . . .	*fö-rě . . .*

Don't forget.

Glem det ikke	Glem det ikke	Glöm det inte
glěm deh ick'-kě	*glěm deh ick'-kě*	*glömm děh in'-tě*

Norwegian	Danish	Swedish

REPAIRS

I want to take these shoes to a shoemaker.

Jeg vil gjerne ta disse skoene til en skomaker	Jeg vil gerne have disse sko til skomageren	Jag vill ta de här skorna till en skomakare
yay vill yair'-ně tah dis'-sě skoh'-ěn-ně till ehn skoh-mah'-ker	*yi vil gair'-ne hah dis'-se skoh til skoh'-mäh-ren*	*yā vill tā děh hair skohr'-nă till en skoh'-mā-kă-rě*

Soles, heels.

Såler, hæler	Såler, hæle	Sulor, klackar
saw'-ler, heh'-ler	*saw'-ler, hai'-le*	*soo'-lŏr, kläck'-ăr*

Rubber.

Gummi	Gummi	Gummi
gŏŏm'-mee	*gŏŏm'-mee*	*gŏŏm'-mee*

This needs mending.

Denne trenger reparasjon	Denne trænger til at blive repareret	Det här behöver lagas
den'-ně treng-ěr rěh-päh-răh-shohn'	*denne train'-er til at blee'-ve rěh-päh-rěh'-ret*	*děh hair beh-hŏ'-ver lah'-găs*

Can you mend this?

Kan De reparere dette?	Kan De reparere dette?	Kan ni laga det här?
kăn dee rěh-päh-rěh'-rě det'-tě	*kan dee rěh-päh-rěh'-re det'-tě*	*kăn nee lah'-gă děh hair*

These spectacles need repairing.

Disse brillene trenger reparasjon	Disse briller trænger til at blive repareret	De här glasögonen behöver lagas
dis'-sě bril'-lě-ně treng'-ěr rěh-päh-răh-shohn'	*disse bril'-ler train'-er til at blee'-ve rěh-päh-rěh'-ret*	*děh hair glahss'-ögon-ěn beh-hŏ'-ver lah'-gas*

I need a new lens, frame.

Jeg trenger en ny linse, innfatning	Jeg trænger til en ny linse, et nyt stel	Jag behöver nya glas, bågar
yay treng'-ěr ehn nü' lin'-sě, in'-făt-ning	*yi train'-er til in nüh lin'-se, it nüt stehl*	*yā beh-hŏ'-ver nü-ă glahss, baw'-găr*

| *Norwegian* | *Danish* | *Swedish* |

They are damaged here.

| De er ødelagt her | De er ødelagt her | De är sönder här |
| *dee air ö'-dĕ-lahgt hair* | *dee air öthe'-lackt hear* | *dĕh ĕh sön'-der hair* |

I want a new case.

| Jeg vil gjerne ha et nytt futteral | Jeg vil gerne have et nyt futteral | Jag vill ha ett nytt fodral |
| *yay vill yair'-nĕ hah ett nütt foot-te-rähl'* | *yi vil gair'-ne hah it nüt foot-tĕh-rähl'* | *yā vill hā ĕtt nütt foh-drähl'* |

Too tight, slack.

| For stramme, løse | For stram, løs | För hårt, löst |
| *for sträm'-mĕ, lö'-sĕ* | *for strähm, lös* | *för hawrt, löst* |

The spectacles are not straight.

| Brillene sitter ikke bent | Brillerne er ikke lige | Glasögonen sitter inte rakt |
| *bril'-lĕ-nĕ sit'-ter ick'-kĕ bĕhnt* | *bril'-ler-ne air ick'-ke lee'-ĕh* | *glahss'-ögon-ĕn sit'-ter ĭn'-tĕ rähkt* |

I want some dark glasses to fit on these.

| Jeg vil gjerne ha noen solbriller til å feste på disse | Jeg vil gerne have nogle mørke briller til at passe disse | Jag vill ha ett par mörka glas som passar till dessa |
| *yay vill yair'-nĕ hah noh'-ĕn sohl'-bril-ler til aw fes'-tĕ paw dis'-sĕ* | *yl vil gatr'-ne hah noh'-le mör'-ke bril'-ler til at pas'-se dis'-se* | *yā vill ha ett par mör-kă glahss som păs'-sar till des'-să* |

My watch has stopped.

| Uret mitt har stoppet | Mit ur er gået i stå | Min klocka har stannat |
| *oor'-ĕt mit hahr stop'-pet* | *meet oor air gaw'-et ee staw* | *min klock-kă här stän-năt* |

My watch is broken.

| Uret mitt er i stykker | Mit ur er gået i stykker | Min klocka är sönder |
| *oor'-ĕt mit air ee stück'-ker* | *meet oor air gaw'-et ee stük'-ker* | *min klock-kă ĕh sön-dĕr* |

The glass is broken.

| Glasset er knust | Glasset er brækket | Glaset är sönder |
| *glăs'-set air knōōst* | *glăss-'set air braik'-ket* | *glahs'-set ĕh sön-dĕr* |

| Norwegian | Danish | Swedish |

The watch needs cleaning.

Norwegian	Danish	Swedish
Uret trenger rensing	Uret trænger til at blive renset	Klockan behöver göras ren
oor'-ĕt treng'-ĕr rĕn'-sing	*oo'-ret train'-er til at blee'-ve rĕn'-set*	*klock-kăn beh-hö'-ver yö'-răs rēhn*

It gains, loses.

Det går for fort, sent	Det vinder, taber	Den går före, efter
deh gawr for fohrt', sēhnt'	*deh vin'-ner, tāh'-ber*	*dĕn gawr fö'-rĕ, ĕf'-tĕr*

Can you regulate it?

Kan De regulere det?	Kan De regulere det?	Kan ni rucka den?
kăn dee rĕh-goo-lēh'-rĕ deh	*kan dee rĕh-goo-lēh'-re deh*	*kăn nee roockă den*

I overwound it.

Jeg trakk det for mye opp	Jeg trak det for meget op	Jag har dragit av fjädern
yay trăhk deh for mü'-ĕh op	*yi trăhk deh for my'-et up*	*yā hār drä'-git äv f-yaid'-ĕrn*

I dropped it.

Jeg slapp det ned	Jeg tabte det	Jag har tappat den
yay slăhp deh nēhḋ'	*yi tăhb'-te deh*	*yā hār tăp-pät dĕn*

A new strap.

En ny rem	En ny rem	Ett nytt armband
ehn nü rĕm	*in nü rĕhm*	*ĕtt nütt ărm'-bănd*

This does not work.

Dette virker ikke	Dette virker ikke	Det här fungerar inte
det'-tĕ veer'-ker ick'-kĕ	*det'-te veer'-ker ick'-ke*	*dĕh hair fŏŏng-gēh'-răr in'-tĕ*

The lock on this case won't work.

Låsen på denne kofferten virker ikke	Låsen på denne taske virker ikke	Låset på den här väskan fungerar inte
law'-sen paw den'-nĕ kohf'-fer-ten veer'-ker ick'-kĕ	*law'-sen paw denne tas'-ke veer'-ker ick'-ke*	*law'-set paw den hair ves'-kăn fŏŏng-gēhr'-ăr in'-tĕ*

Norwegian	Danish	Swedish

I can't wind the film.

Jeg kan ikke rulle filmen fram	Jeg kan ikke dreje filmen	Jag kan inte vrida fram filmen
yay kăn ick'-kĕ rōōl'-lĕ film'-ĕn frăm	*yi kan ick'-ke drei'-eh fil'-men*	*yă kăn in'-tĕ vree'-dă frămm film-ĕn*

I need a new handle.

Jeg trenger et nytt håndtak	Jeg trænger til et nyt håndtag	Jag behöver ett nytt handtag
yay trĕng'-ĕr ett nŭtt hon'-tahk	*yi trĕng'-er til it nŭt hawn'-tāh*	*yă beh-hö'-vĕr ett nŭtt hănd'-tāg*

How long will it take?

Hvor lang tid vil det ta?	Hvor længe vil det tage?	Hur lång tid tar det?
vohr lahng teed' vill deh tah	*vor laing'-ĕh vil deh tāh*	*hōōr long teed tār dĕh*

Can you sew, stitch this?

Kan De sy, stikke dette?	Kan De sy, stikke dette?	Kan ni sy, sy ihop detta?
kăn dee sŭ, stick'-kĕ det'-tĕ	*kan dee sŭ, stick'-kĕ det'-tĕ*	*kăn nee sŭ, sŭ ee-hohp det'-tă*

POLICE

I want to speak to a policeman.

Jeg vil gjerne tale med en politikonstabel	Jeg vil gerne tale med en politibetjent	Jag vill tala med en polis
yay vill yair'-nĕ tah-lĕ meh ehn poh-lee-tee'-kon-stah'-bell	*yi vil gair'-ne tah'-lĕ meth in polee-tee'-bĕht-yent*	*yă vill tā-lă meh en pŏ-lees'*

I wish to register as a foreign visitor, businessman.

Jeg ønsker å registrere som en utenlandsk besøkende, forretningsmann	Jeg ønsker at registrere som en udlændning, forretningsmand	Jag vill anmäla mig som utländsk turist, affärsman
yay ŏn-sker aw regee-strĕh'-rĕ som ehn oot'-ĕn-lahnsk, bĕ-sök'-ĕn-dĕ, for-ret'-nings-männ	*yi ŏn'-sker at regee-strĕ'-rĕ som ooth'-lenning, for-ret'-nings-mann*	*yă vill an-mĕh'-lă may som oot'-lĕnsk too-rist', ăf-fairs'-măn*

Norwegian	Danish	Swedish

Where is the police station?

Hvor er politistasjonen?	Hvor er politistationen?	Var ligger polisstationen?
vohr air po-lee-tee'-stah-shohn'-ĕn	*vor air polee-tee'-stăh-shŏh-nen*	*vär liggĕr pŏ-lees'-stă-shohn'-ĕn*

I am British.

Jeg er britisk	Jeg er britisk	Jag är brittisk
yay air brit'-tisk	*yi air brit'-tisk*	*yā ĕh brit'-tisk*

I am a British citizen.

Jeg er britisk statsborger	Jeg er en britisk statsborger	Jag är brittisk medborgare
yay air brit'-tisk stahts'-bor-gĕr	*yi air in brit'-tisk stahts'-bawr'-ĕr*	*yā ĕh brit'-tisk mĕhd'-bor-yă-rĕ*

I am staying at ...

Jeg bor på ...	Jeg bor på ...	Jag bor på ...
yay bohr paw ...	*yi bohr paw ...*	*yā bohr paw ...*

I intend staying here for ...

Jeg akter å være her i ...	Jeg påtaenker at blive her i ...	Jag ämnar stanna här ...
yay ăk'-ter aw vairĕ hair ee ...	*yi paw'-ten-ker at blee'-ve hear ee ...*	*yā ĕm'-năr stän'-nă hair ...*

Have I to inform you when I am leaving?

Må jeg underrette Dem når jeg reiser?	Skal jeg lade Dem vide når jeg rejser?	Behöver jag underrätta er när jag reser?
maw yay ŏŏn'-der-ret-tĕ dem nawr yay ray'-ser	*skal yi lathe dem vee'-the nawr yi ry'-ser*	*bĕh-hŏ'-ver yā ŏŏn'-der-ret-tă ĕhr nair yā rĕh'-ser*

I have my passport.

Jeg har mitt pass	Jeg har mit pas	Jag har mitt pass
yay hahr mit păss	*yi hahr meet pas*	*yā hăr mitt păss*

Is it worth advertising?

Er det umaken verd å avertere?	Er det værd at avertere det?	Lönar det sig att annonsera?
air deh oo'-mah-ken vaird aw ah-ver-tĕh'-rĕ	*air deh vair at ăh-vĕr-tĕh'-rĕ deh*	*lŏ'-när dĕh say ătt ănn-ong-sĕh'-ră*

Norwegian	Danish	Swedish

Will you inform me if it is found?

Vil De gi meg beskjed hvis det blir funnet?	Vil De lade mig det vide, dersom det bliver fundet?	Vill ni underrätta mig om det återkommer?
vill dee yee may beh-sheh' vis deh bleer fōōn'-net	*vil dee lathe my deh vee'-the, der'-som deh bleer fōōn'-net*	*vill nee ōōn'-děr-ret-tǎ may omm děh aw'-ter-kom-měr*

I shall offer a reward.

Jeg tilbyr dusør	Jeg vil give en dusør	Jag betalar hittelön
yay till'-bür doo-sör'	*yi vil gee in doo-sör'*	*yǎ běh-tǎ'-lǎr hit'-tě-lön*

Shall I call tomorrow?

Skal jeg høre innom i morgen?	Skal jeg høre indenfor i morgen?	Skall jag höra efter i morgon?
skal yay hö'-rě in'-om ee mor'-en	*skal yi höre in'-nen-for ee mor'-en*	*skäll yǎ hörǎ ěf'-ter ee mor'-ron*

ACCIDENTS

Help!

Hjelp!	Hjælp!	Hjälp!
yelp	*yelp*	*yelp*

Quickly.

Hurtig	Hurtig	Fort
hōōr'-tee	*hōōr'-tee*	*fohrt*

There has been an accident.

Der er skjedd en ulykke	Der er sket en ulykke	Det har hänt en olycka
dair air shed ehn oo'-lük-kě	*dair air skeht en oo'-lük-kě*	*děh här hěnt ěn oo'-lückǎ*

Bring a doctor, policeman.

Hent en doktor, politi	Hent en læge, politibetjent	Hämta en doktor, polis
hěnt ehn doctor, poh-lee-tee'	*hent en lai'-ěh, polee-tee'-běh-tyent*	*hěm-tǎ en doktor, pö-lees'*

I don't understand.

Jeg forstår ikke	Jeg forstår ikke	Jag förstår inte
yay for-stawr' ick'-kě	*yi for-stawr' ick'-ke*	*yǎ för-stawr' in'-tě*

Norwegian	Danish	Swedish

Ambulance, nurse.

Sykebil, sykepleierske	Ambulance, sygeplejerske	Ambulans, sköterska
sü'-kĕ-beel, sü'-kĕ-play-ĕr-skĕ	*ähm-bōō-lang'-sĕ, sü'-eh-ply-air-skĕ*	*ăm-boo-lăns', shŏ'-ter-skă*

Does anyone speak English?

Er her noen som snakker engelsk?	Er der nogen der taler engelsk?	Talar någon engelska?
air hair noh'-ĕn som snăk'-ker ehng'-elsk	*air dair noh'-en dair tah'-ler ehng'-elsk*	*tal'-ăr naw'-gon ehng'-elskă*

I don't think it is serious.

Jeg tror ikke det er alvorlig	Jeg tror ikke det er alvorligt	Jag tror inte det är allvarligt
yay trohr ick'-kĕ deh air ahl-vor'-lee	*yi tror ick'-ke deh air al-vor'-leet*	*yă trohr in'-tĕ dĕh ĕh ăll'-văr-lit*

I just want to sit down a while.

Jeg vil bare sitte en liten stund	Jeg ønsker bare at sidde lidt ned	Jag vill bara sitta en stund
yay vill bah'-rĕ sit'-tĕ ehn lee-ten stōōn	*yi ön'-sker băh'-re at sith-thĕ lit neth*	*yă vill bără sit-tă en stoond*

Hurt, injured.

Såret, skadet	Slået, såret	Sårad, skadad
saw'-ret, skah'-det	*slawet, saw'-ret*	*saw'-răd, skă'-dăd*

I am all right.

Jeg er all right	Jeg er all right	Jag mår bra
yay air all right	*yi air all right*	*yă mawr brăh*

Are you all right?

Er det noe i veien med Dem?	Er der noget i vejen med Dem?	Mår ni bra?
air deh noh'-ĕh ee vay'-ĕn meh dem	*air dair noh'-et ee vai'-en meth dem*	*mawr nee brăh*

It was (not) my fault.

Det var (ikke) min feil	Det var (ikke) min skyld	Det var (inte) mitt fel
deh vahr (ick'-kĕ) min fayl	*deh var (ick'-ke) mĕĕn sküll*	*dĕh văr (in'-tĕ) mitt fĕhl*

Norwegian	Danish	Swedish

He did not see (hear) me.

Han så (hørte) meg ikke	Han så (hørte) mig ikke	Han såg (hörde) mig inte
hăhn saw (hör'-tĕ) may ick'-kĕ	*han saw (hör'-te) my ick'-ke*	*hăn sawg (hör'-dĕ) may in'-tĕ*

Where is the nearest doctor, chemist?

Hvor er nærmeste doktor, apotek?	Hvor er nærmeste læge, apotek?	Var är närmaste doktor, apotek?
vohr air nair'-mĕ-stĕ doctor, ah-poh-tehk'	*vor air nair'-mĕs-te lai'-ĕh, ăh-po-tehk*	*văr ĕh nair'-măs-tĕ doktor, ăppŏ-tĕhk'*

First-aid post.

Førstehjelp stasjon	Første hjælps post	Hjälpstation
förs'-tĕ-yelp stah-shohn'	*för'-ste yelps post*	*yelp'-stă-shōhn'*

I am hurt here.

Jeg er skadet her	Jeg er såret her	Jag är skadad här
yay air skah'-det hair	*yi air saw' ret hear*	*yă ĕh skă'-dăd hair*

I can't move.

Jeg kan ikke bevege meg	Jeg kan ikke bevæge mig	Jag kan inte röra mig
yay kăn ick'-kĕ beh-vēh'-gĕ may	*yi kan ick'-ke be-vay'-ĕh my*	*yă kăn in'-tĕ röră may*

It hurts me to move.

Det gjør ondt når jeg beveger meg	Det gør ondt hvis jeg bevæger mig	Det gör ont när jag rör mig
dĕh yŏr ohnt nawr yay beh-vēh'-gĕr may	*deh gör ohnt vis yi be-vay'-ĕr my*	*dĕh yŏr ŏhnt nuir yă rör may*

The pain is here.

Det gjør ondt her	Smerterne er her	Det gör ont här
dĕh yŏr ohnt' hair	*smer'-tĕr-nĕ air hear*	*dĕh yŏr ohnt hair*

Can you bandage this?

Kan De bandasjere dette?	Kan De lægge en bandage på her?	Kan ni lägga ett förband här?
kän dee ban-dah-sheh'-rĕ det'-tĕ	*kan de leg'-gĕ in ban-dăh'-shĕh paw hear*	*kän nee leg'-gă ett för-bănd' hair*

Norwegian	*Danish*	*Swedish*

There is a cut here.

Der er en flenge her	Der er et snitsår	Det är ett sår här
dair air ehn flĕhng'-ĕh hair	*dair air it sneet'-sawr*	*dĕh ĕh ĕtt sawr hair*

I feel faint.

Jeg føler meg svimmel	Jeg føler mig ilde til pads	Det känns som jag skulle svimma
yay fö'-ler may svim'-mel	*yi föh'-ler my ille til pas*	*dĕh chĕnns som yå skool'-lĕ svim'-må*

Press here!

Press her!	Præs her!	Tryck här!
prĕss hair	*press hear*	*trück hair*

That hurts.

Det gjør ondt	Det gør ondt	Det gör ont
deh yör ohnt	*deh gör ohnt*	*dĕh yör ohnt*

Gently, hard.

Forsiktig, hårdt	Forsigtig, hårdt	Försiktigt, hårt
for-sick'-tee, hawrt	*for-sick'-teet, hawrt*	*för-sik'-tit, hawrt*

Someone is drowning.

Der er en som drukner	Der er nogen der er ved at drukne	Någon håller på att drunkna
dair air ehn som drŏŏk'-ner	*dair air noh'-en dair air veth at drŏŏk'-ne*	*naw'-gon hol'-lĕr paw ătt drŏŏnk-na*

THE DENTIST

I want to go to a good dentist.

Jeg vil gjerne gå til en flink tannlege	Jeg ønsker at gå til en god tandlæge	Jag vill gå till en bra tandläkare
yay vill yair'-nĕ gaw till ehn flink' tänn'-leh-gĕ	*yi ön'-sker at gaw til in goth tähn'-lai-ĕh*	*yå vill gaw till en bräh tänd'-lai-kărĕ*

I have lost a filling.

Jeg har mistet en plombe	Jeg har tabt en plombe	Jag har tappat en plomb
yay hahr mis'-tet ehn plom'-bĕ	*yi hahr tähbt in plom'-bĕ*	*yå här tăp'-păt en plomb*

Norwegian	Danish	Swedish

I have toothache.

| Jeg har tannpine | Jeg har tandpine | Jag har tandvärk |
| *yay hahr tănn'-pee-ně* | *yi hahr tăhn'-pee-ně* | *yā hār tănd'-věrk* |

A tooth is broken.

| En tann er brukket | En tand er brækket | Jag har brutit av en tand |
| *ehn tănn air brŏŏk'-ket* | *in tăhn air braik'-ket* | *yā hār broo'-tit ăv ēn tănd* |

I can't see signs of decay.

| Jeg kan ikke se tegn på forfall | Jeg kan ikke se tegn på forfald | Den verkar inte angripen |
| *yay kăn ick'-kě sěh tayn paw for-făhl'* | *yi kan ick'-ke seh tain paw for-făl'* | *děn ver'-kăr in'-tě ănn'-gree-pen* |

Must it come out?

| Må den trekkes? | Behøver den at blive trukket ud | Måste den dragas ut? |
| *maw den trěhk'-kes* | *be-hö'-věr den at blee'-vě trŏŏk'-ket ooth* | *mosstě den drah-găs oot* |

Can I have an injection?

| Kan jeg bli bedøvet? | Kan jeg blive bedøvet? | Kan jag bli bedövad? |
| *kăn yay blee beh-dö'-vet* | *kan yi blee'-vě beh-dö'-vet* | *kăn yā blee beh-dö-văd* |

Can I have a temporary filling?

| Kan jeg få en midlertidig plombe? | Kan jeg få en midlertidig plombering? | Kan jag få en provisorisk fyllning? |
| *kăn yay faw ehn mid'-ler-tee-dee plom'-bě* | *kan yi faw in meeth'-ler-tee-thee plom-běh'-ring* | *kăn yā faw ěn provi-soh'-risk füll-ning* |

The gum is bleeding.

| Tannkjøttet blør | Gummen bløder | Tandköttet blöder |
| *tănn'-chöt-tě blör* | *goom'-men blö'-ther* | *tănd'-chöt-tet blö'-der* |

The gum is sore.

| Tannkjøttet er ømt | Gummen gør ondt | Det gör ont i tandköttet |
| *tănn'-chöt-tě air ömt* | *goom'-men gör ohnt* | *děh yör ohnt ee tănd'-chöt-tet* |

| Norwegian | Danish | Swedish |

I leave on ...

| Jeg reiser på ... | Jeg rejser på ... | Jag far på ... |
| *yay ray'-ser paw ...* | *yi ry'-ser paw ...* | *yā fār paw ...* |

That is much better.

| Det er mye bedre | Det er meget bedre | Det är mycket bättre |
| *deh air mü'-ĕh beh'-drĕ* | *deh air my'-et beth'-rĕ* | *dĕh ĕh mückĕ bet'-trĕ* |

How much do I owe you?

| Hvor mye skylder jeg Dem? | Hvormeget skylder jeg Dem? | Hur mycket är jag skyldig? |
| *vohr mü'-ĕh shül'-lĕr yay dem* | *vor my'-et skyl'-lĕr yi dem* | *hōōr mückĕ ĕh yā shül'-dee* |

Gas.

| Gass | Gas | Bedövning |
| *gås* | *gas* | *bĕh-döv'-ning* |

Gold, ordinary filling.

| Gull, alminnelig plombe | Guld, almindelig plombering | Guld, vanlig fyllning |
| *gōōl, ăhl-min'-nĕ-lee plom'-bĕ* | *gōōl, ăhl-min'-ne-lee plom-bĕh'-ring* | *gōōld, vän'-lee füll'-ning* |

These false teeth are broken.

| Dette gebisset er knust | Disse forlorene tænder er brækkede | De här löständerna är sönder |
| *det'-tĕ geh-bis'-set air knoost* | *disse for-loh'-re-ne ten'-ner air braik'-ke-the* | *dĕh hair lös'-ten-dĕr-nă ĕh sön'-dĕr* |

THE DOCTOR

I must see a doctor.

| Jeg blir nødt til å se en doktor | Jeg bliver nødt til at se en læge | Jag måste gå till en läkare, or doctor |
| *yay bleer nut' till aw sĕh ehn doctor* | *yi bleer nŏth til at sĕh in lai'-ĕh* | *yā mosstĕ gaw till en lai'-kărĕ, doktor* |

Please call a doctor.

| Vær så vennlig å ringe etter en doktor | Vær venlig at tilkalde en læge | Var snäll och ring efter en läkare, doktor |
| *vair saw ven'-lee aw ring-ĕh ĕt'-ter ehn doctor* | *vair ven'-lee at til'-kal-le in lai'-ĕh* | *vär snĕll ock ring ĕf'-tĕr ĕn lai'-kărĕ, doktor* |

| *Norwegian* | *Danish* | *Swedish* |

I don't feel well.

Jeg føler meg ikke bra	Jeg føler mig ikke rask	Jag känner mig inte
yay fö'-ler may ick'-kĕ	*yi föh'-ler my ick'-ke*	bra
brah	rask	*yā chennĕr may in'-tĕ*
		brā

I feel feverish.

Jeg tror jeg har feber	Jeg tror jeg har feber	Jag känner mig febrig
yay trohr yay hahr	*yi trohr yi hahr fĕh'-ber*	*yā chennĕr may*
fĕh'-behr		*fĕhb'-ree*

I feel very weak.

Jeg føler meg svært	Jeg føler mig udmattet	Jag känner mig
svak	*yi föh'-ler my*	mycket matt
yay fö'-ler may svairt'	*ooth'-māt-tet*	*yā chennĕr may*
svahk		*mückĕt mätt*

I have a headache.

Jeg har hodepine	Jeg har hovedpine	Jag har huvudvärk
yay hahr hoh' dĕ pee nĕ	*yi huhr huh'-vĕth-pee-nĕ*	*yā hār hoo'-vod-vĕrk*

Sore throat.

Ondt i halsen	Ondt i halsen	Ont i halsen
ohnt ee häl'-sen	*ohnt ee hähl'-sen*	*ohnt ee häl'-sen*

Earache, toothache.

Ørepine, tannpine	Ørepine, tandpine	Ont i örat, tandvärk
ö'-rĕh-pee'-nĕ,	*ö'-re-pee-nĕ,*	*ohnt ee ör'-āt,*
tänn'-pee-nĕ	*tähn'-pee-nĕ*	*tänd'-vĕrk*

I have a persistent cough.

Jeg har en	Jeg har hoste hele tiden	Jag har en ihållande
vedvarende hoste	*yi hahr hoh'-ste hele*	hosta
yay hahr ehn	*tee'-then*	*yā hār ēn ee'-hol-län-dĕ*
vĕhd'-vah-ren-dĕ		*hohs'-tä*
hŏhs'-tĕ		

I have an infection in . . .

Jeg har en	Jeg har en	Jag har en
infeksjon i . . .	infektion i . . .	infektion i . . .
yay hahr ehn	*yi hahr in*	*yā hār ēn*
in-fek-shohn' ee . . .	*infect-shōhn' ee . . .*	*in-fek-shohn' ee . . .*

Norwegian	Danish	Swedish

E

I have hurt my hand, finger, arm.

Jeg har skadet hånden, fingeren, armen min	Jeg har slået min hånd, finger, arm	Jag har gjort mig illa i handen, fingret, armen
yay hahr skah'-det hon'-nĕn, finger-ĕn, ăr'-mĕn min	*yi hahr slawet meen hawn, fing'-er, arm*	*yā hār yohrt may illă ee hăn'-den, fing'-ret, ăr'-men*

Leg, foot, shoulder.

Legg, fot, skulder	Ben, fod, skulder	Ben, foot, axel
leg, foht, skōŏl'-der	*ben, foth, skōŏl'-ler*	*bēhn, foht, axĕl*

I am (temporarily) deaf.

Jeg er (midlertidig) døv	Jeg er døv (for tiden)	Jag är (tillfälligt) döv
yay air (mid'-ler-tee-dee) döv	*yi air döv (for tee'-then)*	*yā ēh (till-fĕl-lit) döv*

Perhaps the ear needs syringing.

Kanskje øret trenger å renses	Måske trænger øret til at blive sprøjtet	Kanske örat behöver spolas
kăn'-sheh ö'-ret trĕhng-ĕr aw rĕn'-ses	*maw-ske' trĕng'-er ö-ret til at blee'-ve sproy'-tet*	*kăn'-shĕh ö'-răt bĕh-hö'-vĕr spoh'-lăs*

I have a splinter in my finger.

Jeg har en flis i fingeren min	Jeg har en splindt i min finger	Jag har en flisa i fingret
yay hahr ehn flees' ee fing'-ĕr-ĕn min	*yi hahr in spleent ee meen fing'-er*	*yā hār en flee'-să ee fing'-ret*

Take this medicine with water three times a day.

Ta denne medisinen i vann, tre ganger daglig	Tag denne medicin tre gange daglig i vand	Tag den här medicinen med vatten tre gånger om dagen
tah den'-nĕ meh-dee-seen'-ĕn ee vănn, treh gahng'-ĕr dahg'-lee	*tah den'-ne meh-dee-seen' tray gan'-ĕh dahg'-lee ee văhn*	*tă dĕn hair medi-cee'-nĕn mĕh văt'-ten trĕh gongĕr omm dăgĕn*

Before, after, meals.

Før, etter, måltidene	Før, efter, måltiderne	Före, efter, måltider
för, ĕt'-ter, mawl'-tee-de-nĕ	*för, efter, mawl'-tee-ther-nĕ*	*förĕ, ĕf'-ter, mawl'-teed-ĕr*

Norwegian	Danish	Swedish

I have a rash.

Jeg har utslett	Jeg har udslæt	Jag har utslag
yay hahr oot'-slĕt	*yi hahr ooth'-slait*	*yā hār oot'-slāg*

Take this note to the hospital.

Ta dette brevet til sykehuset	Tag denne skrivelse til hospitalet	Tag med den här anteckningen till sjukhuset
tah det'-tĕ brĕh'-vĕ till sü'-kĕ-hoos-ĕh	*tah den'-ne skree'-vel-se til hos-pee-tah'-let*	*tā mĕh dĕn hair änn'-teck-ning-ĕn till shook'-hoo-set*

Must I stay in bed?

Må jeg holde sengen?	Bliver jeg nødt til at ligge i sengen?	Måste jag ligga till sängs?
maw yay hol'-lĕ sehng-ĕn	*blee'-ver yi nŏth til at ligge ee seng'-en*	*mosstĕ yā lig-gă till sĕngs*

Can I eat anything?

Kan jeg spise noe?	Må jeg spise noget?	Får jag äta någonting?
kăn yay spee'-sĕ noh'-ĕh	*maw yi spee'-se noh'-et*	*fawr yā aită naw'-gon-ting*

Should I come back?

Burde jeg komme tilbake?	Skal jeg komme tilbage?	Ska jag komma tillbaka?
boor-dĕ yay kom'-mĕ till-bah'-kĕ	*skal yi kom'-me til-bah'-ĕh*	*skā yā kom'-mă till-bā'-kă*

Will you visit me tomorrow?

Vil De besøke meg i morgen?	Vil De besøge mig i morgen?	Kommer ni och besöker mig i morgon?
vill dee beh-sö'-kĕ may ee mor'-ĕn	*vil dee be-sö'-ĕh my ee mor'-en*	*kom'-mĕr nee ock bĕh-sö'-kĕr may ee mor'-ron*

AT TABLE

Where is the restaurant, dining-room?

Hvor er restauranten, spisesalen?	Hvor er restauranten, spisesalen?	Var är restauranten, matsalen?
vohr air res-too-rahng'-ĕn, spee'-sĕ-sah-len	*vor air res-to-rang'-ĕn, spee'-sĕ-sāh-len*	*vār ēh rĕstau-răng'-ĕn, māt'-sah-len*

Norwegian	Danish	Swedish

When is lunch, dinner served?

Når blir lunsj, middag, servert?	Hvornår bliver der serveret frokost, middag?	Når serveras lunch, middag?
nawr bleer loonsh, mid'-dahg, sehr-vĕhrt'	*vornawr blee'-ver dair sair-veh'-ret froh'-kost, mee'-dāh*	*nair sĕr-vēh'-răs lunch, mid'-dah*

The head waiter.

Hovmesteren	Overtjeneren	Hovmästaren
hohv'-mes-ter-ĕn	*oh'-ĕr-tyay-nĕ-rĕn*	*hawv-mes-tărn*

The waiter.

Kelneren	Tjeneren	Kyparen
kel'-ner-ĕn	*tyay'-nĕ-rĕn*	*chü'-pă-ren*

A table for two.

Et bord til to	Et bord til to	Ett bord för två
ett bohr till toh	*it bohr til toh*	*ĕtt bohrd för tvaw*

Where can we sit?

Hvor kan vi sitte?	Hvor kan vi sidde?	Var kan vi sitta?
vohr kăn vee sit'-tĕ	*vor kan vee seeth'-the*	*văr kăn vee sit'-tă*

A table by the window, the wall.

Et bord ved vinduet, veggen	Et bord ved vinduet, væggen	Ett bord vid fönstret, vid väggen
ett bohr veh vin'-doo-ĕtt, vĕg'-gĕn	*it bohr veth vin'-doo-ĕt, vaig'-gen*	*ĕtt bohrd veed fön'-strĕt, veed vĕg'-gen*

There is a draught here.

Det trekker her	Det trækker her	Det drar hår
deh trĕk'-ker hair	*deh traik'-ker hear*	*dĕh drär hair*

Are you being served?

Blir De servert?	Bliver De serveret?	Blir ni serverade?
bleer dee sehr-vēhrt'	*blee'-ver dee sair-vēh'-rĕt*	*bleer nee sĕr-vēh'-ră-dĕ*

May I have the menu?

Kan jeg få se spiseseddelen?	Må vi se spisekortet?	Kan vi få matsedeln?
kăn yay faw sēh spee'-sĕ-sed-dĕ-len	*maw vee seh spee'-se-kor-tet*	*kän vee faw māt'-sĕh-dĕln*

Norwegian	*Danish*	*Swedish*

We should like . . .

Vi vil gjerne ha . . .	Vi vil gerne have . . .	Vi skulle vilja ha . . .
vee vill yair'-në hah . . .	*vee vil gair'-ne hah . . .*	*vee sköōl'-lë vil'-lä hä . . .*

What do you recommend?

Hva kan De anbefale?	Hvad anbefaler De?	Vad kan ni rekommendera?
vah kän dee ähn'-beh-fah-lë	*vath ähn'-be-fah-ler dee*	*väd kän nee rë-kom-mën-dëh'-rä*

What is this?

Hva er dette?	Hvad er dette?	Vad är detta?
vah air det'-të	*vath air det'-te*	*väd ëh dettä*

What is this in English?

Hva er dette på engelsk?	Hvad hedder dette på engelsk?	Vad är detta på engelska?
vah air det'-të paw ehng'-elsk	*vath heth'-ther det'-te paw ehng'-elsk*	*väd ëh dettä paw ehng'-elskä*

Is it good?

Er det godt?	Er det godt?	Är det gott?
air deh got	*air deh got*	*ëh däh got*

I don't want anything greasy.

Jeg vil ikke ha noe fet mat	Jeg vil ikke have noget der er fedt	Jag vill inte ha någonting fett
yay vill ick'-kë hah noh'-ëh fëht mäht	*yl vil ick'-ke hah noh'-et dair air fit*	*yä vill in'-të hä naw'-gon-ting fet*

I don't like this.

Jeg liker ikke dette	Jeg bryder mig ikke om dette	Jag tycker inte om detta
yay lee'-ker ick'-kë det'-të	*yl brü'-ther my ick'-ke om det-te*	*yä tückër in'-të omm dettä*

Take this away.

Vær så vennlig å fjerne dette	Vær venlig at fjerne dette	Var snell ock tag bort det här
vair saw ven'-lee aw fyair-në det'-të	*vair ven'-lee at fyern det'-te*	*vär snell ock tä bort dëh hair*

This is not clean.

Dette er ikke rent	Dette er ikke rent	Det här är inte rent
det'-të air ick'-kë rëhnt	*det'-te air ick'-ke rent*	*dëh hair ëh in'-të rëhnt*

Norwegian	Danish	Swedish

Can I have something else?

Kan jeg få noe annet?	Kan jeg få noget andet?	Kan jag få något annat?
kăn yay faw noh'-ĕh ăhn'-net	*kan yi faw noh'-ĕt ahn'-net*	*kăn yā faw naw'-got ăn'-năt*

Napkin.

Serviett	Serviet	Servett
sehr-vee-ĕt'	*ser-vee-ĕt'*	*sĕr-vĕtt'*

Would you like some more?

Vil De ha litt mer?	Vil De have noget mere?	Skulle ni vilja ha lite mera?
vill dee hah lit mehr'	*vil dee hah noh'-et meh'-re*	*skŏŏl'-lĕ nee vil'-lă hā leetĕ mēh'-ră*

Would you like something else?

Vil De ha noe annet?	Vil De have noget andet?	Vill ni ha något annat?
vill dee hah noh'-ĕh ăhn'-net	*vil dee hah noh'-et ăhn'-net*	*vill nee hā naw'-got ăn'-năt*

No thank you, I have had sufficient.

Nei takk, jeg er forsynt	Nej tak, jeg har fået nok	Nej tack, jag är nöjd
nay tăkk, yay air for-sünt'	*ny tak, yi hahr faw'-et nok*	*nay tăck, yā ēh nöyd*

Yes please.

Ja takk	Ja tak	Ja tack
yah tăkk	*yah tak*	*yā tăck*

Bring me the bill, please.

Kan jeg få regningen, takk	Vær venlig at give mig regningen	Kan jag få notan (räkningen)
kăn yay faw rayn'-ing-ĕn, tăkk	*vair ven'-lee at ghee my rye-ning-en*	*kăn yā faw noh'-tăn (raik'-ning-ĕn)*

Is the service included?

Er drikkepengene inkludert?	Er drikkepengene indkluderet?	Är det inklusive service?
air drick'-kĕ-pehng-ĕn-nĕ in-kloo-dehrt'	*air drik'-kĕ-peng-ĕh in'-kloo-deh-ret*	*eh deh in-kloh-see'-vĕ sĕr-vees*

Norwegian	Danish	Swedish

The bill is not correct.

Regningen er ikke korrekt	Regningen stemmer ikke	Den här räkningen är inte riktig
rayn'-ing-ĕn air ick'-kĕ correct	*rye'-ning-en stem'-mer ick'-ke*	*dĕn hair raik'-ning-ĕn eh in'-tĕ riktig*

I shall pay for all of us.

Jeg betaler for oss alle	Jeg vil betale for os alle	Jag betalar för oss alla
yay beh-tah'-lĕr for os ăl'-lĕ	*yi vil beh-tah'-le for us alle*	*yā beh-tāh'-lär för oss ăllă*

We shall pay separately.

Vi betaler hver for seg	Vi vil betale hver for sig	Vi betalar var för sig
vee beh-tah'-lĕr vair' for say	*vee vil beh-tah'-le vair for sigh*	*vee bēh-tah'-lär vär för say*

MENU AND UTENSILS

Almonds.

Mandler	Mandler	Mandlar
mănd-ler	*mahn'-ler*	*mănd-lăr*

Apples.

Epler	Æbler	Äpplen
ĕhp'-ler	*aibler*	*ĕpp-lĕn*

Apricots.

Aprikoser	Aprikoser	Aprikoser
ăhp-ree-koh'-ser	*ăhp-ree-koh'-ser*	*ăhp-ree-koh'-ser*

Asparagus.

Asparges	Asparges	Sparris
ahs-păhr'-gĕs	*ăh-spăhrs'*	*spărris*

Bananas.

Bananer	Bananer	Bananer
băh-nah'-ner	*băh-nā'-ner*	*băh-năh'-nĕr*

Beans.

Bønner	Bønner	Bönor
bön'-ner	*bön'-ner*	*bö'-nohr*

Norwegian	*Danish*	*Swedish*

Beef (boiled).

Oksekjøtt (kokt)	(Kogt) oksekød	Oxkött (kokt)
ŏhk'-sĕ-chöt (kohkt)	*(kogt) ŏk'-sĕh-köth*	*ohx-chött (kohkt)*

Beef (roast).

Oksestek	Oksesteg	Rostbiff
ŏhk'-sĕ-stēhk	*ok'-sĕh-stehg*	*rosst-biff*

Beer.

Øl	Øl	Öl
öl	*öl*	*öl*

Biscuit.

Kjeks	Biscuit	Käx, småkakor
chĕks	*biscuit*	*kĕx, smaw'-kä-kor*

Boiled.

Kokt	Kogt	Kokt
kohkt	*kockt*	*kohkt*

Bottle, large bottle.

Flaske, stor flaske	Flaske, stor flaske	Flaska, stor flaska
flăs'-kĕ, stohr flăs'-kĕ	*flas'-ke, stohr flas'-ke*	*flăs'-kă, stohr flăs'-kă*

Brandy.

Konjakk	Cognac	Konjak
kon'-yăck	*kon-yack*	*kon'-yăck*

Bread.

Brød	Brød	Bröd
brö	*bröth*	*bröd*

Butter.

Smør	Smør	Smör
smör	*smör*	*smör*

Cabbage.

Kål	Kål	Kål
kawl	*kawl*	*kawl*

Cake.

Kake	Kage	Kaka
kah'-kĕ	*kah'-ĕh*	*kä'-kă*

Norwegian	*Danish*	*Swedish*

Carrots.

Gulrøtter	Gulerødder	Morøtter
gool'-röt-ter	*gool'-le-röth-ĕr*	*moh'-röt-ter*

Cauliflower.

Blomkål	Blomkål	Blomkål
blom'-kawl	*blohm'-kawl*	*blom'-kawl*

Cheese.

Ost	Ost	Ost
ohst	*ohst*	*ohst*

Chicken, chicken soup.

Kylling, hønsesuppe	Kylling, hønsesuppe	Kyckling, hönssoppa
chül'-ling,	*kül'-ling,*	*chück'-ling,*
hön'-sĕ-sōōp-pĕ	*höhn'-sĕ-sōōp-pĕ*	*hönns'-sop-pä*

Chocolate.

Sjokolade	Chokolade	Choklad
shoh-koh-lah'-dĕ	*cho-ko-läh'-the*	*shŏk-kläd'*

Chop (mutton, pork).

Kotelett, (fåre-, svine-)	Kotelet (lamme-, svine-)	Kotlett (lamm-, fläsk-)
kot'-tĕ-let,	*koh-tĕ-let'*	*kott-let', (lämm-, flĕsk-)*
(faw'-rĕ-, svee'-nĕ-)	*(läm-mĕ-, svee'-nĕ-)*	

Cod.

Torsk	Torsk	Torsk
torsk	*tohrsk*	*torsk*

Coffee.

Kaffe	Kaffe	Kaffe
käf'-fĕ	*kaf'-fĕ*	*käf'-fĕ*

Cold meat.

Koldt kjøtt	Koldt kød	Kallt kött
kolt chöt	*kolt köth*	*källt chött*

Crab.

Krabbe	Krappe	Krabba
kräb'-bĕ	*krap'-pĕ*	*kräb'-bä*

Norwegian	Danish	Swedish

Cream.

| Fløte | Fløde | Grädde |
| *flö-tĕ* | *flö'-the* | *grĕd'-dĕ* |

Cucumber.

| Agurk | Agurk | Gurka |
| *ăh-goork'* | *ăh-goork'* | *goor'-kă* |

Cup.

| Kopp | Kop | Kopp |
| *kop* | *cup* | *kop* |

Dates.

| Dadler | Dadler | Dadlar |
| *dăd'-ler* | *dăth'-ler* | *dăd'-lăr* |

Dessert.

| Dessert | Dessert | Dessert, efterrätt |
| *dĕh-sair'* | *deh-sairt'* | *dĕh-sair', ĕf'-tĕr-rĕtt* |

Dinner.

| Middag | Middag | Middag |
| *mid'-dahg* | *meh'-dāh* | *mid'-dăh* |

Duck.

| And | And | Anka |
| *ăhn* | *ahn* | *ăn-kă* |

Eel.

| Ål | Ål | Ål |
| *awl* | *awl* | *awl* |

Egg.

| Egg | Æg | Ägg |
| *egg* | *egg* | *egg* |

Egg, soft boiled, hard boiled.

| Egg, bløtkokt, hårdkokt | Æg, blødkogt, hårdkogt | Ägg, löskokt, hårdkokt |
| *egg, blöt-kokt, hawr-kokt* | *egg, blöth'-kockt, hawr'-kockt* | *egg, lös'-kohkt, hawrd'-kohkt* |

| Norwegian | Danish | Swedish |

Eggs, fried, poached.

Norwegian	Danish	Swedish
Speilegg, forlorne egg *spayl-egg, for-lohr'-ně egg*	Æg, spejlede, pocherede *egg, spaly'-le-the, poh-che'-rě-the*	Ägg, stekt, förlorat *egg, stēhkt, för-loh'-rät*

Figs.

Fikener *feek'-ner*	Figner *fee'-ner*	Fikon *fee'-kŏn*

Fish.

Fisk *fisk*	Fisk *fissk*	Fisk *fisk*

Fish, fried, boiled.

Fisk, stekt, kokt *fisk, stēhkt, kokt*	Fisk, stægt, kogt *fisk, steckt, kockt*	Fisk, stekt, kokt *fisk, stēhkt, kohkt*

Fork.

Gaffel *gǎf'-fel*	Gaffel *gähf'-fel*	Gaffel *gǎf'-fel*

Fried.

Stekt *stēhkt*	Stægt *steckt*	Stekt *stēhkt*

Fruit.

Frukt *frōōkt*	Frukt *frōōkt*	Frukt *frōōkt*

Fruit pie.

Fruktpai *frōōkt-pie*	Frugt kage *frōōkt kah'-ěh*	Fruktpaj *frōōkt-pie*

Garlic.

Hvitløk *veet'-lök*	Hvidløg *veeth'-löy*	Vitlök *veet'-lök*

Glass.

Glass *glǎss*	Glas *glähs*	Glas *glähss*

Norwegian	Danish	Swedish

Grapes.

Druer	Vindruer	Druvor
droo'-ĕr	*veen'-droo-ĕr*	*droo'-vŏr*

Gravy.

Saus	Sovs	Sås
saws	*sows*	*saws*

Grilled.

Grill-stekt	Stegt	Grillad
grill-stehkt	*steckt*	*grilläd*

Halibut.

Kveite	Helleflynder	Helgeflundra
kvay'-tĕ	*hel'-le-flün-ĕr*	*hell'-yĕ-floon-dră*

Ham.

Skinke	Skinke	Skinka
sheen'-kĕ	*skeen'-ke*	*shin'-kă*

Ham, smoked.

Røkeskinke	Røget skinke	Rökt skinka
rö'-kĕ-sheen-kĕ	*roy'-ĕt skeen'-kĕ*	*rökt shin'-kă*

Herring, pickled, smoked.

Sursild, røkesild	Marinerede sild, røget sild	Sill, inlagd, rökt
soor'-sill, rö'-kĕ-sill	*mă-ree-neh'-rĕ-the sill, roy'-ĕt sill*	*sill, inn'-lägd, rökt*

Hors d'œuvres.

Forrett	Hors d' oeuvres	Smörgåsbord, assiett
for'-ret	*hors d' oeuvres*	*smör-gaws-bohrd, ă-shĕtt'*

Ice.

Is	Is	Is
ees	*ees*	*ees*

Ice cream.

Iskrem	Fløde is	Glass
ees'-krehm	*flö'-the ees*	*gläss*

Norwegian	Danish	Swedish

Jam.

Norwegian	Danish	Swedish
Syltetøy	Syltetøj	Sylt
sül'-tĕ-töy	*sül'-tĕ-toy*	*sült*

Juice, orange, grape, tomato.

Saft, appelsin, grapefrukt, tomat	Saft, appelsin, grapefrugt, tomat	Juice, apelsin, grape, tomat
săhft, ăp-pĕl-seen-', grape'-frōōkt-, toh-maht'	*săhft, ăppĕl-seen', grape'-frōōkt, tohmăt'*	*yoos, ăp-pĕl-seen', grape, toh-maht'*

Kidney.

Nyre	Nyre	Njure
nü-re	*nü-re*	*new'-rĕh*

Knife.

Kniv	Kniv	Kniv
k'-neev	*k'-neev*	*k-neev*

Lamb.

Lamm	Lam	Lamm
lăm	*lăhm*	*lămm*

Lemon.

Sitron	Citron	Citron
see-trohn'	*cee-trohn'*	*see-trōhn'*

Lemonade.

Lemonade, brus	Lemonade	Lemonad, läskedryck
leh-moh-nah'-dĕ, broos	*leh-moh-nah'-the*	*lĕmmŏ-nād', lĕs'-kĕ-drück*

Lettuce.

Salat	Salat	Sallad
sah-lāht'	*săh-lāt'*	*sällăd*

Liqueur.

Likør	Liqueur	Likör
lee-kör	*lee-kör'*	*lee-kör*

Liver.

Lever	Lever	Lever
lēh'-ver	*lēh'-ver*	*lēh'-ver*

Norwegian	Danish	Swedish

Lobster.

Hummer	Hummer	Hummer
hŏŏm'-mer	*hŏŏm'-mer*	*hŏŏm'-mĕr*

Lunch.

Lunsj	Frokost	Lunch
loonsh	*froh'-kost*	*loonsh*

Mackerel.

Makrell	Markræl	Makrill
mäh-krĕll'	*mäh-krell'*	*mäck'-rill*

Marmalade.

Appelsin marmelade	Orange marmalade	Apelsinmarmelad
ăpp-ĕl-seen'	*oh-rang'-sheh*	*ăppĕl-seen'-mär-mĕ-lād'*
mahr-meh-lāh'-dĕ	*mar-mĕ-lāh'-the*	

Meat.

Kjøtt	Kød	Kött
chöt	*köth*	*chött*

Melon, water-melon.

Melon, vannmelon	Melon, vand melon	Melon, vattenmelon
meh-lohn',	*meh-lohn', vahn*	*mĕ-lohn',*
våhn'-meh-lohn'	*meh-lohn'*	*vättĕn-mĕ-lohn'*

Milk.

Melk	Mælk	Mjölk
mĕhlk	*mailk*	*m-yölk*

Mineral water.

Mineralvann	Mineral vand	Mineralvatten
min-neh-rahl' vänn	*mee-neh-rahl' vahn*	*minnĕ-rāl'-vättĕn*

Mushrooms.

Sjampinjong, sopp	Champignons	Champinjoner, svamp
chämp-in-young, sop	*cham'-ping-youngs*	*shamp-in-yoh'-ner,*
		svämp

Mustard.

Sennep	Sennep	Senap
sen'-nep	*sen'-nep*	*sĕhn'-ăp*

Norwegian	*Danish*	*Swedish*

Mutton.

| Fårekjøtt | Fåre kød | Fårkött |
| *faw'-rĕ-chŏt* | *faw'-re köth* | *fawr'-chŏtt* |

Napkin.

| Serviett | Serviet | Servett |
| *søhr-vee-ett'* | *sĕr-vee-et'* | *sĕr-vĕtt'* |

Nuts.

| Nøtter | Nødder | Nötter |
| *nöt-ter* | *nöth'-ther* | *nöt'-ter* |

Olive oil.

| Olivenolje | Oliven olie | Olivolja |
| *o-lee'-ven-oll-yĕ,* | *o-lee'-ven oh'-lee-ĕh* | *ŏleev'-oll'-yă* |

Olives.

| Oliven | Oliven | Oliver |
| *o-lee'-ven* | *o-lee'-ven* | *ŏl-lee'-vĕr* |

Omelette.

| Omelett | Omelet | Omelett |
| *om-mĕh-let'* | *om-mĕh-let'* | *om'-mĕh-let'* |

Onion.

| Løk | Løg | Lök |
| *lök* | *loy* | *lök* |

Orange.

| Appelsin | Appelsin | Apelsin |
| *ăp-pel-seen'* | *ăp-pel-søøn'* | *ăppĕl-seen'* |

Oysters.

| Østers | Østers | Ostron |
| *ŏs'-ters* | *ös'-ters* | *ohs'-tron* |

Peach.

| Fersken | Fersken | Persika |
| *fair'-sken* | *fair'-sken* | *pĕhr'-see-kă* |

Pear.

| Pære | Pære | Päron |
| *pair'-ĕh* | *pai'-rĕ* | *pair'-on* |

| Norwegian | Danish | Swedish |

Peas.

Erter	Ærter	Ärtor
air'-ter	*air'-ter*	*air'-tor*

Pepper.

Pepper	Peber	Peppar
pepper	*pĕh'-ver*	*pĕp'-păr*

Pheasant, partridge.

Fasan, rapphøne	Fasan, raphøne	Fasan, rapphöna
fah-sahn', răpp'-hö-nĕ	*fah-sahn', răp'-höh-nĕ*	*făh-sähn', răpp'-hö-nă*

Pineapple.

Ananas	Ananas	Ananas
ăhn-näh'-năs	*ăhn'-näh-năs*	*ăhn'-näh-năs*

Plate.

Tallerken	Talerken	Tallrik
tah-ler'-kĕn	*tah-ler'-kĕn*	*täll'-rick*

Plum.

Plomme	Blomme	Plommon
plom'-mĕ	*blom'-mĕ*	*plŏhm'-mŏn*

Pork.

Svin	Flæsk	Fläsk
sveen	*flaisk*	*flaisk*

Port wine.

Portvin	Portvin	Portvin
port'-veen	*port'-veen*	*port-veen*

Potatoes, boiled, fried.

Poteter, kokte, stekte	Kartofler, kogte, stegte	Potatis, kokt, stekt
poh-tēh'-ter, kok'-tĕ, stēhk-tĕ	*kăhr-tohf'-lĕr, kok'-te, stēhk'-tĕ*	*pŏh-täht'-is, kohkt, stēhkt*

Potatoes, mashed, chipped.

Potetstappe, franske poteter	Kartofler, mosede, franske	Potatismos, pommes frites
poh-tēht'-stăp-pĕ, frahn'-skĕ poh-tēh'-ter	*kăhr-tohf'-ler, moh'-sĕ-the, fran'-ske*	*pŏh-täht-is-mōhs, pommes frites*

Norwegian	Danish	Swedish

Prunes.

Svisker	Svesker	Sviskon
svis'-ker	*sves'-kĕr*	*svis'-kŏn*

Pudding.

Dessert	Dessert	Pudding
des-sair	*des-sairt'*	*pudding*

Rabbit.

Kanin	Kanin	Kanin
kah'-neen	*kah'-neen*	*kăh'-neen*

Radishes.

Reddiker	Radisser	Radisor
red'-ick-kĕr	*răh-dees'-ser*	*rai'-disŏr*

Raspberries.

Bringebær	Hindbær	Hallon
bring'-ĕh-bair	*hin'-bair*	*hăl'-lŏn*

Rice.

Ris	Ris	Ris
rees	*rees*	*rees*

Roasted

Ovnstekt	Stægt	Stekt
ohvn-stēhkt	*steckt*	*stēhkt*

Roll.

Rundstykke	Rundstykke	Rundstycke, franskbröd
rōōn-stük'-kĕ	*rōōn'-stük-kĕ*	*rōōnd'-stük-kĕ, fränsk'-bröd*

Salad.

Salat	Salat	Sallad
sah'-laht	*săh-lat'*	*săl'-lăd*

Salt.

Salt	Salt	Salt
sahlt	*sahlt*	*săhlt*

Norwegian	Danish	Swedish

Salmon.

| Laks | Laks | Lax |
| *lähks* | *lähks* | *läx* |

Sandwich.

| Smørrbrød | Smørrebrød | Smörgås, sandwich |
| *smör-brö* | *smör'-rĕ bröth* | *smör-gaws, sandwich* |

Sardines.

| Sardiner | Sardiner | Sardiner |
| *sahr-dee'-ner* | *săr-dee'-ner* | *săr-dee'-ner* |

Sauce.

| Saus | Sovs | Sås |
| *saws* | *sows* | *saws* |

Saucer.

| Asjett | Underkop | Tefat |
| *ah-shĕtt'* | *ŏŏn'-nĕr-kop* | *tēh-faht* |

Sausage.

| Pølse | Pølse | Korv |
| *pöl'-sĕ* | *pöl'-sĕ* | *korv* |

Shell fish.

| Skalldyr | Skalddyr | Skaldjur |
| *skăl-dür* | *skal'-dür* | *skăl-yoor* |

Shrimps.

| Reker | Rejer | Räkor |
| *rēh'-ker* | *ry'-ĕr* | *raï'-kohr* |

Snacks.

| En bit mat | Mellemmad | Mellanmål |
| *ehn beet' maht* | *mel'-lem-math* | *mel'-lăn-mawl* |

Sole.

| Flyndre | Rødspætte | Sjötunga |
| *flün'-drĕ* | *röth'-spait-tĕ* | *shö-tŏŏngă* |

Soup.

| Suppe | Suppe | Soppa |
| *sŏŏp'-pĕ* | *sŏŏp'-pĕ* | *sŏp-pă* |

| Norwegian | Danish | Swedish |

Spinach.

Norwegian	Danish	Swedish
Spinat	Spinat	Spenat
spee-naht'	*spee-näht'*	*spĕh-näht'*

Spoon.

Skje	Skø	Sked
shēh	*skēh*	*shēhd*

Stew.

Ragu	Ragu	Stuvning, ragu
rah-goo'	*rah-goo'*	*stoov'-ning, rah-goo'*

Strawberries.

Jordbær	Jordbær	Jordgubbar
yohr'-bair	*yohr'-bair*	*yōhrd-gŏŏb-băr*

Sugar.

Sukker	Sukker	Socker
sŏŏk'-ker	*sŏŏk'-kĕr*	*sucker*

Syrup, fruit-essence.

Sirup, frukt-essens	Sirup, frukt-essens	Sirap, fruktessens
see-rup, frŏŏkt'-ĕh-sĕns	*see'-rup, frŏŏkt'-ĕh-sĕns*	*see'-răp, frŏŏkt-ess-angs ·*

Table, tablecloth.

Bord, bordduk	Bord, borddug	Bord, bordduk
bohr, bohr'-dook	*bor, bor'-dooh*	*bohrd, bohrd-dook*

Tea, teapot.

Te, tekanne	The, the potte	Te, tekanna
teh, teh'-kăn-nĕ	*teh, teh'-pot-te*	*tēh, tēh-kăn-nă*

Toast.

Ristet brød	Ristebrød	Rostat bröd
riss'-tet brö	*ris'-tĕ-bröth*	*ross'-tät bröd*

Tomato.

Tomat	Tomat	Tomat
toh-mäht'	*toh-mät'*	*toh-maht'*

Tongue.

Tunge	Tunge	Tunga
tohng-ĕh	*tohng'-ĕh*	*tōŏng'-gă*

Norwegian	Danish	Swedish

Toothpick.

Tannpirker	Tandpind	Tandpetare
tănn'-pir-kĕr	*tăhn'-pin*	*tănd'-pēh-tah-rĕ*

Tray.

Brett	Bakke	Bricka
brĕt	*bak'-kĕh*	*brick'-kă*

Tunny.

Tunfisk	Tunfisk	Tonfisk
toon'-fisk	*toon'-fisk*	*toon-fisk*

Turkey.

Kalkun	Kalkun	Kalkon
kăl-koon'	*kăhl-koon'*	*kăl-koon'*

Veal.

Kalvekjøtt	Kalvekød	Kalvkött
kăl'-vĕ-chöt	*kal'-ve-köth*	*kălv-chött*

Vegetables.

Grønnsaker	Grøntsager	Grönsaker
grön'-săh-kĕr	*grön'-săh-ĕr*	*grön'-sā-kĕr*

Vegetarian diet.

Vegetariansk diet	Vegetariansk diet	Vegetarisk diet
veg-gĕ-tahr-ee-ăhnsk' dee-ĕtt	*vĕg-gĕ-tahr-ee-ăhnsk' dee-ate'*	*vĕgĕ-tahr'-isk dee-ēht'*

Vinegar.

Eddik	Eddike	Ättika, vinättika
ĕd'-dick	*eth'-thee-kĕ*	*ĕht'-tick-kă, veen'-ĕht'-tick-kă*

Water.

Vann	Vand	Vatten
vănn	*vahn*	*văttĕn*

Whisky and soda.

Whiskypjolter	Whisky og sodavand	Whisky, whiskygrogg
whiskey-pyol'-tər	*whiskey aw soh'-dă-vahn*	*visky, visky-grŏgg*

Norwegian	*Danish*	*Swedish*

Wine, red, white.

Vin, rød, hvit	Vin, rød, hvid	Vin, rött, vitt
veen, rö, veet	*veen, röth, veeth*	*veen, rött, vitt*

Wine, sweet, medium-sweet, medium-dry, dry.

Vin, søt, middels-søt, middels-tørr, tørr	Vin, sød, middelsød, middeltør, tør	Vin, sött, halvsött, halvtorrt, torrt
veen, söt, middels-söt, middels-törr, törr	*veen, söth, meeth'-ĕl'-söth, meeth'-ĕl-tör, tör*	*veen, sött, hälv-sött, hälv-torrt, torrt*

ENTERTAINMENT

Cinema performances in Denmark and Sweden are generally from 7 p.m. until 9 p.m. and from 9 p.m. until 11 p.m. In Norway there is often an extra performance from 5 p.m. until 7 p.m. Seats are often booked in advance. Smoking is forbidden in cinemas and theatres.

Where is the . . . cinema, theatre?

Hvor er . . . kinoen, teateret?	Hvor er . . . biografen, teateret?	Var ligger biografen . . . teatern?
vohr air . . . chee-noh-ĕn, teh-āht'-ĕr-rĕ	*vor uír . . . beeo-grăh'-fen, teh-āht'-ret*	*var lig'-ger beeŏ-grăf'-ĕn . . . tēh-ah'-tern*

Are there any good films, plays, on?

Går der noen gode filmer, skuespill?	Er der nogle gode film, skuespil, på plakaten?	Går det några bra filmer, pjäser?
gawr dair noh'-ĕn goh-ĕh film'-ĕr, skoo'-ĕh-spill	*air dair noh'-lĕ go'-the film, skoo'-ĕh-spil, paw pluh-kāh'-ten*	*gawr deh naw-gra brah filmer, p-yai-ser*

Documentary film, news reel.

Dokumentarfilm, filmavis	Dokumentarisk film, nyheder	Dokumentärfilm, journalfilm
docu-men-tāhr'-film, film'-ăh-vees	*docŏŏ-men-tāh'-risk film, nü'-heh-ther*	*doku-men-tair'-film, shohr-nāl'-film*

What time does the show start?

Når begynner forestillingen?	Hvornår begynder forestilningen?	Hur dags börjar föreställningen?
nawr beh-yün'-ner foh'-rĕ-still-ing-ĕn	*vor-nawr' be-gün'-ner foh'-rĕ-stil-ning-en*	*hoor dags bör-yar fö'-rĕ-stell-ning-ĕn*

Norwegian	Danish	Swedish

When does it end?

Når slutter den?	Hvornår er den forbi?	Hur dags slutar den?
nawr slōōt'-ter den	*vor-nawr' air den for-bee'*	*hoor dăgs sloo-tăr den*

Two performances a day.

To forestillinger pr. dag	To forestilninger daglig	Två föreställningar per dag
toh foh'-rĕ-still-ing-ĕr pĕr dahg	*toh foh'-rĕ-stil-ning-ĕr daw'-lee*	*tvaw för'-eh-stell-ning-ăr pĕr dăg*

Where is the box office?

Hvor er billettkontoret?	Hvor er billetkontoret?	Var är biljettkontoret?
vohr air bil-let'-kon-toh'-rĕ	*vor air bil-let'-kon-toh'-rĕt*	*văr ēh bill-yĕtt'-kon-toh'-ret*

I want to book some seats for this afternoon, this evening, tomorrow.

Jeg vil gjerne bestille noen billetter til i ettermiddag, i aften, i morgen	Jeg vil gerne bestille nogle billetter til i eftermiddag, i aften, i morgen	Jag vill beställa några biljetter till i eftermiddag, till i kväll, i morgon
yay vill yair'-nĕ beh-stil'-lĕ noh'-ĕn bil-let'-tĕr till ee ĕtt'-er-mid-dahg, ee ahf'-ten, ee mor'-ĕn	*yi vil gair'-ne beh-stil'-lĕ noh'-lĕ bil-let'-tĕr til ee efter-mee-dāh, ee ăhf'-ten, ee mor'-en*	*yā vill bēh-stĕl'-lă naw'-gră bill-yet'-ter till ee ĕf'-ter-mid-dăh, ee kvĕll, ee mor'-ron*

I want two seats in the stalls, the balcony.

Jeg vil gjerne ha to billeter til parkett, balkongen	Jeg vil gerne have to billetter til parterret, balkonen	Jag vill ha två platser på parkett, balkong
yay vill yair'-nĕ hah toh bil-let'-ter till păhr-ket', băhl-kong'-ĕn	*yi vil gair'-ne hah toh bil-let'-tĕr til par-ter'-ret, bal-kon'-ĕn*	*yā vill hā tvaw plăt-sĕr paw păr-kĕtt', băl-kong'*

Have you anything better, cheaper?

Har De noe bedre, billigere?	Har De nogle der er bedre, billigere?	Har ni något bättre, billigare?
hahr dee noh'-ĕh bēh'-drĕ, bil'-lee-ĕr-ĕh	*hahr dee noh'-le dair air beth-re, bil'-lee-rĕ*	*hăr nee naw'-got bet'-trĕ, bil'-lee-gă-rĕ*

Norwegian	Danish	Swedish

They are too near, too far back.

De er for langt fremme, bak	De er for langt fremme, for langt tilbage	De är för nära, för långt bak
dee air for lahngt frĕm'-mĕ, bāhk	*dee air for langht frem'-mĕ, for langht til-bāh-ĕh*	*dĕh ēh för nairä, för longt bāk*

I want seats nearer the centre.

Jeg vil gjerne ha noen plasser nærmere midten	Jeg vil gerne have nogle pladser nærmere midten	Jag vill ha platser närmare mitten
yay vill yair'-nĕ ha noh'-ĕn plăhs'-ser nair'-mer-ĕh mit-ten	*yi vil ger'-ne hah noh'-le plah'-sĕr nair'-mĕ-rĕ mit'-ten*	*yă vill hā plăt'-ser nair'-mărĕ mit'-ten*

How much does it cost?

Hvor mye koster det?	Hvor meget koster det?	Hur mycket kostar det?
vohr mŭ-ĕh kos'-ter deh	*vor my'-et kos'-ter deh*	*hoor mückĕ kos'-tăr dĕh*

Give me a programme, please.

Et program, takk	Et program, tak	Ge mig ett program tack
ĕtt proh-grăm', tăkk	*it pro-grahm', tăhk*	*yēh may ĕtt pro-grămm' tack*

I can't find my seat.

Jeg kan ikke finne plassen min	Jeg kan ikke finde min plads	Jag kan inte finna min plats
yay kăn ick'-kĕ fin'-nĕ plăhs'-sen min	*yi kan ick'-ke fin'-nĕ meen plahs*	*yă kăn in'-tĕ finnă min plăts*

When is the interval?

Når er pausen?	Hvornår er der pause?	När är det paus?
nawr air pow'-sen	*vor-nawr' air dair pau'-sĕ*	*nair ĕh dĕh pă'-ŏs*

How long does it last?

Hvor lenge varer den?	Hvor længe vare den?	Hur länge varar den?
vohr lehng-ĕh văhr'-ĕr den	*vor laing'-ĕh vah'-rĕ den*	*hoor lĕngĕ vă-răr den*

No smoking allowed.

Røking forbudt	Rygning forbudt	Rökning förbjuden
rŏk'-ing for-bōōt'	*rü'-ning for-bōōt'*	*rök-ning för-b-yoo'-den*

Norwegian	Danish	Swedish

Way out, way in.

Utgang, inngang	Udgang, indgang	Utgång, ingång
oot-gäng, in-gäng	*ooth'-gang, in'-gang*	*oot'-gong, in'-gong*

Actor, actress.

Skuespiller, skuespillerinne	Skuespiller, skuespillerinde	Skådespelare, skådespelerska
skoo'-ĕh-spil-ler, skoo'-ĕh-spil-ler-in'-nĕ	*skoo'-ĕh-spil-ler, skoo-ĕh-spil-ler-in'-nĕ*	*skaw'-dĕ-spēhl-ărĕ, skaw'-dĕ-spēhl-ĕr-skă*

Choir.

Kor	Kor	Kör
kohr	*kohr*	*kör*

Concert.

Konsert	Koncert	Konsert
kon-sairt	*kon-sairt'*	*kŏn-sair'*

Folk-dancing group.

Leikarring	Folkedans gruppe	Folkdanslag
lay'-kär-ring	*fohl'-kĕ-dans groo'-pe*	*folk'-däns-lāg*

Play.

Skuespill	Skuespil	Pjäs
skoo'-ĕh-spill	*skoo'-ĕh-spill*	*p-yais*

Revue.

Revy	Revy	Revy
reh-vü'	*reh-vü'*	*reh-vü'*

DANCING

I should like to go to a dance.

Jeg vil gjerne gå ut å danse	Jeg vil gerne gå ud at danse	Jag skulle vilja gå ut och dansa
yay vill yair'-nĕ gaw oot aw dän'-sĕ	*yi vil gair'-nĕ gaw ooth at dan'-sĕ*	*ya skōōl'-lĕ vil'-lă gaw oot ock dän-să*

I should like to dance.

Jeg vil gjerne danse	Jeg vil gerne danse	Jag skulle vilja dansa
yay vill yair'-nĕ dän'-sĕ	*yi vil gair'-nĕ dan-sĕ*	*yā skool'-lĕ vil'-lă dän'-să*

Norwegian	Danish	Swedish

I don't dance well.

Jeg danser ikke godt	Jeg danser ikke godt	Jag dansar inte bra
yay dăn'-ser ick'-kě got	*yay dan'-ser ick'-ke got*	*yā dăn'-săr in'-tě brā*

Will you dance with me?

Vil De danse?	Vil De danse?	Vill ni dansa
vill dee dŭn'-sĕ	*vil dee dan'-sĕ*	*vill nee dăn'-sā*

Can you dance the . . . ?

Kan De danse . . . ?	Kan De danse . . . ?	Kan ni dansa . . . ?
kăn dee dăn'-sĕ . . .	*kan dee dan'-sĕ . . .*	*kăn nee dăn'-să . . .*

Waltz, tango, samba.

Vals, tango, samba	Vals, tango, samba	Vals, tango, samba
vahls, tahng-oh, sähm-bă	*vahls, tahn'-go, sähm-bă*	*văls, tăngŏ, sămbă*

The band is very good.

Orkesteret er svært godt	Orkesteret er vældig godt	Det är en mycket bra orkester
or-kes'-těr-rĕ air svairt got	*or-kes'-těr-rĕt air vail'-dee got*	*dēh ĕh en mückĕ brāh orr-kes'-tĕr*

Shall we dance again?

Skal vi danse igjen?	Skal vi danse igen?	Ska vi dansa igen?
skăl vee dăn'-sĕ ee-yen'	*skal vee dan'-sĕ ee-gen'*	*skā vee dăn'-să ee-yen'*

It is very hot in here.

Det er svært varmt her inne	Der er meget varmt her inde	Det är mycket varmt här inne
děh air svairt' vuhrmt hair in'-nĕ	*dair air my'-et vahrmt hair-innĕ'*	*dēh ĕh mückĕ värmt hair in'-nĕ*

Would you like to sit down?

Har De lyst til å sette Dem?	Har De lyst til at sidde ned?	Vill ni sitta?
hahr dee lüst till aw set'-tĕ dĕm	*hahr dee lüst til at sith'-the neth*	*vill nee sit'-tă*

It is cooler outside.

Det er kjøligere ute	Det er køligere udenfor	Det är svalare ute
deh air chŏ'-lee-ĕr-ĕh oo'-tĕ	*deh air köh'-lee-ĕh-rĕ oo'-then-for*	*dēh ĕh svā'-lă-rĕ oo'-tĕ*

Norwegian	*Danish*	*Swedish*

May I see you home?

Får jeg følge Dem hjem?	Må jeg få lov at følge Dem hjem?	Får jag följa er hem?
fawr yay föl'-lĕ dem yem	*maw yi faw law at föl'-lĕ dem yem*	*fawr yā föll'-yă ēhr hĕm*

May I see you again?

Får jeg treffe Dem igen?	Må jeg få lov til at træffe Dem igen?	Får jag träffa er igen?
fawr yay trĕf'-fĕ dem ee'-yen	*maw yi faw law til at tref'-fĕ dem ee-gen'*	*fawr yā tref'-fă ehr ee-yen'*

RADIO

Is there a wireless here?

Fins det en radio her?	Findes der en radio her?	Finns det en radio här?
fins deh ehn rah'-dee-oh hair	*fin'-nes dair in räh'-dio hair*	*finns dēh ĕn rā-dio hair*

Can you get London?

Kan De få London?	Kan man få London?	Kan man få in London?
kăn dee faw Lon-don	*kan man faw Lon'-don*	*kăn mănn faw in London*

I wanted to hear the news.

Jeg ville gjerne høre nyhetene	Jeg ville gerne høre radioavisen	Jag ville gärna höra nyheterna
yay vil-lĕ yair'-nĕ hö-rĕ nü-hēht-ĕn-ĕh	*yi vil'-lĕ gair'-ne höh'-rĕ rah'-dio-äh-vee-sen*	*yā vil'-lĕ yair'-nă hö-ră nü'-hēht-ĕr-nă*

I want to hear some music.

Jeg vil gjerne høre noe musikk	Jeg vil gerne høre noget musik	Jag vill höra lite musik
yay vil yair'-nĕ hö-rĕ noh'-ĕh moo-sick'	*yi vil gair'-ne höh'-rĕ noh'-et mōō-sik'*	*yā vill hö-ră leetĕ moo-seek'*

The wireless is making a lot of noise.

Radioen støyer voldsomt	Radioen laver en masse larm	Radion för ett väldigt väsen
rah'-dee-oh-ĕn stöy-ĕr vol'-somt	*rah'-dioen läh'-vĕr in mas'-se lahrm*	*rā-dion för ĕtt vel-dit vai'-sen*

Norwegian	Danish	Swedish

It disturbs me, at night.

Den forstyrrer meg, om kvelden	Den forstyrre mig, om aftenen	Den stör mig, på natten *dĕn stör may,*
den for-stür'-rer may, om kvĕl'-len	*den for-stür'-rĕ my, um ahft'-nen*	*paw nät'-ten*

Can you turn it down?

Kan De skrue den ned? *kän dee skroo-ĕh den nĕhd*	Kan De skrue den ned? *kan dee skroo'-ĕh den neth*	Kan ni skruva ner den? *kän nee skroo-vä nĕhr dĕn*

Please turn it off.

Vær så vennlig å skrue den av *vair saw ven'-lee aw skroo'-ĕh den ahv'*	Vær venlig at slukke den *vair ven'-lee at sluk'-kĕ den*	Var snäll och stäng av den *vär snĕll ock stĕng äv dĕn*

It is a nuisance.

Den er en plage *den air ehn plah-gĕ*	Den er en plage *den air en plüh'-ĕh*	Det är otrevligt *deh ĕh oo'-trĕhv-lit*

How do I work this set?

Hvordan stiller jeg den inn? *vohr'-dan stil'-ler yay den in*	Hvordan virker denne radio? *vor-dan' veer'-kĕr denne rah'-dio*	Hur gör man med den här radion? *hoor yör män mēh dĕn hair rä-dion*

Long-wave, medium-wave, short-wave.

Langbølge, mellombølge, kortbølge *lahng'-bŏl-gĕ, mel'-lom-bŏl-gĕ, kort'-bŏl-gĕ*	Langbølge, mellembølgo, kortbølge *lahng'-bŏl-ĕh, mel'-lem-bŏl-ĕh, kort'-bŏl-ĕh*	Långvåg, mellanvåg, kortvåg *long'-vawg, mel'-län-vawg, kort'-vawg*

SPORT

Are you interested in sport?

Er De interessert i sport? *air dee in-tĕ-rĕ-sĕhrt' ee spŏrt*	Er De interesseret i sport? *air dee in-tĕ-rĕ-seh'-ret ee sport*	Är ni intresserad av sport? *ĕh nee in-trĕ-sĕh'-räd äv spŏrt*

Norwegian	Danish	Swedish

I like watching games.

Jeg liker å se på sport *yay lee'-ker aw sēh paw spŏrt*	Jeg kan godt lide at se på sport *yi kan got lee'-the at se paw sport*	Jeg tycker om att se på idrott *yā tückĕr omm ătt sēh paw ee'-drŏtt*

What games do you play?

Hva slags idrett driver De? *vah slahgs ee-drĕt dree'-ver dee*	Hvad slags indræt driver De? *vath slaks ee'-drait dree'-ver dee*	Vad för sport utövar ni? *vād för spŏrt oot'-övăr nee*

I don't play any games.

Jeg driver ikke noen idrett *yay dree'-ver ick'-kĕ noh'-ĕn ee-drĕt*	Jeg driver slet ikke idræt *yi dree'-ver slet ick'-ke ee'-drait*	Jag är inte sportig *yā ēh in'-tĕ spor'-tee*

I play tennis, golf.

Jeg spiller tennis, golf *yay spil-ler tennis, golf*	Jeg spiller tennis, golf *yi spil'-ler tennis, golf*	Jag spelar tennis, golf *yā spĕh'-lăr tennis, golf*

Is there a tennis court near here?

Er der en tennisbane i nærheten? *air dair ehn tennis-bah-nĕ ee nair'-hĕ-ten*	Er der en tennis bane i nærheden? *air dair in tennis bah'-nĕ ee nair-hĕ-then*	Finns det en tennisplan i nærheten? *finns dēh ĕn tennis-plăn ee nair'-heh-tĕn*

Is there a golf course here?

Er der en golfbane her? *air dair ehn golf'-bah-nĕ hair*	Er der en golf bane her? *air dair in golf bah'-nĕ hear*	Finns det en golfbana här? *finns dēh ĕn golf-bā-nă hair*

I need a tennis racket.

Jeg trenger en tennis racket *yay trēn-gĕr ehn tennis racket*	Jeg skal bruge en tennis' ketcher *ya skal broo'-ĕh in tennis ket'-cher*	Jag behöver en tennisracket *yā bēh-hö'-vĕr ĕn tennis-racket*

Who won?

Hvem vant? *vem văhnt*	Hvem vandt? *vehm văhnt*	Vem vann? *vĕm vănn*

Norwegian	Danish	Swedish

I need golf clubs.

Jeg trenger golfkøller	Jeg skal bruge nogle golf køller	Jag behöver golfklubbor
yay trĕn-gĕr golf'-köl-ler	*yi skal broo'-ĕh noh'-le golf köl'-lĕr*	*yå bĕh-hö'-ver golf-klubbor*

Tennis balls, golf balls.

Tennisballer, golfballer	Tennis bolde, golf bolde	Tennisbollar, golfbollar
tennis'-băl-ler, golf'-băl-ler	*tennis bol'-dĕ, golf bol'-dĕ*	*tennis-böl-lăr, golf-böl-lăr*

What is your handicap?

Hva er Deres handikap?	Hvad er Deres handicap?	Vad är ert handikapp?
vah air dair-ĕs handicap	*vath air dair'-es handicap*	*våd ĕh ĕhrt handi-kăpp*

I should like to see a football match.

Jeg skulle gjerne se en fotballkamp	Jeg vil gerne se en fodboldkamp	Jag skulle vilja se en fotbollsmatch
yay skŏŏl'-lĕ yair'-nĕ sĕh ehn foht-băl-kahmp	*yi vil gair'-ne seh in foth'-bawld-kamp*	*yå skŏŏl'-lĕ vil'-lå sĕh ĕn foht'-bŏlls-match*

How does one get to the ground?

Hvorledes kommer en til fotballbanen?	Hvordan kommer man til banen?	Hur kommer man till (fotbolls) planen?
vohr-leh-des kom'-mer ĕhn till foht'-băl bah-nen	*vor-dan' kom'-mer man til bah'-nen*	*hoor kom'-mer măn till (foht'-bŏlls) plăn-ĕn*

Two tickets for the stand.

To billetter til tribunen	To billetter til tribunen	Två biljetter på läktaren
toh bil-let'-ter till tree-boon'-ĕn	*toh bil-let'-ter til tree-büh'-nen*	*tvaw bill-yet'-ter paw lĕk'-tărn*

The result was 4–1, 2–0.

Resultatet var 4–1, 2–0	Resultatet var 4–1, 2–0	Resultatet var 4–1, 2–0
reh-sŏŏl-tah'-tĕ vahr fee'-rĕ/ehn, toh/nŏŏl	*reh-sŏŏl-tah'-tet var fee'-rĕ/ehn, toh/nŏŏl*	*rĕsül-tă'-tĕt văr füră/ĕtt, tvaw/nŏll*

Norwegian	*Danish*	*Swedish*

A draw.

Uavgjort	Uafgjordt	Oavgjort
oo'-ahv-yort	*oo'-ahv-g-yort*	*oo'-āv-yohrt*

Horse race.

Hesteveddeløp	Vædeløbet	Hästkapplöpningar
hes'-tĕ-ved-dĕ-löp	*vai'-the-lö-bĕt*	*hĕst'-kăpp-löp'-ning-ăr*

Bet, to bet.

Vedde, å vedde	Væde, at væde	Vadhållning, slå vad
ved'-dĕ, aw ved'-dĕ	*vai'-the, at vai'-the*	or hålla på
		vād'-holl-ning, slaw
		vād, hol'-lă paw

Bicycle, cyclist.

Sykkel, syklist	Cykel, cyklist	Cykel, cyklist
sük'-kel, sük'-list	*sük'-el, sük-leest'*	*sück'-ĕl, sück-list'*

Player.

Spiller	Spiller	Spelare
spil'-ler	*spil'-ler*	*spēhl'-ărĕ*

I should like to go riding.

Jeg vil gjerne ride	Jeg vil gerne ride	Jag skulle vilja rida
yay vill yair'-nĕ ree'-dĕ	*yi vil gair'-ne ree'-the*	*yā skŏŏl'-lĕ vil'-lă*
		ree'-dă

I should like to go for a swim.

Jeg vil gjerne gå å bade	Jeg vil gerne svømme	Jag skulle vilja gå och
yay vill yair'-nĕ gaw	*yi vil gair'-ne svöm'-mĕ*	bada (bada=bathe,
aw bah-dĕ		swim=simma)
		yā skŏŏl'-lĕ vil'-lă gaw
		ock bāh-dă

I should like to go sailing.

Jeg vil gjerne saile	Jeg vil gerne sejle	Jag skulle vilja fara
yay vill yair'-nĕ say-lĕ	*yi vil gair'-ne sigh-lĕ*	ut och segla
		yā skŏŏl'-lĕ vil'-lă fā'-ră
		oot ock sēhg-lă

Can I hire a boat?

Kan jeg leie en båt?	Kan jeg leje en båd?	Kan jag hyra en båt?
kăn yay lay-ĕh ehn	*kan yi lie'-ĕh in bawth*	*kăn yā hü-ră ĕn bawt*
bawt		

Norwegian	Danish	Swedish

Beach-guard, attendant.

Badevakt	Strandvagt, opsyn	Strandvakt, vaktmästare
bah'-dĕ-vahkt	*strahn'-vakt, up'-sün*	*stränd-väkt, väkt'-mĕs-tă-rĕ*

Deep, shallow, water.

Dypt, grunt, vann	Dybt, lavt, vand	Djupt, grunt, vatten
düpt, grŏŏnt, vänn	*dübt, lavt, vahn*	*yōopt, grŏŏnt, vät-ten*

Is it safe, dangerous?

Er det trygt, farlig?	Er det sikkert, farligt?	Är det ofarligt, farligt?
air deh trügt, far'-lee	*air deh sĭk'-kĕrt, fahr'-leet*	*ĕh dĕh oo'-far-lit, far'-lit*

Current.

Strøm	Strøm	Ström
ström	*ström*	*ström*

Are my things safe here?

Er tingene mine trygge her?	Er mine ting sikre her?	Kan jag tryggt lämna mina saker här?
air ting'-ĕn-ĕh mee'-neh trüg'-gĕ hair	*air mee'-nĕ ting sĭk'-rĕ hear*	*kăn yă trüggt lem'-nă mee-nă să'-kĕr hair*

Shooting, fishing.

Jakt, fiske	Jagt, fiskeri	Jakt, fiske
yahkt, fis'-kĕ	*yahkt, fis-kĕr-ree'*	*yăkt, fis'-kĕ*

Do I need a licence?

Behøver jeg lisens?	Behøver jeg et jagttegn?	Behöver jag licens?
bah-hŏ'-ver yay lee-sens'	*be-hŏ'-ver yi it yahkt tien*	*beh-hŏ'-ver yă lee-sens'*

Where do I get a licence?

Hvor får jeg en lisens?	Hvor får jeg et jagttegn?	Var får man en licens?
vohr fawr yay ehn lee-seens'	*vor fawr yi it yahkt'-tain*	*vār fawr măn ĕn lee-sĕns'*

Camp, to camp.

Leir, ligge i telt	Lejr, at ligge i telt	Läger, tälta
layr, lig-gĕ ee telt	*lie'-ĕr, at lig-gĕ' ee telt*	*lai'-gĕr, tel'-tă*

Norwegian	Danish	Swedish

Cartridges.

Norwegian	Danish	Swedish
Patroner	Patroner	Patroner
pah-troh'-ner	*pah-trohn'-ĕr*	*pă-troh'-ner*

To check equipment.

Gå over utstyret	At efterse udstyr	Kontrollera utrustning
gaw aw-ver oot'-stü-rĕ	*at efter'-sĕ ooth'-stür*	*kon-tröl-lēh'-rä oot'-rust-ning*

Danger.

Fare	Fare	Fara
fah-rĕ	*fah'-rĕ*	*fah'-rä*

Guide.

Fører	Fører	Guide, vägvisare
för-ĕr	*föh'-rer*	*guide, vaig'-vee-să-rĕ*

To halt.

Stoppe	Stoppe	Stanna, göra halt
stop'-pĕ	*stop'-pĕ*	*stăn'-nă, yörä hăllt*

Hut.

Hytte	Hytte	Hydda
hüt'-tĕ	*hüt'-tĕ*	*hüd'-dă*

Knife.

Kniv	Kniv	Kniv
k-neev	*k-neev*	*k-neev*

Lamp.

Lampe	Lampe	Lampa
lahm-pĕ	*lam'-pĕ*	*lăm'-pă*

Map.

Kart	Kort	Karta
kahrt	*kort*	*kär'-tă*

Net.

Garn	Næt	Nät
gahrn	*net*	*nait*

Prohibited.

Forbudt	Forbudt	Förbjuden
for-bōōt'	*for-bōōt'*	*för-b-yoo'-dĕn*

Norwegian	Danish	Swedish

Rifle.

Gevær	Riffel	Gevär
geh-vair'	*rif'-fĕl*	*yĕh-vair'*

Rope.

Rep	Reb	Rep
rēhp	*raib*	*rēhp*

Stove.

Primus	Spritapparat	Primus
pree'-mŏŏs	*spreet-ăh-păh-răht'*	*pree'-moos*

Tent.

Telt	Telt	Tält
telt	*telt*	*tĕlt*

Torch.

Lommelykt	Lygte	Ficklampa
lom'-mĕ-lükt	*lüg' tĕ*	*fĭck'-lăm-pă*

MOTORING

Car.

Bil	Bil	Bil
beel	*beel*	*beel*

Garage.

Garasje	Garage	Garage
gah-rah'-sheh	*gah-răh'-shŏh*	*guh-răsh'*

Petrol pump.

Bensin pumpe	Benzin pumpe	Bensinpump
ben-seen' pohm-pĕ	*ben-seen' pŏŏm'-pe*	*bĕn-seen'-pŏŏmp*

Petrol station.

Bensinstasjon	Benzin tank	Bensinstation
ben-seen'-stah-shohn	*ben-seen'-tank*	*bĕn-seen'-stah-shohn'*

Repairs.

Reparasjoner	Reparationer	Reparationer
reh-pah-rah-shoh'-ner	*reh-pah-rah-shōh'-nĕr*	*rĕ-păr-ră-shon'-nĕr*

Norwegian	Danish	Swedish

F

I want some petrol, water, oil.

Norwegian	Danish	Swedish
Jeg vil gjerne ha bensin, vann, olje *yay vill yair'-nĕ ha ben-seen', vănn, ol'-yeh*	Jeg vil gerne have noget benzin, vand, olie *yi vil gair'-ne hah noh'-et ben-seen', vahn, oh'-lee-ĕ*	Jag vill ha bensin, vatten, olja *yā vill hā bĕn-seen', văt'-ten, oll'-yă*

Give me . . . litres.

Gi meg . . . liter *yee may . . . lee-tĕr*	Giv mig . . . liter *ghee my . . . leet'-ter*	Ge mig . . . liter *yĕh may . . . lee-tĕr*

Do I need oil as well?

Trenger jeg olje også? *trehng-ĕr yay ol'-yeh os-saw*	Trænger jeg også til olie? *treng'-ger yi aw'-saw til oh'-lee-ĕ*	Behöver jag olja också? *bēh-hö'-ver yā oll'-yă ock-saw*

That will do.

Det er nok *deh air nock*	Det er nok *deh air nock*	Det räcker *deh reck'-ĕr*

I need air in the tyres.

Jeg vil gjerne ha luft i dekkene *yay vill yair'-nĕ ha looft ee dek'-kĕ-nĕ*	Jeg vil gerne have luft i dækkene *yi vil gair'-ne hah looft ee daik'-kē-ne*	Jag behöver luft i ringarna *yā beh-hö'-ver lŏŏft ee ring'-ăr-nă*

The tyres are a bit flat.

Dekkene er litt flate *dek'-kĕ-nĕ air lit flāh-tĕ*	Dækkene er lidt flade *daik'-kĕ-nĕ air lit flā'-the*	Ringarna är lite platta *ring'-ăr-nă ĕh lee-tĕ plăt-tă*

I don't know what is wrong.

Jeg vet ikke hva som er i veien *yay vēht ick'-kĕ vah' som air ee vay'-ĕn*	Jeg ved ikke hvad der er i vejen *yi veth ick'-ke vath dair air ee vy'-ĕn*	Jag vet inte vad som är fel *yā vēht in'-tĕ vād sŏm ĕh fĕhl*

The trouble is here.

Feilen er her *fay'-len air hair*	Det er her der er noget galt *deh air hear dair air noh'-et galt*	Felet är här *fĕhl'-ĕt ĕh hair*

Norwegian	*Danish*	*Swedish*

Puncture.

Punktering	Punktering	Punktering
pŏŏnk-teh'-ring	*pŏŏnk-tēh'-ring*	*pŏŏnk-tēh'-ring*

This does not work.

Dette virker ikke	Dette virker ikke	Detta fungerar inte
det'-tĕ vir-ker ick'-kĕ	*det'-te veer'-ker ick'-ke*	*dĕt-tă fōōng-gēh'-răr in'-tĕ*

The engine will not start.

Motoren vil ikke starte	Motoren vil ikke starte	Motorn vill inte starta
moh-toh'-ren vill ick'-kĕ stahr-tĕ	*moh'-toh-ren vil ick'-ke star'-tĕ*	*mōh-tŏrn vill in'-tĕ stăr'-tă*

The lights won't work.

Lysene virker ikke	Lygterne virker ikke	Ljuset fungerar inte
lüs'-ĕh-nĕ vir-ker ick'-kĕ	*lüg'-tĕr-nĕ veer'-ker ick'-ke*	*yoo'-set fōōng-gēh'-răr in'-tĕ*

The engine, steering, starter.

Motoren, styringen, selvstarteren	Motoren, styringen, selvstarteren	Motorn, styrinrättningen, startmotorn
moh-toh'-ren, stür'-ing-ĕn, sel'-stahr-ter-ĕn	*moh'-toh-ren, stü'-ring-ĕn, sel'-start-tĕ-rĕn*	*mōh'-tŏrn, stür'-in-rĕtt'-ning-ĕn, stărt'-mōh-tŏrn*

The wheels, brakes.

Hjulene, bremsene	Hjulene, bremserne	Hjulen, bromsarna
yoo'-lĕ-nĕ, brem'-sŏ-nĕ	*yoo'-lĕ-nĕ, brem'-sĕr-nĕ*	*yool'-ĕn, brom'-săr-nă*

Can I leave it here?

Kan jeg la den stå her?	Kan jeg efterlade den her?	Kan jag lämna den här?
kăn yay lah den staw' hair	*kan yi efter'-lā-the den hear*	*kăn yă lĕm'-nă dĕn hair*

An overhaul of the car.

Ettersyn/service av bilen	Et eftersyn/service af bilen	En översyn service av bilen
ĕtt'-ĕr-sün/service ahv bee'-len	*it efter'-sün/service af bee'-len*	*ĕn ŏ'-vĕr-sün service ăv bee'-len*

Norwegian	*Danish*	*Swedish*

To clean, wash.

Å pusse, vaske	At pusse, vaske	Göra ren, tvätta
aw pōōs'-sĕ, vahs-kĕ	*at poos'-sĕ, vahs'-ke*	*yŏ'-rä rēhn, tvĕt-tä*

Can you give me a tow?

Kan De taue meg?	Kan De trække min bil?	Kan ni bogsera mig?
kăn dee tuw-ĕh may	*kan dee traik'-kĕ meen beel*	*kăn nee bōōg-sēh'-rä may*

Can you give me a lift?

Kan De la meg få sitte på?	Kan De tage mig med?	Kan ni ge mig en lift?
kăn dee lah may faw sit'-tĕ paw	*kan dee tah my meth*	*kăn nee yēh may ĕn lift*

Is there a car-ferry?

Er der en bilferje?	Er der en bilfærge?	Finns det en bilfärja?
air dair ehn beel'-fair-yĕ	*air dair in beel fairg'-ĕh*	*finns dēh ĕn beel-fair'-yä*

Ferry-boat.

Ferje	Færge	Färja
fair'-yĕ	*fair'-ĕh*	*fair'-yä*

You have to make for the bridge at . . .

De må kjøre til broen ved . . .	De skal køre til broen ved . . .	Ni måste fara till bron vid . . .
dee maw chŏ-rĕ till broh'-ĕn veh . . .	*dee skal kŏre til bro'-ĕn veth . . .*	*nee moss'-tĕ fä'-rä till brōhn veed . . .*

Accelerator, brake.

Gasspedal, bremse	Accellerator, bremse	Gaspedal, broms
gās-pĕ-dāl', brĕm'-sĕ	*ăc-cel-lĕ-rah'-tohr, brehm'-sĕ*	*gās-pĕ-dāl', brŏmm*

Battery, carburettor.

Batteri, forgasser	Batteri, karburator	Batteri, karburator
băt'-tĕ-ree', for-găs'-ĕr	*bat-tĕ-ree', kahr-bōō-rah'-tor*	*băt-tĕ-ree', kär-boo-räh'-tor*

Clutch.

Clutch	Kobling	Koppling
clutch	*kohb'-ling*	*kopp'-ling*

| Norwegian | Danish | Swedish |

Gear, first, second, third, fourth.

Norwegian	Danish	Swedish
Gir, første, annet, tredje, fjerde *geer, förs'-tĕ, ähn'-net, tray'-ĕ, fyair'-ĕ*	Gear, første, andet, tredie, fjerde *gear, för'-ste, ahn'-ĕt, treh'-ye, fyer'-rĕ*	Växel, ettan, tvåan, trean, fyran *vexĕl, ĕtt'-än, tvaw'-än, trēh'-än, fü'-ran*

Neutral, reverse gear.

Fri, revers gir *free, reh-vĕrs' geer*	Fri-, bak-gear *free-, bak'-gear*	Nolläge, backen *noll-'lai-gĕ, bäck'-en*

Direction-indicator.

Retningsviser *ret'-nIngs-vee-ser*	Retningsviser *ret'-nIngs-vee-sĕr*	Körriktningsvisare *chur'-rikt-nings-vee'- sä-rĕ*

Horn.

Bilhorn *beel-hohrn*	Horn *hohrn*	Bilhorn *beel-hohrn*

Motor-cycle, lorry, scooter.

Motorsykkel, lastebil, scooter *moh'-tohr-sük-kel, lähs'-tĕ-beel, scooter*	Motorcykel, lastvogn, scooter *motor-sük'-kel, läst'-vogn, scooter*	Motorcykel, lastbil, scooter *moh'-tŏr-sückĕl, lässt'-beel, scooter*

Number plate.

Nummerskilt *nŏŏm'-mer-sheelt*	Nummerplade *nŏŏm'-mĕr-plā-the*	Nummerplåt *nŏŏm'-mer-plawt*

Radiator.

Radiator *rah-dee-ah'-tohr*	Radiator *ra-dee-āh'-tor*	Kylare *chü'-lå-rĕ*

Sparking-plug.

Tennplugg *ten-plŏŏg*	Tændstift *tain'-stift*	Tändstift *tĕnd'-stifft*

Speedometer.

Speedometer *speed-oh-mĕh'-ter*	Speedometer *spee-do-meter'*	Hastighetsmätare *häs'-stig-hēhts-maï'- tä-rĕ*

Spring.

Fjær *fyair*	Fjeder *fye'-ther*	Fjäder, fjädring *f-yaï'-dĕr, f-yaid'-ring*

Norwegian	Danish	Swedish

Windscreen, windscreen-wiper.

Frontglass, vinduspusser	Forrude, vinduesvisker	Vindruta, vindrutetorkare
front-glăss, vin'-doos-pŏŏs-ser	*for'-rŏŏ-the, veen'-dŏŏs-viss'-kĕr*	*vind'-roo-tă, vind'-roo-tĕ-törr'-kă-rĕ*

The car skidded.

Bilen gled	Bilen skređ	Bilen slirade
bee'-len gleh	*beel'-en skreth*	*bee'-lĕn slee'-ră-dĕ*

I did not see (understand) the sign, signal.

Jeg så (forsto) ikke skiltet, signalet	Jeg så ikke (forstod ikke) skiltet, signalet	Jag såg (förstod) inte tecknet, signalen
yay saw (for-stoh') ick'-kĕ shil'-tĕ, sig-nah'-lĕ	*yi saw ick'-ke (for-stoth' ick'-ke) skil'-tet, see-nă'-lĕt*	*yă saw (för-stohd') in'-tĕ teck'-net, sig-nă'-len*

I am a foreigner.

Jeg er utlending	Jeg er udlænding	Jag är utlänning
yay air oot'-len-ning	*yi air ooth'-lain-ning*	*yă ĕh oot'-len-ning*

Here is my driving-licence.

Her er mitt førerkort	Her er mit kørekort	Här är mitt körkort
hair air mit för'-ĕr-kort	*hear air meet kö'-rĕ-kort*	*hair ĕh mitt chör'-kohrt*

I am not used to driving here yet.

Jeg er ikke vant til å kjøre her ennå	Jeg er endnu ikke vandt til at køre her	Jag är inte van att köra här ännu
yay air ick'-kĕ văhnt till aw chö'-rĕ hair ĕn-naw	*yi air in'-noo ick'-ke vahnt til at kö'-rĕ hear*	*yă ĕh in'-tĕ văn ătt chö'-ră hair ĕnn'-noo*

I forgot to keep to the right (Norway, Denmark), left (Sweden).

Jeg glemte å holde til høire	Jeg glemte at holde til højre	Jag glömde att hålla till vänster
yay glĕm'-tĕ aw hol-lĕ till höy'-rĕ	*yi glem'-te at hol'-lĕ til hoy'-rĕ*	*yă glömm'-dĕ ătt hol'-lă till ven'-stĕr*

He was driving too fast.

Han kjørte for fort	Han kørte før hurtigt	Han körde för fort
hăn chör'-tĕ for fohrt	*han kör'-te for hoor'-teet*	*hăn chör'-dĕ för fohrt*

Norwegian	*Danish*	*Swedish*

He overtook me on the bend.

Han kjørte forbei meg i svingen	Han kørte uden om mig i svinget	Han körde om mig i kurvan
hän chör'-tĕ for-bee' may ee sving'-ĕn	*han kör'-te oo'-then um my ee sving'-et*	*hän chör'-dĕ omm may ee koor'-van*

He was on the wrong side of the road.

Han var på gale siden av veien	Han var på den gale side af vejen	Han var på fel sida av vägen
hän vahr paw gah'-lĕ see-den ahv vay-ĕn	*han var paw den ga'-lĕ see'-the af vy'-ĕn*	*hän vär paw fēhl see'-dă av vai'-gĕn*

ROAD SIGNS

Crossroads.

Veikryss	Korsvej	Vägkorsning
vay-krüs	*kors'-vy*	*vaig'-kors-ning*

Danger.

Fare	Fare	Fara
ah'-rŏ	*fah'-rĕ*	*fă'-ră*

Dangerous bend.

Farlig kurve	Farligt sving	Farlig kurva
ăhr'-lee kŏŏr'-veh	*fahr'-lit sving*	*far-lee koor'-vă*

Diversion, detour.

Omkjørsel	Omkørsel	Omläggning av väg
om'-chör-sel	*om'-kör-sel*	*omm'-leg-ning äv vaig*

Drive with care.

Kjør forsiktig	Kør forsigtigt	Kör försiktigt
chör for-sick'-tee	*kör for-sick'-teet*	*chör för-sik'-tit*

First-aid post.

Førstehjelp stasjon	Første-hjælpspost	Hjälpstation
förs'-te-yelp stah-shohn'	*för'-ste yelps posst*	*yelp-stă-shohn'*

Keep right, left.

Hold til høyre, venstre	Hold til højre, venstre	Håll till höger, vänster
hol till höy'-rĕ, vens'-trĕ	*hol til hoy'-rĕ, ven'-strĕ*	*holl till hö'-gĕr, ven'-stĕr*

Norwegian	Danish	Swedish

Level-crossing.

Planovergang	Jernbaneoverskæring	Varning för tåg.
plāhn'-ohver-gahng	*yern'-bah-nĕ-aw-ĕr-skai'-ring*	Järnvägsövergång
		vār'-ning fŏr tawg,
		yairn'-vaigs-över'-gong

Maximum speed.

Maksimalfart	Maksimal hastighed	Högsta hastighet
măck-see-māhl'-fährt	*măhk-see-māhl'*	*högg'-stă hăss'-tig-hĕht*
	hahs'-tee-heth	

No entrance.

| Innkjørsel forbudt | Indkørsel forbudt | Ingen infart |
| *in'-chŏr-sel for-bŏŏt'* | *in'-kŏr-sĕl for-bŏŏt'* | *ing-ĕn inn'-fărt* |

No parking.

Parkering forbudt	Parkering forbudt	Parkering förbjuden
păr-kĕh'-ring for-bŏŏt'	*par-kĕh'-ring for-bŏŏt'*	*păr-kĕhr'-ing*
		fŏr-b-yoo'-dĕn

No through road.

| Gjennomkjørsel forbudt | Gennemkørsel forbudt | Ej genomfart |
| *yen'-nom-chŏr-sel for-bŏŏt'* | *gen'-nem-kŏr-sĕl for-bŏŏt'* | *ay yĕh'-nom-fărt* |

One-way street.

| Enveiskjøring | Ensrettet kørsel | Enkelriktad gata |
| *ĕhn'-vays-chŏr-ing* | *ens'-ret-tet kŏr'-sĕl* | *ĕn'-kel-rik-tăd gā-tă* |

Road closed.

| Veien er sperret | Vejen er spærret | Vägen avstängd |
| *vay-en air sper'-ret* | *vy'-ĕn air spair'-rĕt* | *vaigĕn āv-stĕngd* |

Road up; repairs.

| Veiarbeide, reparasjoner | Vejarbejde, reparationer | Vägarbete |
| *vay'-ahr-bay-dĕ, reh-pah-rah-shoh'-ner* | *vy'-ar-by-dĕh, reh-pah-rah-shōh'-ner* | *vaig'-ărr-bēh'-tĕ* |

Stop.

| Stopp | Holdt, stop | Stopp |
| *stop* | *holt, stop* | *stop* |

| *Norwegian* | *Danish* | *Swedish* |

COUNTRIES, NATIONALITIES, PLACES

America, American.

Amerika, amerikansk	Amerika, amerikansk	Amerika, amerikansk
ah-mēh'-ree-kah,	*ah-mēh'-ree-kah,*	*ă-mēh'-ree-kă,*
ah-meh-ree-kāhnsk'	*ah-meh-ree-kānsk'*	*ă-mēh-ree-kānsk'*

Australia, Australian.

Australia, australsk	Australien, australsk	Australien, australisk
au-strah'-lee-ăh,	*au-strah'-lee-ĕn,*	*au-strä'-lee-en,*
au-strahlsk	*au-strahlsk*	*au-strä'-lisk*

British.

Britisk	Britisk	Brittisk
bree'-tisk	*bree'-tisk*	*brittisk*

Canada, Canadian.

Kanada, kanadisk	Kanada, kanadisk	Kanada, kanadensisk
kăn-nă-dă, kah-nă'-disk	*kăh'-nă-dă,*	*kăn'-ădă,*
	kah-nă'-disk	*kănă-děn'-sisk*

Denmark, Danish.

Danmark, dansk	Danmark, dansk	Danmark, dansk
dăhn'-mahrk, dahnsk	*dan'-mark, dan'-sk*	*dănn'-mărk, dănsk*

England, English.

England, engelsk	England, engelsk	England, engelsk
ehng'-lăhn, ehng'-ĕlsk	*ehng'-lăhn, ehng'-ĕlsk*	*ehng'-lănd, chng'-ĕlsk*

France, French.

Frankrike, fransk	Frankrig, fransk	Frankrike, fransk
frăhnk'-ree-kĕ, frăhnsk	*frăhn'-kree, frăhn'-sk*	*frănk'-ree-kĕ, frănsk*

Great Britain.

Storbritannia	Storbritanien	Storbritannien
stohr'-bree-tăn-yă	*stohr'-bree-tahn-yen*	*stohr-bree-tăn'-yen*

Germany, German.

Tyskland, tysk	Tyskland, tysk	Tyskland, tysk
tüsk'-lăhn, tüsk	*tüsk'-lăhn, tüsk*	*tüsk'-lănd, tüsk*

Norwegian	*Danish*	*Swedish*

Ireland, Irish.

Irland, irsk	Irland, irsk	Irland, irländsk
eer'-lähn, eersk	*eer'-lähn, eersk*	*eer'-länd, eer'-lĕndsk*

Norway, Norwegian.

Norge, norsk	Norge, norsk	Norge, norsk
nor'-gĕ, norsk	*nor'-ĕh, norsk*	*norr'-yĕ, norsk*

Scotland, Scottish.

Skottland, skotsk	Skotland, skotsk	Skottland, skotsk
skot'-lähn, skotsk	*scot'-lähn, scotsk*	*skott'-länd, skotsk*

South Africa, South African.

Syd-Afrika, Syd-afrikansk	Syd Afrika, Syd Afrikansk	Sydafrika, sydafrikansk
süd' ah'-free-kah, süd' ah-free-kahnsk'	*süth af'-ree-kah, süth' af-ree-kahnsk'*	*süd'-ah-frikă, süd'-ah-free-känsk'*

Spain, Spanish.

Spania, spansk	Spanien, spansk	Spanien, spansk
spähn'-yă, spahnsk	*spähn'-yen, spähnsk*	*spähn'-yen, spänsk*

Sweden, Swedish.

Sverige, svensk	Sverrig, svensk	Sverige, svensk
svĕhr'-yĕ, svehnsk	*svair'-ree, sven'-sk*	*svĕr'-yĕ, svĕnsk*

U.S.A.

De Forenede Stater (USA)	De Forenede Stater (USA)	Förenta Staterna (USA)
dee for-ĕh'-nĕ-dĕ stah'-ter (oo-ess-āh)	*dee for-ĕh'-nĕ-the stah'-ter (oo-ess-āh)*	*fur-ēhn'-tă stā'-tĕr-nă (oo-ess-āh)*

TIME

DAYS OF THE WEEK

Sunday.

Søndag	Søndag	Söndag
sön'-dahg	*sön'-dāh*	*sönn'-dăh*

Monday, Tuesday.

Mandag, tirsdag	Mandag, tirsdag	Måndag, tisdag
măhn'-dahg, teers'-dahg	*mahn'-dāh, teers'-dāh*	*monn'-dăh, tees'-dăh*

| *Norwegian* | *Danish* | *Swedish* |

Wednesday, Thursday.

| Onsdag, torsdag | Onsdag, torsdag | Onsdag, torsdag |
| *ohns'-dahg, tohrs'-dahg* | *oons'-dāh, tors'-dāh* | *ohns'-dāh, tohrs'-dāh* |

Friday, Saturday.

| Fredag, lørdag | Fredag, lørdag | Fredag, lördag |
| *frēh'-dahg, lör'-dahg* | *frēh'-dāh, lör'-dāh* | *frēh'-dāh, lör'-dāh* |

MONTHS

January, February.

Januar, februar	Januar, Februar	Januari, februari
yàhn'-oo-ahr,	*yah'-noo-ähr,*	*yăn-noo-ār'-ee,*
feh'-broo-ahr	*feh'-broo-ähr*	*feb-rōō-ār'-ee*

March, April.

| Mars, april | Marts, April | Mars, april |
| *māhrs, äh-preel'* | *māhrts, äh-preel'* | *mārsh, ä-prill'* |

May, June.

| Mai, juni | Mai, Juni | Maj, juni |
| *my, yoo'-nee* | *my, yoo'-nee* | *my, yoo'-nee* |

July, August.

| Juli, august | Juli, August | Juli, augusti |
| *yoo'-lee, ow-gōōst'* | *yoo'-lee, aw-gōōst'* | *yoo'-lee, ă-goos'-tee* |

September, October.

September, oktober	September, Oktober	September, oktober
sep-tem'-ber,	*sep-tem'-ber,*	*sep-tem'-ber,*
ŏk-toh'-ber	*ock-toh'-ber*	*ock-toh'-ber*

November, December.

November, desember	November, December	November, december
noh-vem'-ber,	*no-vem'-ber,*	*noh-vem'-ber,*
deh-sem'-ber	*de-sem'-ber*	*deh-sem'-ber*

SEASONS AND HOLIDAYS

Season (of the year).

Årstid	Årstid	Årstid
awrs'-teed	*awrs'-teeth*	*awrs'-teed*
Norwegian	Danish	Swedish

A holiday, holidays.

En fridag, ferie	En fridag, ferie	Helgdag, semester
ehn' free-dahg, *fēh'-ree-ĕh*	*in free'-dāh, feh'-ree-ĕh*	*hell'-dāh, sĕh-mĕs'-ter*

Christmas.

Jul	Jul	Jul
yool	*yool*	*yool*

Easter.

Påske	Påske	Påsk
paws'-kĕ	*paw'-skĕ*	*pŏssk*

Spring, summer.

Vår, sommer	Forår, sommer	Vår, sommar
vawr, som'-mĕr	*fohr'-awr, som'-mĕr*	*vawr, som'-măr*

Autumn, winter.

Høst, vinter	Efterår, vinter	Höst, vinter
höst, vin'-ter	*ehf'-tĕr-awr, vin'-tĕr*	*höst, vin'-ter*

GENERAL TIME PHRASES

Day, week.

Dag, uke	Dag, uge	Dag, vecka
dahg, oo'-kĕ	*dāh, oo'-ĕh*	*dahg, vĕck'-kă*

Fortnight.

Fjorten dager	To uger (fjorten dage)	Fjorton dagar
fyohr'-ten dah'-ger	*toh oo'-ĕr, fyor'-ten dāh'-ĕh*	*fyohr'-tonn dăh'-găr*

Month.

Måned	Måned	Månad
maw'-ned	*maw'-neth*	*maw'-năd*

Three months.

Tre måneder	Tre måneder	Tre månader
treh' maw-ned-ĕr	*trĕh maw'-nĕ-ther*	*trĕh maw'-nă-dĕr*

Year, two years.

År, to år	År, to år	År, två år
awr, toh' awr	*awr, toh awr*	*awr, tvaw awr*

Norwegian	Danish	Swedish

Morning, afternoon, evening, night.

Norwegian	Danish	Swedish
Morgen, ettermiddag, aften, natt *mor'-ĕn,* *ĕtt'-ĕr-mid-dahg,* *ähf'-ten, näht*	Morgen, eftermiddag, aften, nat *mor'-en,* *efter'-mee-dāh,* *ähf'-ten, näht*	Morgon or förmiddag, eftermiddag, kväll, natt *mor'-ron, för'-middă,* *ĕf'-ter-middă,* *kvĕll, nătt*

Today, yesterday.

Norwegian	Danish	Swedish
I dag, i går *ee dahg, ee gawr*	I dag, i går *ee däh, ee gawr*	I dag, i går *ee däg, ee gawr*

Day before yesterday.

Norwegian	Danish	Swedish
I forgårs *ee for'-gawrs*	I forgårs *ee for'-gawrs*	I förrgår *ee förr-gawr*

Yesterday evening, morning.

Norwegian	Danish	Swedish
I gåraftes, i gårmorges *ee gawr-ăhf'-tes,* *ee gawr-mor'-ĕs*	I går aftes, i går morges *ee gawr ähf'-tes,* *ee gawr mor'-ĕs*	I går kväll, morse *ee gawr kvĕll, mor'-sĕ*

Tomorrow.

Norwegian	Danish	Swedish
I morgen *ee mor'-ĕn*	I morgen *ee mor'-ĕn*	I morgon *ee mör'-rŏn*

Tomorrow morning, afternoon.

Norwegian	Danish	Swedish
I morgen tidlig, i morgen ettermiddag *ee mor'-ĕn teed'-lee,* *ee mor'-ĕn* *ĕtt'-er-mid-dahg*	I morgen tidlig, i morgen eftermiddag *ee mor'-en teeth'-lee,* *ee mor'-en* *efter'-mee-dāh*	I morgon förmiddag, eftermiddag *ee mör'-rŏn för'-middă,* *ĕf-ter-middă*

Day after tomorrow.

Norwegian	Danish	Swedish
I overmorgen *ee aw'-ver-mor-en*	I overmorgen *ee oh'-ĕr-mor'-en*	I övermorgon *ee över'-mör-rŏn*

Last week.

Norwegian	Danish	Swedish
Forrige uke *for'-ree-ĕh oo'-kĕ*	Sidste uge *sis'-tĕ oo'-ĕh*	Förra veckan *för'-ră vĕck'-kăn*

Last month, last year.

Norwegian	Danish	Swedish
Forrige måned, i fjor *for'-ree-ĕh maw'-ned,* *ee fyohr*	I sidste måned, år *ee sis'-tĕ maw'-neth,* *awr*	Förra månaden, året *för'-ră maw'-nă-dĕn,* *äw'-ret*

Norwegian	Danish	Swedish

A month, week ago.

Norwegian	Danish	Swedish
En måned, uke siden	For en måned, uge siden	För en månad, sedan, för en vecka sedan
ehn maw'-ned, oo'-kě see-den	*for in maw'-neth, oo'-ěh see'-then*	*för ěn maw'-năd sěh'-dăn, för en věck'-kă sěh'-dăn*

Every day, daily.

Norwegian	Danish	Swedish
Hver dag, daglig	Hver dag, daglig	Varje dag, dagligen
vair dahg, dahg'-lee	*vair dāh, dăhv'-lee*	*văr'-yě dahg, dahg'-lee-gěn*

I have been here since Sunday.

Norwegian	Danish	Swedish
Jag har vært her siden søndag	Jeg har været her siden i søndag	Jag har varit här sedan i söndags
yay hahr vairt' hair see-den sön'-dahg	*yi hahr vairet hear see'-then ee sön'-dāh*	*yā hār vă'-rit hair sěh'-dăn ee sönn'-dăs*

I have been here four days.

Norwegian	Danish	Swedish
Jeg har vært her i fire dager	Jeg har vært her i fire dage	Jag har varit här i fyra dagar
yay hahr vairt' hair ee fee'-rě dahg-ěr	*yi hahr vairet hear ee fee'-rě dāh'-ěh*	*yā hār vă'-rit hair ee fü-ră dahr*

THE CLOCK

What time is it?

Norwegian	Danish	Swedish
Hva er klokken?	Hvad er klokken?	Vad är klockan?
vah air klock'-ken	*vath air klock'-ken*	*văd ěh klock'-ăn*

It is one o'clock.

Norwegian	Danish	Swedish
Klokken er ett	Klokken er et	Klockan är ett
klock'-ken air ětt	*klock'-ken air it*	*klock'-ăn ěh ětt*

It is ten o'clock.

Norwegian	Danish	Swedish
Klokken er ti	Klokken er ti	Klockan är tio
klock'-ken air tee	*klock'-ken air tee*	*klock'-ăn ěh tee'-oh*

Quarter past two.

Norwegian	Danish	Swedish
Et kvarter over to	Et kvarter over to	Kvart över två
ětt kvahr-ter' oh'-ver toh	*it kvahr-těr' oh'-ěr toh*	*kvărt över tvaw*

Norwegian	Danish	Swedish

Quarter to nine.

| Kvart på ni | Et kvarter i ni | Kvart i nio |
| *kvahrt paw nee* | *it kvahr'-tĕr ee nee* | *kvärt ee nee'-oh* |

It is twelve o'clock.

| Klokken er tolv | Klokken er tolv | Klockan är tolv |
| *klock'-ken air tol* | *klock'-ken air tol* | *klock'-än ēh tolly* |

It is half-past twelve.

| Den er halv ett | Den er halv et | Den är halv ett |
| *den air hăhl' ĕtt* | *den air hahl it* | *den ēh hälly ĕtt* |

It is twenty past five.

| Den er tyve minutter over fem | Den er tyve minutter over fem | Den är tjugo över fem |
| *den air tü'-vĕ mee-nŏŏt'-ter oh'-ver fehm* | *den air tü'-vĕ mee-nŏŏt'-tĕr oh'-ĕr fem* | *den ēh choo'-gŏh övĕr fĕm* |

It is ten to three.

| Den er ti minutter på tre | Den er ti minutter i tre | Den är tio i tre |
| *den air tee' mee-nŏŏt'-ter paw treh* | *den air tee mee-nŏŏt'-tĕr ee tray* | *den ēh tee'-oh ee trēh* |

SOME PUBLIC NOTICES

Address.

| Adresse | Adresse | Adress |
| *ah-dres'-sĕ* | *ah-dres'-sĕ* | *ăddrĕss'* |

Admission free.

| Fri adgang | Fri indgang | Fritt inträde |
| *free ahd'-gahng* | *free in'-gang* | *fritt' inn'-trai-dĕ* |

Auction.

| Auksjon | Auction | Auktion |
| *ow-shohn'* | *auk-shōhn'* | *äk-shohn'* |

Boarding-house.

| Pensjonat | Pension | Pensionat |
| *pahng-shoh-naht'* | *pahng-shohn'* | *pän-shoh-naht'* |

| Norwegian | Danish | Swedish |

Booking-office.

| Billettkontor | Billet kontor | Biljettkontor |
| *bil-let'-kon-tohr'* | *bil-let' kon-tōhr'* | *bill-yett'-kon-tōhr'* |

Bus.

| Buss | Bus | Buss |
| *bŏŏs* | *bŏŏs* | *bŏŏs* |

Closed.

| Lukket | Lukket | Stängt |
| *lŏŏk'-ket* | *lŏŏk'-kĕt* | *stĕngt* |

Cold.

| Kaldt | Koldt | Kallt |
| *kahlt* | *kolt* | *källt* |

Consulate.

| Konsulat | Konsulat | Konsulat |
| *kon-soo-laht'* | *kon-soo-lăt'* | *kon-soo-laht'* |

Customs.

| Toll | Told | Tull |
| *tol* | *tol* | *tŏŏll* |

Danger.

| Fare | Fare | Fara |
| *fah'-rĕ* | *fä'-rĕ* | *fä'-ră* |

Do not lean out.

| Len Dem ikke ut | Læn Dem ikke ud | Luta er inte ut |
| *lēhn dem ick'-kĕ oot* | *lain dem ick'-ke ooth* | *loo'-tă ĕhr in'-tĕ oot* |

Drinking water.

| Drikkevann | Drikke vand | Dricksvatten |
| *drick'-kĕ-vănn* | *drik'-kĕ vahn* | *dricks'-văt-ten* |

Embassy.

| Ambassade | Ambasade | Ambassad |
| *ăm-băh-sah'-dĕ* | *am-bă-sāh'-the* | *ămm-bă-säd'* |

Exit.

| Utgang | Udgang | Utgång |
| *oot'-gahng* | *ooth'-gang* | *oot'-gong* |

| Norwegian | Danish | Swedish |

Express.

| Ekspress | Ekspress | Express, snälltåg |
| *express* | *ex-press'* | *express', snell-tawg* |

Fire Brigade.

| Brannvesen | Brandvæsen | Brandkår |
| *brähn-věh-sěn* | *brahn'-vai-sěn* | *brănn-kawr* |

Forbidden.

| Forbudt | Forbudt | Förbjudet |
| *for-bōōt'* | *for-bōōt'* | *för-b-yoo'-dět* |

For hire, to let.

| Til leie | Til leje | Uthyres, att hyra |
| *till lay'-ěh* | *til lai'-ěh* | *oot'-hü-rěs, ätt hü'-ra* |

Free, vacant.

| Fri, ledig | Fri | Ledig (tom) |
| *froo, lěh' dee* | *free* | *lěh-dee (tohm)* |

Full board.

| Full pensjon | Full Pension | Helpension |
| *full' pahng-shohn'* | *full pahng-shohn'* | *hěhl-pǎn-shohn'* |

Gentlemen (lavatory).

| Herrer | Herrer | Herrar |
| *hěhr'-er* | *hair'-rě* | *hěr'-rǎr* |

Information.

| Informasjon | Oplysning | Upplysningar, information |
| *in-for-mah-shohn'* | *up'-lüs-ning* | *ōōp'-lüs-ning-ǎr, inn-formǎ-shohn* |

Knock.

| Bank på | Bank på | Knacka |
| *bǎhnk paw* | *bank paw* | *knǎckǎ* |

Ladies (lavatory).

| Damer | Damer | Damer |
| *dah'-mer* | *da'-mer* | *dǎ-měr* |

| Norwegian | Danish | Swedish |

Lavatory.

Norwegian	Danish	Swedish
W.C./toalett *veh.ceh./toh-ah-let'*	W.C./Toilet *veh.seh./to-a-let'*	W.C./Toalett *veh.seh./toh-ă-let'*

Name.

Navn *nahvn*	Navn *navn*	Namn *nămmn*

Open.

Åpen *aw'-pen*	Åben *aw'-pen*	Öppen *öp'-pen*

Poison.

Gift *yeeft*	Gift *geeft*	Gift *yeeft*

Post Office.

Postkontor *post'-kon-tohr*	Postkontor *posst'-kon-tohr'*	Postkontor *posst'-kon-tohr'*

Press.

Press, trykk *prěss, trück*	Tryk *trück*	Tryck *trück*

Pull.

Trekk *trěkk*	Træk *traik*	Drag *drāh*

Push.

Skubb *skŏŏb*	Skub *skŏŏb*	Skjut *shoot*

Repairs (roads).

Veiarbeide *vay'-ahr-bay-dě*	Vejarbejde *vy'-ar-by-dě*	Vägarbete *vaig'-ărr-bēh-tě*

Sale.

Salg *sahlg*	Salg *salg*	Realisation *rēh-ă-lis-să-shohn'*

Signature.

Underskrift/signatur *ŏŏn'-der-skrift/ sig-nah-toor'*	Underskrift *ŏŏn'-ner-skrift*	Signatur, underskrift *sing-nă-toor', ŏŏn'-děr-skrift*

Norwegian	Danish	Swedish

Smoking, no smoking.

Norwegian	Danish	Swedish
Røking, røking forbudt	Rygning, rygning forbudt	Rökning tillåten, förbjuden
rök'-ing, rök'-ing for-boōt'	*rü'-ning, rü'-ning for-boōt'*	*rök-ning till-law'-ten, för-b-yoo'-dĕn*

Travel Agency.

Norwegian	Danish	Swedish
Reisebyrå	Rejsebureau	Resebyrå
ray'-sĕ-bü-raw	*ry'-sĕ-bü-ro*	*rēh'-sĕ-bü-raw*

Norwegian	*Danish*	*Swedish*

ABBREVIATIONS

Norwegian

K.N.A.	Kongelig Norsk Automobilklub Royal Norwegian Automobile Club	km	kilometer
		m	meter
		gt.	gate street
A/S	Aksjeselskap Limited Company	D.N.T.	Den Norske Turist-forening Norwegian Tourist Association
Co.	Kompani Company		
N.S.B.	Norske Statsbaner Norwegian State Railways	Eft.	Efterfølgere Successors (commerce)
Frk.	Frøken Miss	S.A.S.	Scandinavian Airlines System
hk	hestekrefter horse-power	1. etasje	ground floor
do.	ditto ditto	2. etasje	first floor
		3. etasje	second floor
kg	kilogram	Kr.	kroner

Danish

K.D.A.K.	Kongelig Dansk Automobil Klub Royal Danish Automobile Club	m	meter
		gd.	gade street
A/S	Aktieselskab Limited Company	D.T.F.	Dansk Turist Forening Danish Tourist Association
Co.	Company		

D.S.B.	Danske Stats Baner Danish State Railways	Eft.	Efterfølgere Successors (commerce)
Frk.	Frøken Miss	S.A.S.	Scandinavian Airlines System
hk	hestekræfter horse-power	1. etage	ground floor
do.	ditto ditto	2. etage	first floor
kg	kilogram	3. etage	second floor
km	kilometer	kr.	kroner

Swedish

K.A.K.	Kungliga Automobilklubben Royal Swedish Automobile Club	Tga.	Telegramadress Telegram address
		hk	Hästkrafter Horse-power
M.	Motormännens Riksförbund The Motorists Association	do or d:o	Dito Ditto
		kg	Kilogram
A.B.	Aktiebolag Co. Ltd.	km	Kilometer
		m	Meter
Co.	Kompani Company	gat. or g.	Gata Street
S.J.	Statens Järnvägar Swedish State Railways	B.v.	Bottenvåningen Ground floor
Frk.	Fröken (this abbr. is seldom used) Miss	S.T.F.	Svenska Turist Föreningen Swedish Tourist Association

NUMERALS

	Norwegian	Danish	Swedish
0	Null *nöol*	Nul *nöol*	Noll *nöll*
1	En (or ett) *ehn*	En (or et) *ayn*	Ett (or en) *ĕtt, ĕnn*
2	To *toh*	To *toh*	Två *tvaw*
3	Tre *trēh*	Tre *trēh*	Tre *trēh*
4	Fire *fee'-rĕ*	Fire *fee'-rĕ*	Fyra *fü'-ră*

	Norwegian	*Danish*	*Swedish*
5	Fem *fĕhm*	Fem *fĕm*	Fem *fĕm*
6	Seks *sex*	Seks *seks*	Sex *sex*
7	Syv *silv*	Syv *silv*	Sju *shoo*
8	Otte *ot'-tĕ*	Otte *oh'-tĕ*	Åtta *ot'-tă*
9	Ni *nee*	Ni *nee*	Nio *nee'-ŏ*
10	Ti *tee*	Ti *tee*	Tio *tee'-ŏ*
11	Elleve *el'-vĕ*	Elve *el'-vĕ*	Elva *ell'-vă*
12	Tolv *tol*	Tolv *tol*	Tolv *tollv*
13	Tretten *trĕt'-ten*	Tretten *trait'-ten*	Tretton *trĕt'-tonn*
14	Fjorten *fyor'-ten*	Fjorten *fyor'-ten*	Fjorton *f-yohr'-tonn*
15	Femten *fem'-ten*	Femten *fem'-ten*	Femton *fĕm'-tonn*
16	Seksten *sex'-ten*	Sejsten *sy'-sten*	Sexton *sex'-tonn*
17	Sytten *süt'-ten*	Sytten *süt'-ten*	Sjutton *shoo'-tonn*
18	Atten *ăht'-ten*	Atten *ăht'-ten*	Aderton *ăr'-tonn*
19	Nitten *nit'-ten*	Nitten *nit'-ten*	Nitton *nit'-tonn*
20	Tyve *tü'-vĕ*	Tyve *tü'-vĕ*	Tjugo *choo'-goh*
21	En og tyve *ehn' aw tü-vĕ*	Enogtyve *ayn'-aw-tü-vĕ*	Tjugoett *choo-goh-ĕtt'*
22	To og tyve *toh' aw tü-vĕ*	Toogtyve *toh'-aw-tü-vĕ*	Tjugotvå *choo-goh-tvaw'*
30	Tredve *tred'-vĕ*	Tredve *treth'-vă*	Trettio *trĕ'-tee-oh*
40	Førti *för'-tee*	Fyrre *für'-rĕ*	Fyrtio *fur'-tee-oh*
50	Femti *fehm'-tee*	Halvtreds *hăhl-tress'*	Femtio *fĕm'-tee-oh*

	Norwegian	Danish	Swedish
60	Seksti *sex'-tee*	Treds *tress*	Sextio *sex'-tee-oh*
70	Sytti *süt'-tee*	Halvfjerds *hähl-fyers'*	Sjuttio *shööt'-tee-oh*
80	Åtti *ot'-tee*	Firs *feers*	Åttio *ott'-tee-oh*
90	Nitti *nit'-tee*	Halvfems *hähl-fems'*	Nittio *nit'-tee-oh*
100	Hundre *hōōn'-dreh*	Hunderede *hoon'-rĕ-the*	Hundra *hōōn'-drä*
200	To hundre *toh'-hōōn-dreh*	Tohunderede *toh'-hoon-rĕ-the*	Tvåhundra *tvaw'-hōōn-drä*
1000	Tusen *too'-sen*	Tusind *too'-sin*	Tusen *too'-sĕn*
2000	To tusen *toh'-too-sen*	Totusind *toh'-too-sin*	Tvåtusen *tvaw'-too-sen*

A million

En million *ehn mil-lee-ohn'*	En million *ayn mil-lee-ohn'*	En miljon *ĕnn mill-yohn'*

First, second

Første, annen *förs'-tĕ ähn'-nen*	Første, anden *för'-ste, ahnen*	Första, andra *för'-stä, änn'-drä*

Third, fourth

Tredje, fjerde *tray'-ĕh, fyair'-ĕh*	Tredie, fjerde *treh'-ye, fyer'-rĕ*	Tredje, fjärde *trēhd'-yĕ, f-yair'-dĕ*

Fifth, sixth

Femte, sjette *fehm'-tĕ, shĕt'-tĕ*	Femte, sjete *fem'-tĕ, syet'-tĕ*	Femte, sjätte *fem'-tĕ, shet'-tĕ*

A quarter, two-thirds.

En fjerdedel,
  to tredjedeler
ehn' fyair'-ĕh-dĕhl,
  toh' tray-ĕh-dĕhl-ĕr
	En fjerdedel,
	  to trediedel
	in fyeh'-rĕ-dĕl,
	  toh treh'-yĕ-dēl
		En kvart(s),
		  en fjärdedel,
		  två tredjedelar
		enn kvärt(s),
		  en f-yair'-dĕ-dēhl,
		  tvaw trēhd'-yĕ-dĕhl-är

Half, a third

Halv, en tredjedel *hähl, ehn tray'-ĕh-dĕhl*	Halvdel, en trediedel *hähl, in treh'-yĕ-dēl*	Halv, en tredjedel *hällv, en trēhd'-yĕ-dĕhl*

Norwegian	Danish	Swedish

WEIGHTS AND MEASURES

The metric system is used in Scandinavia. The following tables give approximate equivalents:

WEIGHT

100 gram	=	3½ oz.
1 kilogram	=	2 lb. 3 oz.

CAPACITY

1 liter	=	1¾ pints
4½ liter	=	1 gallon

LENGTH

1 centimeter (cm)	=	⅜ inch
2½ centimeter (cm)	=	1 inch
30 centimeter (cm)	=	1 foot
91 centimeter (cm)	=	1 yard
1 meter (m)	=	39 inches
1 kilometer (km)	=	0.62 mile
1.6 kilometer (km)	=	1 mile

TEMPERATURE

To convert degrees Centigrade into degrees Fahrenheit, multiply by 9, divide by 5 and add 32. Thus, 20° C.=68° F. (20×⅘+32=68°).

INDEX

The words printed in capitals refer to Sections, in which the subject is dealt with at length.

HALT
sign

All
Vehicles
Prohibited

STOP
Customs

No
Parking
I on even days
II on odd days

Use of
Horn
Prohibited

Speed
Limit

DANGER

Tunnel

Loose
Chippings

Slippery
Road

Cross
Roads
with
minor road

Cross
Winds

PRIORITY
ROAD

END
of priority.
Give way to
traffic from
right.

DANGER
Give way to
traffic from
right.
(France)

PRIORITY
ROAD.

Level
Crossing

Minimum
Speed
Limit

END
of
Minimum
Speed

Keep
Right

Switch
on
headlights

Snow
Chains or
Tyres
Compulsory

Cycle path
Compulsory

First
Aid

First
Aid

Information

Subway
or
Bridge

Pedestrian
Crossing

Mechanical
Help

Filling
Station